Force.com Platform Fundamentals

An Introduction to Custom Application Development in the Cloud

Version 9.2, August 2016

Written by
Phil Choi
Chris McGuire
Caroline Roth

With contributions by
Dave Carroll
Nick Tran
Andrea Leszek
Brian Donnelly

Get acquainted with the native functionality of the Force.com platform by creating
a recruiting application. Design and create objects, customize the app's user
interface, control access to data, collaborate with Chatter, automate processes,
and report on your data.

Force.com Platform Fundamentals

ISBN: 978-0-9789639-3-4

CONTENTS

Contents

Contents

Contents

As users of the Internet, we're all familiar with the fascinating, innovative, creative, and sometimes silly ways in which it has changed how we work and play. From social networking sites to wikis to blogs, and more, it's exciting to watch the innovations taking place that are changing the ways we communicate and collaborate.

While these changes have certainly impacted how we work with content, a similar set of Internet-driven ideas and technologies is changing how we build and work with business applications. While yesterday's business applications required thousands, if not millions, of dollars and sometimes years of professional services help to set up and customize, the technologies offered by the Internet today make it much easier to create, configure, and use business applications of all kinds. Indeed, the power of the Internet has given us the ability to solve new kinds of business problems that, because of complexity or cost, had previously remained out of reach.

Just as the changes that moved publishing technology from paper to bits made it possible for us to have information about anything in the whole world right at our fingertips, the changes in application technology make it similarly possible to imagine a robust, enterprise-class application for almost any business need. Sound pretty good? Then you're probably wondering: "What's the magic that makes this possible?"

Welcome to the Cloud!

These new ways of building and running applications are enabled by the world of *cloud computing*, where you access applications, or *apps*, over the Internet as utilities, rather than as pieces of software running on your desktop or in the server room. This model is already quite common for consumer apps like email and photo sharing, and for certain business applications, like customer relationship management (CRM).

Because almost all apps these days are delivered via a Web browser, it's increasingly hard to tell which applications are "traditional software," and which are run in the cloud. As with the Internet, applications that run in the cloud have grown so ubiquitous that almost every business user interacts with at least one, whether it's an email service, a Web conferencing application, or a sales system.

Platforms for Cloud Computing

A new twist, the *platform in the cloud*, is making the delivery of application functionality even more interesting. Increasingly, applications that run in the cloud are starting to look less like websites and more like platforms, meaning they are starting to sprout Application Programming Interfaces (APIs), code libraries, and even programming models. Collectively, these new kinds of development technologies can be thought of as platforms to run apps in the cloud.

Similar to traditional platforms, cloud computing platforms provide tools that allow developers to leverage existing functionality to create something new; however, because these platform tools are accessed freely over the Internet rather than through an operating system or package that was installed on a local machine, developers don't need to worry about the logistics of putting together an executable that will be installed on a user's machine. Anyone with a Web browser can access the app!

The possibilities presented by this new type of platform have emerged quickly, spurred on by the popularity of *mash-ups*—a website or application that combines tools from multiple cloud computing platforms to create new functionality. Some of the cloud computing platform tools used in today's mash-ups include innovations like Google's search API, which allows developers to use the power of that search engine in their applications, eBay's APIs for auctions and listings, or Amazon.com's system for creating entirely new storefronts. For example, almost any real estate website or application these days uses a mapping service such as Google Maps under the hood, illustrating how these new APIs are now commonly running alongside the more traditional database, app server, or operating system platforms.

About This Book

This book Introduces you to the Force.com platform, Salesforce's platform for building and running business applications in the cloud.

To illustrate the technologies available on the Force.com platform, and to show you just how easy it is to create your own business application with the platform, this book walks you through the process of creating a new recruiting application that runs in the cloud. To follow along you won't need to learn any programming languages or hack your way through cryptic configuration documents—instead, you'll just need to point-and-click your way through a Web interface, following the easy step-by-step instructions in the book.

> Note: Want an online version of this book? Go to
> `https://developer.salesforce.com/page/Force_Platform_Fundamentals`.

Intended Audience

This book can be easily understood by anyone from a business user to a professional developer. However, to get the most out of the book, it helps to be familiar with basic Internet and database concepts, such as tables and fields.

While the book focuses primarily on using the declarative, point-and-click functionality of the Force.com platform, Moving Beyond Point-and-Click App Development on page 325 introduces you to the platform's user interface programming tools. To fully understand that chapter, you should be familiar with HTML and JavaScript. However, all the code you need is provided, so even if you're not an experienced developer, you can still follow along to gain a deeper understanding of what can be done with the Force.com platform.

Chapter Contents

If you're already familiar with the Force.com platform, you can skip around to the chapters in which you're most interested:

Chapter	Description
Introducing the Force.com Platform	Learn about the technologies behind the Force.com platform, including the AppExchange directory.
About the Sample Recruiting App	Learn about the recruiting application that we'll be building in this book and the fictitious company for whom we'll be building it.
Reviewing Database Concepts	Review database concepts such as tables, records, fields, keys, and relationships.
Building a Simple App	Create the first custom object in our recruiting app, and add several basic fields.
Enhancing the Simple App with Advanced Fields, Data Validation, and Page Layouts	Add picklists, dependent picklists, validation rules, and formula fields to the custom object, and then edit the layout of the object's detail page.
Expanding the Simple App Using Relationships	Add five more custom objects to our recruiting app, and associate them with one another using relationships.
Securing and Sharing Data	Set up rules for who can read, create, edit, and delete records in the app.
Collaborating with Chatter	Enable Chatter for your organization so users can keep up with the information they care about.
Automating Business Processes	Define workflow rules and approval processes that assign tasks, update fields, and send emails when certain criteria are met.
Analyzing Data with Reports and Dashboards	Create custom reports, charts, and dashboards that give users a bird's-eye view of recruiting data.
Moving Beyond Point-and-Click App Development	Learn how to use Visualforce to extend the functionality of the platform by creating a mash-up

Chapter	Description
	with Google maps and adding a tool for mass updating records.
Learning More	Find out where you can get more information about developing on the platform.
Glossary	Look up the definition of any term you find unfamiliar.

Note: This book contains lots of screenshots. Because the Force.com platform is a rapidly developing platform, the screenshots might vary slightly from what you see on the screen, but don't worry! These differences should be minor and won't affect your understanding of the system.

Choosing Your Development Environment

To follow along with the exercises in this book, you'll need a Salesforce account. If you're a Salesforce customer, you can use a Force.com *sandbox*. A sandbox is a copy of your Salesforce org that you can use for testing configurations and training users without compromising the data in your production org. Professional, Enterprise, Unlimited, and Performance Editions come with free sandboxes. Users of other editions can use Developer Edition to do the exercises.

If you're new to Salesforce, or if you don't want to use a sandbox, go to `http://sforce.co/WBtUN7` and sign up for a free Developer Edition account. Developer Edition is a fully functional version of Salesforce that you can use to develop Salesforce apps. Since it's free, there are limits on the amount of users, bandwidth, and storage you're allowed, but it includes all the features in Salesforce. When you sign up, you become part of the growing community of Force.com platform developers around the world.

Note: Although Developer Edition orgs include all the features in Salesforce, these orgs are more limited than sandbox orgs. Developer Edition orgs, for example, are limited to two registered users. If you're using a Developer Edition version of Salesforce, you might not be able to complete some of the exercises in this workbook.

Sending Feedback

Questions or comments about anything you see in this book? Suggestions for topics that you'd like to see covered in future versions? Go to the Salesforce Developers discussion boards at `community.salesforce.com/sforce?category.id=developers` and let us know what you think! Or email us directly at developerforce@salesforce.com.

About Salesforce Developers

Salesforce Developers is a community of developers who customize and build applications that run in the cloud and are built with the Force.com platform. Salesforce Developers members have access to a full range of resources, including sample code, toolkits, an online developer community, and the test environments necessary for building apps. The Salesforce Developers website includes an online version of this book and has information about the Dreamforce event that we hold every year for Force.com platform developers. If you need more info, have a question to ask, are seeking a toolkit or sample, or just want to dig a little deeper into Force.com platform development, Salesforce Developers is where it all comes together.

To find out more about the resources available on the Salesforce Developers website, see developer.salesforce.com, and review the Learning More chapter.

Salesforce Trailhead

Trailhead is the easiest—and most fun—way to learn Salesforce. With more than 30 trails made up of more than 100 modules, Trailhead allows you to learn the Force.com platform and other aspects of Salesforce at your own pace. Trailhead uses interactive challenges that you complete in your own Developer Edition org to test your skills at the end of each unit. When you complete modules, you earn badges that you can display proudly on your Salesforce Developers profile. Check out Trailhead at https://trailhead.salesforce.com.

Salesforce Training & Certification

A number of examples in this book have been provided by Salesforce Training & Certification and are drawn from the expert-led training courses available around the world. Salesforce Training & Certification courses provide an opportunity to get hands-on experience with the Force.com platform and Salesforce applications, and prepare you to become Salesforce certified. Register for courses at www.salesforce.com/training.

CHAPTER 1   Introducing the Force.com Platform

In this chapter ...

- The Basics of an App's User Interface
- The Benefits of a Force.com App
- The Technologies Behind a Force.com Platform App

Force.com is a platform for creating and deploying next-generation cloud apps. Because there are no servers or software to buy or manage, you can focus solely on building apps that include built-in social and mobile functionality, business processes, reporting, and search. Your apps run on a secure, proven service that scales, tunes, and backs up data automatically.

Why use Force.com:

- **Proven** — More than 100,000+ companies trust Force.com, including many industry leaders. They've built 220,000+ apps that run in accredited, world-class data centers with backup, failover, disaster-recovery, and an uptime record exceeding 99.9%. You can see real-time system performance data at trust.salesforce.com.

- **Agile** — Force.com requires minimal coding. Assemble your apps in building-block fashion using our visual tools and library of components. Streamline development with sandbox environments, and integrate your apps using open APIs.

- **Social** — Work more effectively with your colleagues using your own secure social network. Force.com includes pre-built components for feeds, profiles, conversations, updates, and file sharing. All components are available through REST APIs that can be easily integrated into any custom app.

- **Mobile** — Run your business from your phone using the Salesforce1 mobile app. Build native mobile apps powered by a secure cloud database, with rock-solid APIs. Or build mobile-optimized browser apps, using our UI framework and HTML5 to support any device with one code base. Or mix native and HTML in a hybrid cocktail that gives you the best of both worlds. Force.com has what you need to securely deliver apps on mobile devices.

The Basics of an App's User Interface

You and your users may access Salesforce through two interfaces: the full Salesforce site, as accessed from your desktop computer, and the mobile app. Throughout this guide, we'll walk through tasks and see the impact of those customizations in both environments. If you haven't used Salesforce before, you'll find it worthwhile to log in and spend a bit of time clicking around both the full site and the mobile app. Most Salesforce editions (including Developer Edition) have a basic Salesforce Sales app, so we'll start by looking at that. The interface for these tasks has a lot in common with the interface of the app we're planning to build.

> Note: Haven't signed up for Developer Edition yet? Go to `http://sforce.co/WBtUN7`.

Apps in the Full Site Include Tabs, Fields, and Links

As you can see when you start clicking around, there are a few key elements that form the foundation of the Sales app and of most applications created with the platform.

Tabs

Across the top of the app is a set of *tabs* that segment the app into different parts. Each tab corresponds to a type of object, such as an account or contact, and within a tab you can perform actions on particular records of that tab's type. For example, when you click on the Accounts tab, you can create a new record for the "Acme" account. You can also edit existing accounts, or use a *list view* to filter lists of accounts by certain criteria. Most app development work revolves around creating tabs and defining the data and behaviors that support them.

Fields

Displayed within each record is a selection of *fields*, which is how the Force.com platform houses and organizes information. For example, a contact record includes fields such as `Last Name`, `Home Phone`, `Mailing City`, `Title`, `Birthdate`, `Reports To`, and `Account`. When developing a new app, you can customize which fields appear for a given type of record—such as for contact records—as well as how they are organized. In a Force.com platform app, users enter information with writable fields on an *edit page* and view that information with read-only fields on a *detail page*.

Links

Finally, because Force.com platform apps are delivered in a Web browser, they use *links* to provide navigation to related data. For example, on an account detail page, there are links to related records, such as the contacts who belong to the account and the sales user who manages the account. Other links take you to recently visited records and to areas of the app where users can set personal preferences. Links provide navigation within an app and to external Web sites.

Now let's look at how these elements appear in a mobile context, like Salesforce1. We still see collections of fields, and tapping links navigates us to the indicated record or external website. That said, tabs don't exist in the mobile app.

Menu Items

Instead of tabs, mobile users access objects from items in the *navigation menu*. Like a tab, each menu item in the Recent section corresponds to a type of object, such as an account or contact. Objects are surfaced based on which objects you've viewed or worked with recently. Tapping **Show More** displays all the objects available based on your profile and permissions. When you tap one of these items, such as Accounts, you can create a new record or look your recently visited records. To edit an existing record, you first need to tap the record to open it.

Menu items also include things like Tasks, Dashboards, and Chatter, most of which we'll talk about later in this guide.

The Salesforce1 Mobile App Includes Menu Items, Fields, and Links

The Benefits of a Force.com App

To better understand what the platform is best suited for, let's look beyond the core elements of tabs, fields, and links, and into the types of applications they enable. Two huge benefits start to come into focus when you look at Force.com platform apps: they're data-centric and collaborative.

Data-Centric Apps

Because the platform is centered around a database, it allows you to write apps that are *data-centric*. A data-centric app is an application that is based on structured, consistent information such as you find in a database or XML file. We can find these data-centric apps everywhere, in small desktop databases like Microsoft Access or FileMaker, all the way to the huge systems running on database management systems like Oracle or MySQL. Unlike applications that are built around unstructured data, like plain text documents or HTML files, data-centric apps make it easy to control, access, and manage data.

For example, consider an exercise such as trying to determine the total sales for a month from a set of Microsoft Word-based contracts versus a set of contracts in a simple database. Whereas it takes a lot of effort to open each Word document, find the contract total, and then add them all together, if this data is stored in the database of a data-centric app, we can more efficiently get the same result by issuing a single query.

While most people don't need a data-centric application to keep track of anything other than contacts, photos, or music, companies of all sizes constantly need to query and aggregate their large amounts of data to make fast business decisions. As a result, the data-centric nature of the Force.com platform makes it the perfect platform to build and host business applications.

Collaborative Apps

Because the platform can be accessed by multiple users at the same time, it allows you to write apps that are *collaborative*. A collaborative app is an application with data and services that are shared by multiple users in different locations. Unlike more traditional forms of software that are installed on a single machine and are hard to access from a distance, collaborative apps on the platform can be accessed from anywhere in the world with only a Web browser. This makes it easy for teams to work together on activities like selling a product, managing a project, or hiring an employee.

In addition to easy access over a Web browser, a number of built-in platform features also facilitate productive group collaboration:

* Use the platform's **security and sharing model** to finely control a user's access to different data.
* Use **workflow rules** to automatically assign tasks, update data, or send e-mail alerts when certain business events occur, such as the creation of a new record or a change in the value of a record field.
* Use **approval processes** to set up a sequence of steps necessary for a record to be approved, including who must approve it at each step.

Collectively, these features provide a framework for sharing apps across groups, divisions, and entire corporations without relinquishing administrative control over sensitive data.

The Technologies Behind a Force.com Platform App

Now that we've talked about the kinds of apps the platform can build, let's review some of the technologies behind the platform. These technologies have a big impact on what the platform supports and what it's like to develop on it.

Table 1: Key Technologies Behind the Platform

Technology	Description
Multitenant architecture	An application model in which all users and apps share a single, common infrastructure and code base.
Metadata-driven development model	An app development model that allows apps to be defined as declarative "blueprints," with no code required. Data models, objects, forms, workflows, and more are defined by metadata.
API Access	Several application programming interfaces (APIs) provide direct access to all data stored in Force.com from virtually any programming language and platform. • The SOAP API and REST API integrate your organization's data with other applications • The RESTful Bulk API (also available using Data Loader) loads or deletes large numbers of records • The Metadata API manages customizations in your organization (also available using the Force.com Migration Tool) • The Chatter REST API accesses Chatter feeds and social data • The Streaming API provides notifications reflecting data changes in your organization
Apex	The world's first on-demand programming language, which runs in the cloud on the Force.com platform servers.
Visualforce	A framework for creating feature-rich user interfaces for apps in the cloud.
Mobile Access	With Salesforce mobile apps, you can access custom apps built using the Force.com platform's point-and-click development tools. Your users can access those apps on their mobile devices—and you don't have to learn any mobile programming languages.
AppExchange directory	A Web directory where hundreds of Force.com apps are available to Salesforce customers to review, demo, comment upon, and/or install. Developers can submit their apps for listing on the AppExchange directory if they want to share them with the community.

A Multitenant Architecture

In a *multitenant architecture*, all users share the same infrastructure and the same version of the Force.com platform. In contrast to their single-tenant counterparts, such as client-server enterprise applications or email servers, multitenant architectures release upgrades automatically and simultaneously for all users. Consequently, no one has to worry about buying and maintaining their own physical stack of hardware and software, or making sure that their applications always have the latest patch installed.

Besides the Force.com platform, several popular, consumer-based applications also use a multitenant architecture, including eBay, My Yahoo!, and Google Gmail. Multitenant architecture allows these applications to be low-cost, quick to deploy, and open to rapid innovation—exactly the qualities for which Salesforce has also become known.

On-Demand, Multitenant Applications that Run in the Cloud

The platform's multitenant architecture also impacts how developers use the platform to create new applications. Specifically, it defines a clear boundary between the platform and the applications that run on it. A boundary is important because it allows applications to define their own components without jeopardizing the functionality of the core platform or the data stored by other users.

A Metadata-Driven Development Model

The Force.com platform uses a *metadata-driven development model* to help app developers become more productive in putting together apps. It means that the basic functionality of an app—that is, the tabs, forms, and links—are defined as metadata in a database rather than being hard-coded in a programming language. When a user accesses an app through the Force.com platform, it renders the app's metadata into the interface the user experiences.

As a result of metadata-driven development, the Force.com platform app developers work at a much higher level of abstraction than if they developed applications using Java or C#, and are shielded from having to worry about low-level system details that the platform handles automatically. At the same time, Force.com platform developers can also leverage advanced features that the platform provides by default.

Customizing your app's metadata might sound intimidating, but as you'll see in this book, the platform's user interface makes it easy. Anyone who is familiar with using a Web browser can quickly get up to speed, even if he or she doesn't know any programming languages.

> **Tip:** Developers can use the *Force.com Metadata API* to programmatically manage their app's setup. The Force.com Metadata API provides an alternative to the platform's user interface by allowing developers to directly modify the XML files that control their organization's metadata. Developers can also use the Metadata API to migrate configuration changes between organizations, and create their own tools for managing organization and application metadata. For more information, see *Metadata API Developer Guide*.

Although at first glance metadata-driven development may seem somewhat esoteric, it's exactly the same model for how Web browsers work. Instead of hard coding the definition of a Web page in a free-form programming language, a Web page author first defines the page as HTML, which is itself a kind of metadata. When a user requests a page, the Web browser renders the page using the metadata provided in the HTML tags. Even though the HTML/browser combination does not allow authors as much formatting power as they might get in a regular publishing tool, it simplifies the work of publishing content to a wide audience and increases the Web page author's overall productivity.

Likewise, the Force.com platform vastly simplifies the work of building an app and increases a developer's overall productivity. And, like Web pages that use JavaScript or Flash to add functionality to HTML pages, the Force.com platform also provides ways for more advanced developers to add custom functionality to the apps you build.

APIs

The platform's metadata-driven development model allows app developers to quickly build a lot of functionality with tools provided by the platform; however, sometimes app developers want to modify the actual data in an app and use third-party services to create more customized app behaviors. To do this, they can use a number of APIs to integrate with the platform. The core set of APIs include Force.com SOAP API and REST API, the Bulk API, Streaming API, and Metadata API. You can call these APIs from a wide variety of client-side languages - and toolkits are also available to ease the integration. For more information, see "Which API Do I Use?" in the Salesforce Help.

Our APIs provide straightforward, powerful, and open ways to programmatically access the data and capabilities of any app running on the platform. They allow programmers to access and manipulate apps from any server location, using any programming language that supports Web services, like Java, PHP, C#, or .NET. For more information, see https://developer.salesforce.com/page/Integration.

Apex

As you might expect from the company that delivered the world's first cloud computing platform, Salesforce also introduced the world's first cloud computing programming language, Apex. Apex, whose syntax is similar to Java, the most popular programming language for Web apps, runs on the Force.com platform servers. Apex is specifically designed for building business applications to manage data and processes within the larger context of the Force.com platform. The language provides a uniquely powerful and productive approach to creating functionality and logic, allowing developers to focus just on the elements specific to their application, while leaving the rest of the "plumbing" to the Force.com platform.

The majority of this book is intended for readers who don't necessarily code, so Apex is beyond the scope of what we'll discuss here; however, you can learn everything there is to know at `developer.salesforce.com/page/Apex`.

Custom User Interface

At the front of any great business application is a great user interface that's easy to use, powerful, and suited exactly for the tasks, users, and devices the application serves. Visualforce is a complete framework for creating such user interfaces, enabling any kind of interface design and interaction to be built and delivered entirely in the cloud. The user interfaces you build with Visualforce can extend the standard Force.com platform look and feel, or replace it with a completely unique style and set of sophisticated interactions. Because Visualforce markup is ultimately rendered into HTML, designers can use Visualforce tags alongside standard HTML, JavaScript, Flash, or any other code that can execute within an HTML page on the platform. And that's only the beginning: you can also use Visualforce pages to combine data from multiple Force.com platform objects, or blend data from Web services into your applications, as we discuss in Moving Beyond Point-and-Click App Development on page 325.

In Winter '16, Salesforce unveiled Lightning Experience, a new user interface that makes the Force.com platform faster and easier to use than ever before. In Lightning Experience, you can use the Lightning Component framework to create dynamic, single-page web apps across platforms. The Lightning Component framework includes ready-to-use components—like the App Launcher component and the Recent Items component—that you can combine with components you develop yourself as you build your app.

Because Lightning Experience is still being continuously developed and improved, this book references ·
Salesforce Classic. To learn more about Lightning Experience, try the Get Started with Lightning Experience
trail at https://trailhead.salesforce.com/trail/lex_admin_implementation.

Mobile Access

As the primary points of Internet access shift from desktops and laptops to smartphones and tablets, apps
that don't provide mobile access to critical data will quickly become obsolete. Don't let your app get
trampled by the mobile stampede! Instead, use the Salesforce1 app or Salesforce Classic Mobile to deliver
your Force.com customizations to your mobile users.

So how do you decide which mobile app to use? Salesforce1 and Salesforce Classic Mobile are each apps
themselves. Downloadable versions of these apps install on mobile devices and use the native functionality
of the device. When users log in on a mobile device, they can access and update their data via an interface
specially designed for mobile device screens. Both apps allow you to work with most standard Sales objects,
some standard Service objects, and all custom objects.

Salesforce1

Administrators don't have to create special configurations for mobile users to access their organization's
data. What users see is controlled by their profile and user permissions, and the app respects any
customizations made in the full Salesforce site. In addition, this app includes Chatter, so your users can
keep collaborating while on the go.

Salesforce1 is supported on Apple® iPhones® and iPads®, as well as Android™ phones. If your organization
prohibits installing the downloadable app to corporate-issued devices, Salesforce1 is also available
from a mobile web browser.

When you're ready to take your app mobile, see the *Salesforce1 App Admin Guide* or the *Salesforce Classic
Mobile Implementation Guide*.

AppExchange

The final piece of technology that differentiates the Force.com platform from other platforms is the
AppExchange. The AppExchange is a Web directory where apps built on the Force.com platform are
available to Salesforce customers to browse, demo, review, and install. Developers can submit their apps
for listing on the AppExchange directory if they want to share them with the community.

To fully appreciate the benefits of the AppExchange, take a quick tour at
`http://sites.force.com/appexchange`. There you'll see the hundreds of innovative and
exciting apps that exist today, including everything from payroll management to telephony integration,
service and support surveys, adoption dashboards, and beyond. Some of these apps have been created

inhouse at Salesforce, but most are built by partners and individual developers who have chosen to take advantage of the Force.com platform.

CHAPTER 2 About the Sample Recruiting App

The goal of this book is to show you how easy it is to create powerful, multifaceted applications that solve common business problems. To do so, let's walk through the steps of creating a simple application for a make-believe company called Universal Containers.

Like many companies that have grown rapidly, Universal Containers has been experiencing a few growing pains, especially in its Human Resources department. In this book, we're going to build a Recruiting app for the company that allows it to move away from the Microsoft Word documents and Microsoft Excel spreadsheets that it has traditionally used to an application that's available on demand.

By the time we finish building the Recruiting app in this book, you should feel confident enough to build a custom application in the cloud that suits your own company's needs. So let's get started!

About Universal Containers

First, let's learn a little more about our fictional company, Universal Containers.

Universal Containers is a rapidly growing international supplier of container products. The company produces every kind of container from simple overnight letter mailers to custom equipment packaging to large cargo shipping containers. In addition, Universal Containers develops and maintains its own proprietary software to facilitate the design of its various types of containers. As such, Universal Containers has a very diverse group of employees, including facilities and operations professionals, software and design engineers, financial accountants, and legal and human resources personnel.

Historically, the Human Resources department has used Microsoft Word documents and Microsoft Excel spreadsheets to manage the recruiting and hiring process for new employees. However, over the last two quarters it's become evident that unless this process is replaced by one that is more collaborative, reliable, and scalable, the department won't be able to meet its hiring goals for this fiscal year. Universal Containers needs a centralized application that can bring all of its recruiting and hiring processes together, and the company has hired us to solve this problem. Our approach will be to leverage their Salesforce account and build a recruiting application on the Force.com platform. We're going to introduce Universal Containers to the world of cloud computing!

Considerations for the Recruiting App

After meeting with Megan Smith, Universal Containers' vice president of Human Resources, we've drawn up a few requirements for the new Recruiting app. The app needs to:

- Track positions in all stages of the process, from those that are open to those that have been filled or canceled.
- Track all of the candidates who apply for a particular position, including the status of their application (whether they've had a phone screen, are scheduled for interviews, have been rejected or hired, or have passed on an offer that was presented).
- Track the posting of jobs on external employment websites, such as Monster.com.
- Allow employees to post reviews for candidates whom they've interviewed.
- Provide security for the recruiting data so that it's not mistakenly viewed, edited, or deleted by employees who shouldn't have access.
- Automatically inform the relevant recruiter about the next steps that should be taken when a decision has been made about an applicant.
- Automatically inform all employees of new positions that have been posted.
- Make sure that a new job opening has executive approval before it becomes active.

- Include reports that give users an overview of recruiting status.
- Allow recruiters to map the locations of all candidates who are applying for a position, to better understand relocation expenses.
- Make it easy to perform several similar tasks at once, like rejecting multiple job applications.
- Automatically post open positions on Universal Containers' public website.

An app that meets these requirements is going to greatly increase the efficiency of Universal Containers' recruiting and hiring processes.

Building the App: Our Design

Let's take a look at the different parts of the Force.com platform that we'll use to implement Universal Containers' Recruiting app. We'll learn about all of these things in a lot more detail in later chapters, but for now, this quick preview will give you an idea about what's in store.

Custom Objects

Custom objects are the native components that model the data we need to store in our Recruiting app. Similar to a database table, a custom object is composed of several fields that store information such as a job applicant's name, or the maximum salary for a particular position. However, unlike traditional database tables, we don't need to write any SQL in order to create custom objects. We can simply point and click in the platform to create as many objects as we need.

For our Recruiting app, we'll be creating six custom objects to track recruiting-related data:

- Position
- Candidate
- Job Application
- Review
- Job Posting
- Employment Website

Most of these objects will be displayed as tabs in our application and menu items in Salesforce1. When a user clicks one of the tabs, he or she will have access to individual instances of that particular object, as shown in the following screenshot.

One of the powerful features of a custom object is the fact that it can have relationships with other objects in the system. For example, for every review written by an interviewer and entered into the system, we'll want to associate it with the job application of the candidate who was being interviewed. Again, we won't need to write any SQL to make this happen—thanks to the platform, defining a relationship will be as simple as a few clicks of the mouse.

Security and Sharing Rules

Another important function that we'll need to build into our app is the ability to restrict access to data that particular users shouldn't see, without preventing other users from performing their jobs effectively. We're going to implement this requirement with a group of components that we've grouped under a single term: *security and sharing rules*.

With security and sharing rules, we'll first specify which custom objects a particular user should be allowed to create, view, or edit (for example, Candidate and Position), and then which instances of those objects should be accessible (for example, the records for candidate John Smith or the Senior Sales Manager position). Controlling our data either with the wide brush of object-level security or with the more detailed brush of record-level security will give us a lot of power and flexibility in controlling what users can and can't see.

Automated Processes

Three of our requirements involve automating business processes, such as triggering an alert email to a recruiter whenever a job application's status has changed, and submitting new job openings for executive approval. Once again, the Force.com platform makes these requirements easy for us to implement natively with the built-in *Process Builder* and *approval process* components.

Process Builder and approval processes allow us to create business logic based on rules:

- Process Builder can assign tasks to users, update fields, or send email alerts.
- Approval processes allow users to submit sensitive records like new contracts or purchase orders to other users for approval.

For example, in our Recruiting app, we can create a process that triggers an event whenever the status of a job application has changed to Reject or Extend an Offer, as illustrated below.

Process When a Job Application's Status Has Changed

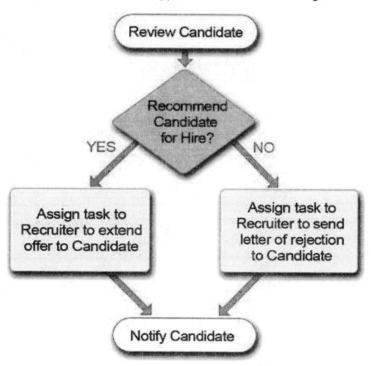

When a hiring manager makes a decision to either extend an offer to or reject the candidate, changing the status of the application triggers the appropriate task to be assigned to the recruiter for that position. Based upon the hiring manager's decision, the recruiter performs the appropriate follow-up task.

Similarly, we can define an automatic approval process that sends all new positions to the appropriate management for approval. If the position is approved, its status automatically changes to Open - Approved and recruiters can start the hiring process. If the position is rejected, its status automatically changes to Closed - Not Approved and the position won't be filled.

Custom Reports and Dashboards

Finally, we need to give users a way to inspect the status of all positions and job applicants in the Universal Containers recruiting program. Managers need to delve into the intricate details of how each recruiter is performing, while executives just want a high-level overview of how departments are doing with staffing goals.

We can meet these requirements using reports and dashboards. Using report builder, we can create detailed reports with filters, conditional highlighting, subtotals, and charts. With dashboard builder, we can quickly create a dashboard of up to 20 different components on a single page.

Visualforce

We'll be able to use point-and-click tools to satisfy nearly all of our Recruiting app use cases; however, there are a few use cases, such as the mapping of candidate locations and the posting of positions on Universal Containers' public jobs site, that will require us to use Visualforce, the Force.com platform's tag-based markup language that allows you to build sophisticated, custom user interfaces for apps. We won't address these use cases until the very last chapter, and when we do, this book will provide all the code you need.

Although we haven't yet gone into detail about how any of this stuff is going to work, you can probably see now just how flexible and powerful the Force.com platform can be when you're creating a custom app.

In the next chapter, we'll start out by building our first custom object. We'll swiftly get a feel for how the platform interface works, and it won't be any time at all before you're building app components easily and quickly. When it's this easy, you can't help but become an expert!

CHAPTER 3 Reviewing Database Concepts

Now that we've introduced the power of the Force.com platform and learned about the requirements of the Recruiting app that we're going to build, let's take a moment to talk about databases and why a simple understanding of database concepts can help you realize the full potential of the platform and make your app development a whole lot easier.

As you know, the underlying architecture of the platform includes a database where your data is stored. This means that all of the information you enter is stored in that database and then retrieved from the database whenever you view it within your app.

Historically, companies were required to buy, build, and maintain their own databases and IT infrastructures in order to distribute and run their applications. Cloud computing on the Force.com platform provides an alternative and makes it easy for you, as a company or as a sole developer, to build and deliver your app. Part of the simplicity of the cloud computing model is that the technical responsibilities of maintaining and running all of the database hardware and software is handled by the hosting company (in this case, Salesforce), so you can focus on developing your app.

It's worth pointing out that although your data is stored in a database and a simple understanding of database concepts is helpful, you don't need to be a database developer to build an app on the platform. We won't be doing any traditional database programming in the course of developing our app.

What's a Database?

In simple terms, a *database* is an organized collection of information. Common examples include a phone book, a library catalog, an employee directory, a catalog of the MP3s you own, or in the case of our Recruiting app, information about the open positions at a company, the people who are applying for those positions, and the managers at our company who are in charge of hiring each position.

Typically, you use a database to collect information about people, things, or concepts that are important to you and whatever project you're working on. In standard database language, the category of a person, thing, or concept you want to store information about is referred to as an *entity*, although in standard Force.com platform terminology, we refer to this as an *object*.

In a database, each entity is represented by a *table*. A database table is simply a list of information, presented with rows and columns, about the category of person, thing, or concept you want to track. So in a phone book, you might have a table to store information about residences and another table to store information about businesses; or in a library catalog, you might have one table to store information about books and another to store information about authors.

In our Recruiting app, we'll have one table to store information about open positions, another table to store information about the candidates applying for the positions, and a table to store information about hiring managers. (Our Recruiting app will have more than just this, but we'll get to that later.)

In very simplistic terms, a Force.com platform object is similar to a database table in that you'll have a separate object for each person, thing, or concept about which you want to collect information. In reality, a Force.com platform object is much more than this because the full functionality of the platform is behind each object. Each object automatically has built-in features like a user interface, a security and sharing model, workflow processes, and much more that you'll learn about in the rest of this book.

> Note: As we introduce database concepts, "object" and "table" will be used interchangeably because they are similar. Just remember that a Force.com platform object is much more than just a database table.

It's important to understand that a single database table, or Force.com platform object, should contain only one type of information. You don't want to lump all of your information into one table, so you wouldn't store positions, candidates, and hiring managers all in the same place. Not only is this not good database design, but it doesn't allow you to relate objects to one another. For example, if all of our data were in one table, how would we ever know which candidates were applying for which positions, or which managers were in charge of hiring for which positions?

As we define our app, it's important for us to keep this in mind and ask ourselves questions like, "What kind of information do we want to store? Can we separate our information into distinct categories so that each object holds only one type of person, thing, or concept?" The answers to these questions will guide us as we design the structure of our application.

What's in a Database?

As we mentioned, a database table presents your information in rows and columns. Let's take a look at how a table of positions might look:

Position Information in a Table

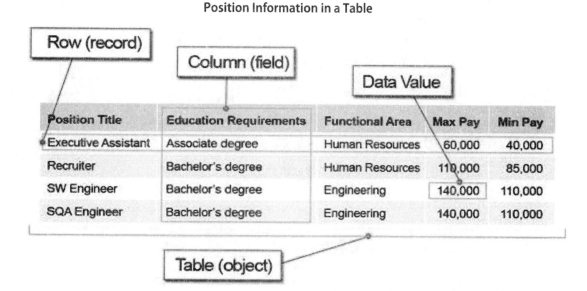

Each row in the table represents the information about a specific instance of the object, for example, the Recruiter position or the SW Engineer position. In standard Force.com platform terminology, we call this a *record*. For every object you want to track in your app, you'll have multiple records to represent each individual item about which you're storing information. It's common for users who are new to the platform to confuse the meanings of object and record. It'll make your development a lot easier if you remember that an object is a category of information, such as a position or candidate, and the record is a single instance of an object, such as a SW Engineer.

> **Note:**   As a side note here, we'll mention that the platform includes a set of built-in objects when you first start using it; we call these *standard objects*. One example of a standard object is the User object, which stores information about each person who is a user of the app, like our hiring managers. You can also build your own objects to store information that's unique to your app; we call these *custom objects*. Both standard objects and custom objects are not really all that different—one kind is prebuilt for you, and the other you build yourself. We'll talk more about these later as you start to build your app.

Now let's look at the columns in the table. Each column lists a particular piece of information such as the Position Title or Max Pay. We refer to these as *fields*. Every object has a set of fields that you use to enter the information about a particular record. For each field in the table, a single item of data that you enter, such as Human Resources in the Functional Area, is referred to as a *data value*.

Just like objects, fields come in two varieties: standard and custom. The standard fields are the ones that are built into the platform and automatically added for you. The custom fields are the ones you define to store specific pieces of information that are unique to your app. Fundamentally, there is no difference between standard and custom fields. Both are simply columns in the database table. We'll talk more about standard and custom fields later when you begin building your app.

What's a Relational Database?

Now you have some information stored in your database, but so what? You could easily make a list of positions using Microsoft Excel or some other spreadsheet software. For each position, you could even list the hiring manager in a field called Hiring Manager, like:

Position Information with Hiring Manager Field

Position Title	Education Requirements	Functional Area	Max Pay	Min Pay	Hiring Manager
Executive Assistant	Associate degree	Human Resources	60,000	40,000	Phil Katz
Recruiter	Bachelor's degree	Human Resources	110,000	85,000	Megan Smith
SW Engineer	Bachelor's degree	Engineering	140,000	110,000	Andrew Goldberg
SQA Engineer	Bachelor's degree	Engineering	140,000	110,000	Ben Stuart

But what if a hiring manager is responsible for hiring more than one position? You would need to have duplicate records for the same hiring manager so you could capture every position for which that hiring manager is responsible, like:

Position Information with Duplicate Hiring Managers

Position Title	Education Requirements	Functional Area	Max Pay	Min Pay	Hiring Manager
Executive Assistant	Associate degree	Human Resources	60,000	40,000	Phil Katz
Recruiter	Bachelor's degree	Human Resources	110,000	85,000	Megan Smith
Senior Recruiter	Bachelor's degree	Human Resources	115,000	95,000	Megan Smith
SW Engineer	Bachelor's degree	Engineering	140,000	110,000	Andrew Goldberg
Senior SW Engineer	Bachelor's degree	Engineering	140,000	110,000	Andrew Goldberg
SQA Engineer	Bachelor's degree	Engineering	140,000	110,000	Ben Stuart

This is not a good database design! Using this approach, data is repeated unnecessarily. In addition, there is really no way to capture additional information about our hiring managers, like their email addresses or phone numbers. And if we try to add information about which candidates are applying for each position, you can imagine that our simple table will quickly become extremely complex and unmanageable.

As we mentioned before, you want to create separate database tables, or objects, for each person, thing, or concept you want to track. A better way to model our scenario here would be to create one object for positions, one object for candidates, and one object for hiring managers. (Luckily, the platform has a standard object that we'll be able to use to represent our hiring managers—the User object.)

Once we have our data separated into discrete objects, we can easily relate objects to each other. This is what a relational database is all about! A *relationship* is an association between two or more tables. For example, we can relate positions to hiring managers so we know which positions each hiring manager is responsible for.

Positions Related to Hiring Managers

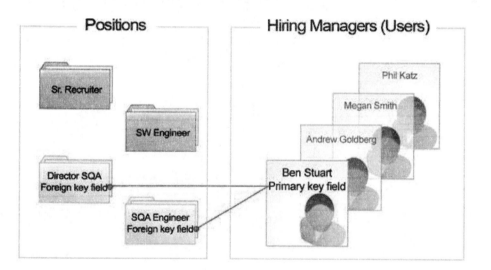

From a technical standpoint, each table in a relational database has a field in which the data value uniquely identifies the record. This field is called the *primary key*. The primary key is one part of what defines the relationship; the other part is the *foreign key*. A foreign key is a field whose value is the same as the primary key of another table. You can think of a foreign key as a copy of a primary key from another table. The relationship is made between two tables by matching the values of the foreign key in one table with the values of the primary key in another.

Primary and foreign keys are fundamental to the concept of relationships because they enable tables to be related to each other. As you begin building your app, you won't really need to think too much about primary keys and foreign keys. The important concept to understand here is that in a relational database, objects are related to each other through the use of common fields that define those relationships.

Summary of Database Concepts

At this point, we're ready to dive into the building of our Recruiting app. But first let's recap what we've learned about databases. Whether this was your first introduction to databases or whether you're already an experienced database developer who's new to the Force.com platform, the important things to remember are:

- A *database* is an organized collection of information.
- A database table stores information about a single type of person, thing, or concept—such as a job position. In the Force.com platform, we use the term *object* here (even though an object is much more than this, as you'll see).
- A database row, or *record* in Force.com platform terms, represents a single instance of an object—such as the SW Engineer position.
- A *field* stores a particular piece of information on a record.
- *Relationships* define the connection between two objects, and objects are related to each other through the use of common fields.

Now that we've got that all covered, let's get started building our first object!

CHAPTER 4   Building a Simple App

In this chapter ...

Just as traditional programming books first teach you how to write a simple "Hello World" program before getting into more complicated things, in this chapter, we're going to create a very simple version of the Recruiting app to show you just how easy it is to get started with the Force.com platform. Along the way we'll orient ourselves to the platform's user interface (where we'll be doing most of our work), and we'll learn how to create and configure our first custom object. Although easy and straightforward, the tasks we complete here will be the first step in developing a full-featured Recruiting app. So let's dive right in!

Get Familiar with the Setup Area

Since we're going to spend most of our time working in the Setup area of the platform, let's first become familiar with what it is and how to navigate to it.

The Setup area is a place to build and customize applications and to administer and monitor organizations and users, all in one. We perform almost every task we need to create our app in the Setup area, so most of the "Try It Out" sections of the book are going to start with an instruction like "From Setup, enter *Apps* in the `Quick Find` box, then select **Apps**." This is a short way of saying:

1. Depending on your organization settings, you'll access the Setup area in one of two ways. Look at the header at the top of the page.

   If you see **Setup** in the header, click it.

   If you don't see **Setup** in the header, click your name, then select **Setup**.

2. Once you're in the Setup area, you'll see a menu on the left side of the page. From that menu, enter *Apps* in the `Quick Find` box, then select **Apps**.

The text that you enter and the page name that you click (in this example, **Apps**) will change depending on the task you're performing.

The Setup Area

The navigational sidebar includes expandable lists of all the tools that are available in the Setup area. The tools include options for setting up, maintaining, and customizing your organization and for building, extending, and managing apps.

> **Tip:** Since you'll be developing apps in Force.com, you might want to make the Setup area your default landing page when you log in. To do this:
>
> 1. At the top of the page, click the down arrow next to your name. From the menu under your name, select **My Settings** or **Setup**—whichever one appears.
>
> 2. From the left panel, select one of the following:
>
>   - If you clicked **My Settings**, select **Display & Layout** > **Customize My Pages**.
>   - If you clicked **Setup**, select **My Personal Information** > **Personal Information**, then click **Edit**.
>
> 3. Select **Make Setup My Default Landing Page**.
>
> 4. Click **Save**.

Now that we know what we're looking at, let's start creating our simple app.

Introducing Apps

What should we do first? If we were writing a software application, the first thing we'd need to do is build a project where we could store all the code that we were going to write. With the Force.com platform, the first thing we need to do is create a new app.

Like a programming project, an *app* is little more than a container for all of the objects, tabs, and other functionality that we're going to build as part of our Recruiting application. It consists simply of a name, a logo, and an ordered set of tabs. The simplest app contains only one tab—the Home tab—and a default logo. As we define more tabs in the remainder of this book, we can add them to the app later.

Let's start clicking through the process of actually creating a simple app now. Log in to your Salesforce account so you can follow along!

 Note: Because the platform is continually evolving, you might find that the screenshots you see in this book vary slightly from what you see on your screen. These changes should be minor and shouldn't affect your understanding.

Try It Out: Define an App

1. Open a browser and go to `www.salesforce.com`.
2. Click **Log in to Salesforce**.
3. Enter your username and password.
4. From Setup, enter `Apps` in the `Quick Find` box, then select **Apps**.
5. If you see an introductory splash page, simply click **Continue**.

     Note: Many parts of the application have these splash pages to help you understand what you can do with the platform. If you never want to see a particular page again, just select **Don't show me this page again**.

Welcome to the Apps list page! Like many of the setup tools, the starting page for the Apps tool consists of a list of all the apps that are currently enabled for your organization. Depending on which edition you're using or have installed from the AppExchange, you'll probably already have some standard apps listed here.

Beyond the Basics

There are actually two ways to create an app. The **Quick Start** button creates an app with one custom object and associated tab. With the **New** button, you create an app with a logo, add existing

---

tabs, and specify the app's visibility for your profiles. In this book we'll use the **New** button, but feel free to try out the **Quick Start** button later.

6. Click **New**. The New Custom App wizard appears.

7. If you are a new user, select **Custom app**.

8. In the `App Label` field, enter *Recruiting*.

The app label is the name that represents our app in the Force.com app menu that appears at the top right of all pages. Users can use this menu to switch back and forth between apps.

Notice that a vertical red bar appears just to the left of this `Label` field. This red bar indicates that you must provide a value for this field in order to save your work. If you don't enter a value here and try to proceed, an error message is displayed.

Required Fields Highlighted in Red

New Custom App   Help for this Page ?

Step 2. Enter the Details   Step 2 of 5

Fill in the fields below to define the custom app.

Error: Invalid Data.
Review all error messages below to correct your data.

Custom App Information | = Required Information

App Label   [   ]
               Error: You must enter a value
               Example: HRforce, Financeforce, Bugforce

9. Click your mouse inside the `App Name` field.

The app name is what developers use to identify an app when writing code for the Force.com platform. We won't do anything in this book that uses the app name, but the field is required, so it needs a value. Fortunately, when you enter a value in the `App Label` field, the same value should automatically appear in the `App Name` field. If it doesn't, enter *Recruiting* in the `App Name` field now.

10. In the `Description` field, enter *Manage positions, candidates, and job applications, and track job postings on employment websites.*

11. Click **Next**.

The next screen in the New Custom App wizard allows you to specify the image file to use for this app's logo. Whenever the app is selected in the Force.com app menu, this logo appears in the upper-left corner of all pages. Since we're just creating a simple app, let's accept the default logo that's already provided. We can always change it later.

12. Click **Next**.

As we said before, an app is a container for an ordered collection of tabs, and this step of the New Custom App wizard allows us to specify which tabs we want to include in our new app. The `Available Tabs` list shows us the standard and custom tabs that are available for us to choose, and the `Selected Tabs` list shows us which tabs are already included, listed in the order that they should be displayed. You'll notice that one tab, the Home tab, is already included in our app by default. This is because the Home tab is required in every app, and must always be in the first position; however, you can use the `Default Landing Tab` drop-down menu to select which tab is first displayed when the app opens.

Again, since we're just creating a simple app, let's accept the defaults and move on. We'll add more tabs later.

13. Click **Next**.

Now that we've defined some of the basic features of our app, you might be wondering what remains to be done in the New Custom App wizard—shouldn't we already be done? It turns out that one crucial step remains: we need to define the users who can access our app.

In this step of the New Custom App wizard, we can choose which user profiles should have access to the app. We'll learn more about profiles in Securing and Sharing Data on page 145. For now, just understand that every user is assigned to a profile, and profiles control which apps the users assigned to that profile can view.

14. Select the `Visible` checkbox next to the Standard User and System Administrator profiles.

15. Click **Save**.

That's it!

Look at What We've Done

Now that we've made it back to the Apps list page, let's see what we've just done. First of all, we've got a new entry in the Apps list—our Recruiting app! It shows up in the list in the same order it's going to appear in our Force.com app menu. In fact, let's go look at the Force.com app menu now.

Force.com App Menu

> 💡 **Tip:** If you want to change the position of our app in this menu, do so from the Apps list page by clicking **Reorder** and rearranging the available apps as you see fit.

Now select the Recruiting app from the menu and see what happens—our app is launched with a single Home tab! We've created the Recruiting app's Home tab, and we've added it to the Force.com app menu. That's how easy it is to get started.

You'll notice that the approach we're taking here is iterative: we'll build part of the app, look at what we've accomplished, and then add to it. This sequence not only reflects the fact that we're leading you through the steps of building an app in this book, but you'll also find that in building Force.com platform apps in general, this iterative process is common.

During the course of this book, you'll also notice that unlike with traditional coding projects, your app is always functional. There's no build or compile phase, and as a result, you'll almost never be chasing down syntax bugs or other typos. In fact, with this simple one-tab app, you can already utilize all of the built-in functionality that comes with the platform, including search, calendar events and tasks, user preferences, and a familiar user interface.

Introducing Objects

Now that our app is functional (but rather boring), let's make it a little more interesting by introducing our first object.

As you might remember from the last chapter, an *object* is very similar to a database table in the Force.com platform. The platform comes with a number of standard objects, like contacts, accounts, and cases, which support default apps like Salesforce Sales and Salesforce Call Center. We can also define custom objects that allow us to store information specific to our Recruiting app.

Whether they're standard or custom, Force.com platform objects not only provide a structure for storing data but they also power the interface elements that allow users to interact with the data, such as tabs, the layout of fields on a page, and lists of related records. Because any object can correspond to a tab, and an ordered collection of tabs makes up an app, objects make up the heart of any app that we create with the platform.

With custom objects being so important—they have lots to do with how our app will look, behave, and feel—what we do with custom objects and how we use them quickly becomes essential to creating a successful app. The design of the data model behind an app is typically the biggest factor in its success or failure.

That's enough talk about objects for now. Let's go define one!

The Position Custom Object

The first custom object that we'll create for our Recruiting app reflects a typical recruiting task: describing a position. Recruiters at Universal Containers need to keep track of all the positions they're hiring for, such as a Senior Developer, Sales Engineer, or Benefits Specialist. They'll need easy access to all positions in the system through a tab, and they'll need to include certain information for each position, such as its minimum and maximum salary range, the position's location, and its hiring manager. In Force.com platform terms, we'll create a custom object, create a custom tab for that object, and then define some custom fields.

Try It Out: Define the Position Custom Object

To create the Position custom object, we'll go back to the Setup area.

1. From Setup, enter *Objects* in the `Quick Find` box, then select **Objects**.
2. On the Custom Objects page, click **New Custom Object**.

Unlike defining a custom app, which we did through the New Custom App wizard, defining a custom object is confined to just one page. You'll find that the platform uses wizards or single pages depending on the amount of information that needs to be specified.

Custom Object Definition Page

New Custom Object   Help for this Page

 Permissions for this object are disabled for all profiles by default. You can enable object permissions by explicitly editing
custom profiles. Tell me more!   Don't show this message again

Custom Object Definition
Edit   [Save] [Save & New] [Cancel]

Custom Object Information   ǀ = Required Information

The singular and plural labels are used in tabs, page layouts, and reports.
Label | Position | Example: Account
Plural Label | Positions | Example: Accounts
Starts with vowel   ☐
sound

The Object Name is used when referencing the object via the API.
Object Name | Position | Example: Account

Description | This object stores information about the open job positions at our company. |

---

3. In the Label field, enter *Position*.

4. In the Plural Label field, enter *Positions*.

5. The Object Name field is defaulted to *Position*. Let's leave it as is.

The Label and Plural Label of a custom object are what users see in all of the object's related user interface elements, such as the object's tab or in search results headings. Object labels work best as nouns, and the plural label is always used to label a custom object's tab (if you create a tab for your object).

The value of a custom object's Object Name represents the unique name for the object when it's referenced in other areas of the platform, such as formulas and Visualforce pages. This value is helpfully auto-generated based on the value that you enter for the Label, except that all spaces and punctuation are replaced with underscore characters. We'll talk more about formulas and Visualforce later in this book. For now, keep in mind that the Object Name value must be unique across all objects defined in your organization.

 Note: Within the platform, Object Name is actually stored with ___c appended to the end as a suffix (for example, Position___c). This identifies it as a custom object.

6. In the Description field, enter *This object stores information about the open job positions at our company.*

7. For the Context-Sensitive Help Setting, accept the default. If you later want to provide customized help documentation for your users about this object, you can come back and choose the Open a window using a custom Visualforce option.

The `Record Name` is the label for the field that identifies individual position records in the system. Salesforce automatically populates `Record Name` with the custom object label followed by *Name*. In this case, the field is populated with *Position Name*. A custom object cannot be saved without this identifying field.

> **8.** In the `Data Type` drop-down list, select Text.

The `Data Type` drop-down list allows you to select the type of value used for this identifying field: either Text or Auto-Number. Some objects, like Positions or Accounts, can be identified with a text field because there will always be a name for a position or account available. Other objects, like a Case (used in the standard Call Center app) are harder to identify with a single text field, so we assign them auto-numbers instead.

 Tip: Whenever possible, it's best to use text as the data type for an identifying field so that users can more easily identify a particular record when several of them appear together in a single list.

To illustrate how custom object and record name labels work together in the app, let's fast forward a bit to see where each label will appear once we've defined our Position custom object, its tab, and a single Sr. Developer position record.

Custom Object and Record Name Labels

Home	Positions

Search
Search All ⌄   [Go!]
☐ Limit to items I own
Advanced Search...

Custom Object Plural Label

Positions
Home

View: All ⌄ [Go!]   Edit | Create New View

Help for this Page

Recent Positions   [New]   Recently Viewed ⌄

Position Title

Sr. Developer

Create New... ⌄

Recent Items
- Sr. Developer
- Dave Carroll
- Grand Hotels & Resorts Ltd.
- Admin User

Record Name Label

Recycle Bin

Let's move on.

> **9.** Select `Allow Reports`, `Allow Activities`, `Allow Search`, and `Track Field History`.

Note: `Allow Search` is selected by default in Developer Edition orgs.

These checkboxes actually enable some really robust functionality.

Allow Reports

Selecting this option makes the data in the position records available for reporting purposes. The platform comes with a large number of standard reports, and users can also create custom reports by using a simple yet powerful report builder. (To find out more about reports, see Analyzing Data with Reports and Dashboards on page 281.)

Allow Activities

Selecting this option allows users to associate tasks and scheduled calendar events with a particular position. For example, a user can create a task, such as "Update salary range for Sr. Developer position," and specify attributes such as priority, due date, and status. The user can then handle the task or assign it to someone else. (To find out more about tasks, see "Activities" in the Salesforce Help.)

Track Field History

Selecting this option allows the platform to automatically track edits to position records, such as who changed the value of a field, when it was changed, and what the value of the field was before and after the edit. History data is available for reporting, so users can easily create audit trail reports when this feature is enabled. (To find out how to select which data is tracked, see "Track Field History for Custom Objects" in the Salesforce Help.)

In general, select these options if there's any chance that they might be useful for whatever custom object you're defining.

10. In the Deployment Status area, select `Deployed`.

 Note: This step assumes that you're working in a development environment. If you're not, and if you don't want users to see the Position object after you click **Save**, select `In Development`. Setting the status to `In Development` hides position records from all users except those with the "Customize Application" user permission (that is, just about anyone who isn't a System Administrator).

11. In the Object Creation Options area, select the `Add Notes & Attachments related list to default page layout` and `Launch New Custom Tab Wizard after saving this custom object` checkboxes.

These two options are available only when you're creating a new custom object. If you later decide to go back and edit some of the details about your custom object, you won't see them. But what do they do?

* Enabling notes and attachments for an object means you can attach external documents to any position record, in much the same way that you can add a PDF or photo as an attachment to an email. It's handy functionality, so select it.

* Launching the New Custom Tab wizard does exactly what it says—it's a shortcut to launching the tab wizard after we've saved our Position object, and will save us a few clicks if we know that we need a tab.

41

All set? Let's go ahead and save our Position custom object now.

That's all there is to it! As promised, the New Position Tab wizard is displayed instead of the list of custom objects that we'd normally see. Let's take a moment to talk about why we should even be defining a tab for our Position object in the first place. What's so great about tabs, anyway?

Introducing Tabs

If you're familiar with the Force.com platform, you know that clicking tabs is how you navigate around an app. Every tab serves as the starting point for viewing, editing, and entering information for a particular object. When you click a tab at the top of the page, the corresponding home page for that object appears. For example, if you click the Accounts tab, the Accounts tab home page appears, giving you access to all of the account records that are defined in your organization. Click the name of a particular account record and you'll view all of the record's information in its associated detail page.

What's really powerful about building an app with the platform is that you can create custom tabs that look and behave just like the tabs for standard objects that are already provided. From the perspective of your end users, any customizations that you make appear perfectly seamless, and as a developer, you don't have to do anything special to make it work that way! Let's see how quickly we can create a tab for our Position object.

Try It Out: Define the Positions Tab

To create a custom tab for our Position object, we're going to use the New Custom Object Tab wizard that was so helpfully launched for us when we clicked **Save** after defining the object. However, in case you forgot to select the `Launch New Custom Tab Wizard after saving this custom object` option or if you're coming back to work that you previously saved, have no fear! There's another way to launch the wizard.

1. From Setup, enter *Tabs* in the `Quick Find` box, then select **Tabs**.

2. In the Custom Object tabs area, click **New**.

Easy. Now that we're all on the same page, let's get started working through the wizard.

3. In the `Object` drop-down list, select Position.

If you launched the wizard directly after defining the custom object, the Position object is automatically selected for you.

4. Click the `Tab Style` 🔍 icon to launch the Tab Style Selector as shown in the following screenshot.

Every object that appears as a tab must have a unique color scheme and icon. This color scheme is what identifies the object, not only on its tab but also in different places in the user interface, such as in related lists and search results.

Custom Object Tab Setup Page and Tab Style Selector

In the Tab Style Selector, you can choose a predefined color and icon or you can create your own. To keep things simple, we're going to select an existing style.

5. Click the **Hide values which are used on other tabs** link to make sure you choose a unique style.

6. Click any colored box to choose a color scheme and icon.

Leave the `Splash Page Custom Link` drop-down list set to `--None--`. We'll learn more about custom links in Moving Beyond Point-and-Click App Development on page 325.

7. In the `Description` field, enter `A tab and color scheme for the Position custom object.`

8. Click **Next**.

9. Click **Next** again to accept the default user profile visibility.

Just as we controlled access to our Recruiting app by selecting user profiles in the New Custom App wizard, we can also control access to our Positions tab by selecting user profiles here. We'll learn more about user profiles and what they do in Securing and Sharing Data on page 145. For now, just know that accepting the defaults will make the tab visible to all users.

10. Deselect all of the `Include Tab` checkboxes except the one for our Recruiting app.

In performing this step, we're providing access to the Positions tab only when someone has access to our Recruiting app. Unless an employee is interested in recruiting, he or she probably doesn't need to see this tab.

11. Select the `Append tab to users' existing personal customizations` checkbox.

If you don't select this option, any users who have personalized their tab display will not immediately see the Positions tab. Also, if you've already created a new tab and didn't turn this option on, you have to first delete the existing tab and then recreate it with this option turned on to automatically push the tab to existing users. What a pain! Do yourself a favor and just always keep this option selected.

12. Click **Save**.

You'll notice when the page refreshes that the Positions tab has automatically been added next to the Home tab at the top of the page. If you don't see the Positions tab, click **All Tabs** (**+**) to see more.

Look at What We've Done

To truly appreciate what we've just built with a few clicks, let's take a look at what we've done.

1. First, click the Positions tab to display the Positions tab home page, as shown in the following screenshot. Although the list is empty because we haven't yet created any records, you can see how this page will become the gateway to viewing, creating, editing, and deleting all of the positions that we create in our Recruiting app. It looks just like the tab home page of any other standard object.

The Positions Tab Home Page

2. Now, check out the contents of the **Create New...** drop-down list in the left sidebar. As promised, our custom object has been seamlessly incorporated into the platform with the other standard objects like Event and Task. An end user need never know that the Positions tab was created with a custom object, because it shows up alongside the standard objects as well.

3. Select Position from the **Create New...** drop-down list, or click **New** in the Positions tab home page. Voilà—it's the Position edit page! Sadly, though, our position still doesn't have much room for data. At this point, all we have is a field for `Position Title` (the record identifier) and `Owner`, a default field that appears on every object to identify the user who created the object.

4. Click **Cancel**. It doesn't do much to create a position record with hardly any interesting data. We need more fields! And sure enough, that's what we'll get to next. First, though, we'll revisit our Position custom object and orient ourselves to what else is available through a custom object detail page in the Setup area.

5. Notice the arrow icon (■) on the right side of the page. Click it to open the Force.com quick access menu. When you're building apps, the quick access menu makes it easy to switch between object records and setup pages. This menu appears from the list pages and record detail page for any object, so you can easily jump to the setup pages for an object and its tabs, fields, and more. You'll get a chance to try out the quick access menu in a little while.

Force.com Quick Access Menu

> ![Note icon] **Note:** You can see this menu because you have the "Customize Application" permission, which allows you to create apps, objects, tabs, and fields. Users who don't build apps, like those with the Standard User profile, won't see this menu.

Becoming Familiar with Setup Detail Pages and Related Lists

You may recall when we first introduced the concept of objects that we learned: "Whether they're standard or custom, Force.com platform objects not only provide a structure for storing data but they also power the interface elements that allow users to interact with the data, such as tabs, the layout of fields on a page, and lists of related records." If you've been following along closely, you might have been wondering why we didn't get to define any fields (other than the identifier field of Position Title) or user interface elements (other than the Positions tab) when we created our Position object. If fields and user interface elements are a part of the definition of what a custom object is all about, where do we get to define them?

It turns out that the Force.com platform differentiates between the initial creation of certain components and details related to those components. In other words, the information that we see when we define or edit a custom object is different from the information that we see when we view a custom object that's already defined. Let's go back to our custom object list page to see how this difference is reflected in the platform interface.

1. From Setup, enter `Objects` in the `Quick Find` box, then select **Objects**.

Here we are back in the custom object list page. You'll notice in the row for Position there are three links that we can click.

Edit

> This link takes us back to the Custom Object edit page where we originally defined our Position object.

Del

> This link deletes the custom object, including any records, tabs, reports, or other components associated with that object.

Position

> This link takes us to the custom object detail page for our Position object.

Custom Object List Page: Edit, Delete, and Detail Links

We're already familiar with the edit page from when we defined our Position object, and we certainly don't want to delete our object. Let's go ahead and open up the detail page to see what we can do there.

2. Click **Position**.

As you can see, the Custom Object edit page that we filled out when we defined our Position object was just the tip of the iceberg. The top two areas of the Position detail page include all of the information that we originally specified, plus a few standard fields that the platform includes with every object. Below those areas are several additional groupings of data that allow us to do more with our Position object.

In Force.com platform terms, those groupings of data are called *related lists*, and they're a big part of what makes the platform so powerful. A related list is a list of records or other components that are associated with whatever we're viewing. Related lists appear in both the main application and in the Setup areas and represent a relationship between the items that appear in the related list and the object or record that we're viewing in the detail area. We'll learn a lot more about relationships in Expanding the Simple App Using Relationships on page 97, but for now, just understand that anything that appears in an object's related list is directly related to that object.

Now that we've found out where we can continue customizing our Position custom object, let's use the Custom Fields & Relationships related lists to create some more fields in our Position object.

Position Custom Object Detail Page

Introducing Fields

We're ready to add more fields to our Position custom object, but first, let's talk briefly about what a field is and how it fits into the world of the Force.com platform.

As you might remember from the last chapter, a *field* is like a database column. The primary characteristic of a field is its data type—some fields hold text values, while others hold currency values, percentages, phone numbers, email addresses, or dates. Some fields look like checkboxes, while still others are drop-down lists or record lookups from which a user makes a selection.

The data type of a field controls the way the field is ultimately displayed in the user interface and how data entered into the field is stored in the platform. To get a better feel for how the fields will look, let's take a sneak peak at what the Position object is ultimately going to look like and the types of custom fields we're going to create for it:

Position Custom Object Fields

There are a lot of fields here that we need to define, some more complicated than others. To keep things simple, let's go through and create the simple text, currency, checkbox, and date fields. We can tackle the more complicated picklist and custom formula fields in Enhancing the Simple App with Advanced Fields, Data Validation, and Page Layouts on page 57.

Try It Out: Add Text Fields

First let's define a few text fields. We already created a basic text field for `Position Title` when we defined our Position custom object. Looking at our screenshot, the only text fields that remain are the text fields under the Description heading. We'll start by defining the `Job Description` field.

1. From Setup, enter `Objects` in the `Quick Find` box, then select **Objects**.

2. Click **Position**.

3. In the Custom Fields & Relationships related list, click **New**.

Every time you create a custom field, you'll first choose a data type from the field type selection page.

The platform allows us to choose between different types of text fields.

- Basic text fields allow users to enter any combination of letters and numbers on a single line, up to as many as 255 characters.
- Text area fields also have a 255-character limit but also allow carriage returns so the text can be formatted on separate lines.
- Long text fields allow as many as 131,072 characters, on separate lines.
- Rich text fields allow user to enter as many as 131,072 characters of formatted text, including images and hyperlinks.
- Encrypted text fields allow users to enter any combination of letters and numbers that are stored in encrypted form, up to as many as 175 characters.

Since job descriptions can be lengthy, let's choose a long text area.

4. Choose the `Text Area (Long)` data type, and click **Next**.

 Tip: Carefully consider the data type you choose for each of your custom fields, because once you set it, it isn't always the best idea to change it later. See "Notes on Changing Custom Field Types" in the Salesforce Help for details.

The second page of the custom field wizard allows us to enter details about our long text area field. The fields that appear in this step change depending on the data type that we selected in the previous page.

5. In the `Field Label` field, enter `Job Description`.

Like the other labels we've seen in the platform so far, `Field Label` specifies the text that appears when the field is rendered in the user interface. Notice that when we enter a value for `Field Label`, `Field Name` is automatically populated with the same text but with all spaces and punctuation replaced by underscores. The value for `Field Name` is a unique name that is used to refer to the field when writing a custom formula or using the API.

Note: Within the platform, `Field Name` is actually stored with `__c` appended to the end as a suffix (for example, `Job_Description__c`). This identifies it as a custom field.

The `Length` field allows us to restrict the maximum number of characters that are allowed. Since we don't get any benefit from this kind of restriction, leave this value set to 131,072.

6. In the `Length` field, enter `131,072`.

7. In the `# Visible Lines` field, enter `3`.

This field allows us to specify how large our text box will appear on the page.

8. In the `Description` and `Help Text` fields, enter *High-level description of the job and its duties.*

While the description is displayed only in the details for this custom field in Setup, this help text is displayed on record detail and edit pages when users hover over the field's label. Its purpose is to assist users in filling out the field correctly. It's optional to add help text for a field, but it's a good idea if you have fields that you think might confuse users.

There's no obvious default value for a text field, so just leave `Default Value` blank.

9. Click **Next**.

The third page of the Custom Field wizard allows us to restrict access to this field from certain user profiles. We'll learn more about profiles and field-level security in Securing and Sharing Data on page 145, so for now, just accept the defaults.

10. Click **Next**.

The last page of the wizard allows us to automatically place our field on the Position page layout. Again, we'll learn about page layouts in the next chapter, so for now, just accept the defaults.

11. Click **Save & New**.

Instead of clicking **Save** and returning to the Position object detail page, clicking **Save & New** saves a few clicks and allows us to finish up the other text area fields that we need. Here's what you need to know to define them.

Table 2: Position Object Long Text Area Fields

Data Type	Field Label	Length	# Visible Lines	Default Value
Text Area (Long)	Responsibilities	131,072	3	Leave unspecified
Text Area (Long)	Skills Required	131,072	3	Leave unspecified
Text Area (Long)	Educational Requirements	131,072	3	Leave unspecified

Now that we've wet our feet with text fields, let's quickly create a few more fields of other types. You'll find that with few exceptions, they're all very similar to one another.

Try It Out: Add Currency Fields

To keep track of a position's salary range, we need to add two currency fields: `Min Pay` and `Max Pay`. Note that unlike some fields, once we define these as currency fields, we won't be able to change them to any other type.

Defining a currency field is almost identical to defining a text field, with a few slight differences.

- The `Length` of a currency field actually corresponds to the number of digits to the left of the decimal point. An additional `Decimal Places` field handles the number of digits that should be displayed to the right.

- In the Details page of the wizard, a new checkbox called `Required` is displayed. We can select this option if we want to force our users to enter a value for this field when creating a new position.

Everything else should be familiar to you, so go ahead and use the custom field wizard to define the following fields:

Table 3: Position Object Currency Fields

Data Type	Field Label	Length	Decimal Places	Required	Default Value
Currency	Min Pay	7	2	Leave unchecked	Leave unspecified
Currency	Max Pay	7	2	Leave unchecked	Leave unspecified

Try It Out: Add Checkbox Fields

Here are some easy ones. The Position object requires a few checkbox fields: one to indicate if travel is required for the position, and four others to indicate which programming languages are required. By default, these values should be unchecked. (Note that similar to currency fields, once you define a field as a checkbox, you can't change it to any other type.)

Use the custom field wizard to define these fields.

Table 4: Position Object Checkbox Fields

Field Type	Field Label	Default Value
Checkbox	Travel Required	Unchecked
Checkbox	Java	Unchecked
Checkbox	JavaScript	Unchecked
Checkbox	C#	Unchecked
Checkbox	Apex	Unchecked

Try It Out: Add Date Fields

Finally, before we close out this chapter, let's add three date fields to our Recruiting app to track the date a position opens, the date it closes, and the date by which it should be filled. Date fields are great because they automatically include a popup calendar interface from which users can select a day without any typing—yet another built-in feature that we can leverage in our app without any extra work!

Once again we'll use the custom field wizard to define these three fields:

Table 5: Position Object Date Fields

Field Type	Field Label	Required	Default Value
Date	Open Date	Unchecked	Leave unspecified
Date	Hire By	Unchecked	Leave unspecified
Date	Close Date	Unchecked	Leave unspecified

Look at What We've Done

We've defined text, currency, checkbox, and date fields for our Position object. Let's take a look by going to the Positions tab and clicking **New**.

Position Object Fields

Check out all the fields we've just made! Each field got added to the page in the order that we created it, and we may want to adjust the layout later, but it's definitely functional. Wasn't that easy?

Taking Our Simple App Mobile

Remember that mobile app we mentioned earlier? Salesforce1 hooks into your Salesforce organization and presents all your customizations and data in a mobile-friendly user interface. That means that anything you do in the full site will be reflected automatically in this mobile app, so your users will have access to the information they need, no matter where they are! This will be especially useful for our recruiters, who sometimes travel to find the best candidates for Universal Containers' open positions. Let's take a look at how the Positions tab and its fields appear in mobile.

Before we begin, make sure you have access to Salesforce1. You can do this with a downloadable app or the mobile browser app.

- To use the downloadable app, go to `www.salesforce.com/mobile`, and select the appropriate platform for your device to download Salesforce1 directly to your device.
- To use the mobile browser app, navigate to `login.salesforce.com` from your mobile browser. Salesforce will recognize that you're working from a mobile device and redirect you to the Salesforce1 mobile browser app.

1. Open Salesforce1 from your mobile device.

2. Enter your Salesforce credentials and tap **Log in to Salesforce**.

Notice that there isn't a home tab. With our current configuration, the first thing that appears for users is the first item in the *navigation menu*. We'll go over how to select which page appears when users first open Salesforce1 later in Analyzing Data with Reports and Dashboards on page 281.

3. Tap ☰ to open the navigation menu.

Now is a good time to talk about how apps and tabs work in Salesforce1. Earlier, we learned that each tab is represented through a menu item in the Recent section of the Salesforce1 navigation menu. Salesforce apps, such as the Sales app or a custom app, don't appear in Salesforce1, because the mobile app figures out which records you look at most often. Rather than using the Force.com app menu to customize the tabs a user sees regularly, the smart search items under the Recent section reorder based on the user's history of recent objects. Since our organization is new and we haven't added any data yet, we see the default objects for now: accounts, cases, contacts, files, leads, and opportunities.

We don't see our custom object in this list, so let's look at the full list of smart search items.

4. Tap **Show More**.

5. Tap **Positions**.

6. Tap **New** to check out how our fields look in Salesforce1.

Just like in the full site, all the fields we made are here, and we can easily create a new position from our mobile device. That means we don't have to duplicate our effort to create a pleasant mobile experience for our users. It just works!

Create Position Page in Salesforce1

Once again, welcome to the power of the Force.com platform. First we created a new Recruiting app with a single Home tab, then we created a Position object and tab, and now we've just added a few fields, all in less than 15 minutes of clicking around. From start to finish we always had a fully functional app, and we never had to spend any time compiling or debugging our "code!"

In the next chapter, we'll enhance our simple Recruiting app even further by adding some additional fields that are more complex, defining validation rules to help our data stay clean, and then moving the fields around in a page layout so users can more easily find and enter the information they need. Let's keep going!

CHAPTER 5 Enhancing the Simple App with Advanced Fields, Data Validation, and Page Layouts

In the last chapter, we got our Recruiting app off to a quick start by defining the Position custom object, tab, and several simple fields. This simple version of our app had the same look and feel as any other page on the Force.com platform, and we were able to whip it together in a matter of minutes.

In this chapter, we're going to enhance the Positions tab: first by defining a few more advanced fields, then by defining a couple of validation rules to make sure our data stays clean, and finally by moving our fields around within a page layout. These additions will help change the detail page of our Positions tab from a somewhat flat and inelegant user interface to something that users find powerful and intuitive to use. Let's get started!

Adding Advanced Fields

In this section, let's revisit the custom field wizard to help us create fields with more sophisticated functionality: picklists, dependent picklists, and fields that leverage custom formulas. We'll see how the platform's user interface helps guide us through the setup of these more complicated fields.

Introducing Picklists

When viewing the preview of what we wanted our Positions page to ultimately look like, there were several fields that were specified with drop-down lists. In Force.com platform terms, these fields are called *picklists*, and they consist of several predefined options from which a user can select.

Picklists come in two flavors: a standard picklist, in which a user can select only one option, and a multi-select picklist, in which a user can select multiple options at a time. For the purposes of our Position object, we need to define standard picklists for a position's location, status, type of job, functional area, and job level.

Location Picklist Field

Try It Out: Add Picklists

Let's walk through the creation of the `Location` picklist field. Then, as in the previous chapter, we'll give you the information that you need to create the others on your own.

1. From Setup, enter `Objects` in the `Quick Find` box, then select **Objects**.

2. Click **Position**.

3. In the Custom Fields & Relationships related list, click **New**.

4. Select the `Picklist` data type, and click **Next**.

5. In the `Field Label` text box, enter `Location`.

6. In the large text area box just below, enter the following picklist values, each on its own line:

   - San Francisco, CA
   - Austin, TX
   - Boulder, CO
   - London, England
   - New York, NY
   - Mumbai, India
   - Sydney, Australia
   - Tokyo, Japan

7. Select the `Use first value as default value` checkbox.

This option allows us to populate the field with a default value. If you select it, the field defaults to the first value that you specify in the list of possible picklist values. Otherwise, the field defaults to None on all new position records. Because most positions at Universal Containers are based at its headquarters in San Francisco, CA, this should be the default.

8. Accept all other default settings for field-level security and page layouts.

9. Click **Save & New**.

Easy! Now specify the remaining picklists according to the table below:

Table 6: Status, Type, Functional Area, and Job Level Picklist Values

Data Type	Field Label	Picklist Values	Sort Alphabetically?	Use First Value as Default?
Picklist	Status	New Position Pending Approval Open - Approved Closed - Filled Closed - Not Approved Closed - Canceled	No	Yes
Picklist	Type	Full Time Part Time	No	No

Data Type	Field Label	Picklist Values	Sort Alphabetically?	Use First Value as Default?
		Internship		
		Contractor		
Picklist	Functional Area	Finance	Yes	No
		Human Resources		
		Information Technology		
		Retail Operations		
		Warehousing		
		Miscellaneous		
Picklist	Job Level	FN-100	Yes	No
		FN-200		
		FN-300		
		FN-400		
		HR-100		
		HR-200		
		HR-300		
		HR-400		
		IT-100		
		IT-200		
		IT-300		
		IT-400		
		RO-100		
		RO-200		
		RO-300		
		RO-400		
		WH-100		
		WH-200		
		WH-300		

Data Type	Field Label	Picklist Values	Sort Alphabetically?	Use First Value as Default?
		WH-400		
		MC-100		
		MC-200		
		MC-300		
		MC-400		

Introducing Field Dependencies

Now that we've made all those picklists, answer this question: How many times have you clicked on a drop-down list and found far too many values to choose from? For example, maybe you were selecting Uruguay from a list of countries, and every country in the world was on the list. That meant that you had to scroll all the way down to the countries that started with the letter U. What a pain!

Fortunately, the folks who built the Force.com platform have encountered that situation a few times themselves, and as a result, they've given us a tool to help us avoid this problem with our own picklist fields: *field dependencies*.

Field dependencies are filters that allow us to change the contents of a picklist based on the value of another field. For example, rather than displaying every value for Country in a single picklist, we can limit the values that are displayed based on a value for another field, like Continent. That way our users can find the appropriate country more quickly and easily.

Picklist fields can be either *controlling* or *dependent* fields. A controlling field controls the available values in one or more corresponding dependent fields. A dependent field displays values based on the value selected in its corresponding controlling field. In the previous example, the Continent picklist is the controlling field, while the Country picklist is the dependent field.

Try It Out: Create a Dependent Picklist

Looking at the picklists that we've created, it's quickly obvious that our users might get frustrated with the length of our `Job Level` picklist. Let's make our users happy by turning `Job Level` into a dependent field of the `Functional Area` picklist. Doing this will allow users to see only the four relevant job level values when a department is selected in the `Functional Area` picklist:

1. From Setup, enter `Objects` in the `Quick Find` box, then select **Objects**.

2. Click **Position**.

3. In the Custom Fields & Relationships related list, click **Field Dependencies**.

4. Click **New**.

5. For the `Controlling Field` drop-down list, choose Functional Area.

6. For the `Dependent Field` drop-down list, choose Job Level.

7. Click **Continue**.

A field dependency matrix displays with all the values in the controlling field across the top header row and the dependent field values listed in the columns below. For each possible value of the controlling field, we need to include the values that should be displayed in the dependent picklist when that controlling value is selected. In the field dependency matrix, yellow highlighting shows which dependent field values are included in the picklist for a particular controlling field value.

Field Dependency Matrix

To include a dependent field value, you simply double-click it. To exclude a dependent value from the list, double-click it again.

For example, let's try it out by including the values that should be displayed in the `Job Level` picklist whenever Finance is selected in the `Functional Area` picklist:

8. In the column labeled Finance, double-click FN-100, FN-200, FN-300, and FN-400.

Those four fields should now be shaded yellow in the `Finance` column.

Instead of double-clicking every `Job Level` value, we can also use SHIFT+click to select a range of values or CTRL+click to select multiple values at once. Once those values are highlighted in blue, we can click **Include Values** to include them, or **Exclude Values** to remove them. Let's try it out.

9. In the column labeled Human Resources, single-click HR-100 and then press and hold the SHIFT key while clicking HR-400.

10. Click **Include Values**.

Now we have values selected for both the Finance and Human Resources columns!

11. Continue highlighting the appropriate values for all of the remaining columns, as described in the following table.

💡 Tip: To get to all of the values that you need to modify for this step, you'll need to click **Previous** or **Next** to see additional columns.

Table 7: Functional Area and Job Level Field Dependency Matrix

Functional Area (Controlling picklist field)	Job Level (Dependent picklist field)
Finance	FN-100
	FN-200
	FN-300
	FN-400
Human Resources	HR-100
	HR-200
	HR-300
	HR-400
Information Technology	IT-100
	IT-200
	IT-300
	IT-400
Retail Operations	RO-100
	RO-200
	RO-300

Functional Area (Controlling picklist field)	Job Level (Dependent picklist field)
	RO-400
Warehousing	WH-100
	WH-200
	WH-300
	WH-400
Miscellaneous	MC-100
	MC-200
	MC-300
	MC-400

12. Click **Preview** to test the results in a small popup window.

13. Click **Save**.

Look at What We've Done

Now that we've created all those picklists, let's revisit the Positions tab to see what we have so far.

1. Go to the Positions tab.

2. Click **New**.

3. In the Functional Area picklist, select Finance.

4. Open the Job Level picklist.

Dependent Picklist Fields

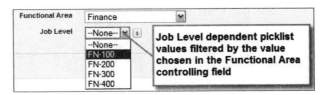

Our Recruiting app users are going to be very happy that they no longer have to deal with a long, onerous picklist. Now let's go add a field that's even more powerful and complex than a dependent picklist: a custom formula field.

Introducing Custom Formula Fields

Up to this point, the fields that we've defined have all had one thing in common—they each require a user to give them a value. Fields like that are very helpful for storing and retrieving data, but wouldn't it be great if we could somehow define a "smart" field? That is, what if we could define a field that looked at information that was already entered into the system and then told us something new about it?

Fortunately, *custom formula fields* give us the ability to do just that. Just as you can use a spreadsheet program like Microsoft Excel to define calculations and metrics specific to your business, we can use custom formula fields to define calculations and metrics that are specific to our Recruiting app.

For example, on our Position object, we've already created fields for minimum pay and maximum pay. If Universal Containers gives out yearly bonuses based on salary, we could create a custom formula field that automatically calculated the average bonus that someone hired to that position might receive.

How would we perform this calculation if we were using a spreadsheet? The columns in our spreadsheet would represent the fields that we defined on our Position object, and each row of the spreadsheet would represent a different position record. To create a calculation, we'd enter a formula in a new column that averages the values of Min Pay and Max Pay in a single row and then multiplies it by a standard bonus percentage. We could then determine the average bonus for every position record row in our spreadsheet.

Custom formulas work in a very similar way. Think of a custom formula like a spreadsheet formula that can reference other values in the same data record, perform calculations on them, and return a result. However, instead of using cell references, you use *merge fields*, which serve as placeholders for data that will be replaced with information from your records, user information, or company information. And, instead of typing fields, operators, and functions, you can click to select them.

The net result is that anyone can quickly and easily learn to create formula fields. And, as with all platform tools, the cloud computing delivery model makes it easy to experiment. You can create a formula, view the results, and change the formula again and again, as many times as you want! Your underlying data is never affected.

> **Tip:** For more guidance on creating custom formulas, check out
> http://www.salesforce.com/us/developer/docs/usefulFormulaFields/.

Calculating How Long a Position Has Been Open

Let's think about another custom formula field that we could create for our Position object—a custom formula field that calculates how many days a position has been open. To do this, let's first think about the logic that we should use to define the field, and then we can go through the process of creating it in our Recruiting app.

Let's think about the data that we need to make this calculation: we need to know the current date and the date the position was created. If we could somehow subtract these two, we'd have the number of days that the position has been open. Fortunately, it's easy to get both of these values.

- For the current date, we can use the platform's built-in TODAY() function. TODAY() returns today's date.

- For the date that the position was opened, we can use the Open Date field that we defined in the last chapter.

When using fields in formulas, you can't just refer to a field by its name. Instead, you need to refer to it by its merge field name, also called its API name. The format of the API name is typically the name of the field but with underscores instead of spaces. For custom fields, the API name is suffixed with two underscores and the letter "c," like this: Open_Date__c. This naming convention in the platform helps distinguish between standard and custom fields.

 Tip: You don't need to memorize the API names of fields you want to use in formulas. Simply use the field picker in the formula editor to insert fields and the platform automatically inserts the API name for you. If you ever want to know the API name of a specific field and you aren't using the formula editor, you can view the field's detail page.

Now that we have our two dates, we want to subtract them: TODAY() - Open_Date__c. Even if the two dates span different months or years, the platform is sophisticated enough to know how to handle all the intricacies of such a calculation behind the scenes. We just have to provide the dates, and the platform can do all the rest.

So far so good, but one problem still remains—what if the position has already closed? Our formula only works if we assume the position is still open. Once it closes, however, the value of our current formula will continue to increment every day as TODAY() gets farther and farther away from the original Open Date. If we can, we want to use the Close Date field in the formula instead of TODAY() after a position closes. How can we do this?

Once again, we can dip into the extensive library of platform functions. The `IF()` function allows us to perform a test and then return different values depending on whether the result of the test is true or false. The `IF()` function's syntax looks like:

```
IF(logical_test,
        value_if_true,
        value_if_false)
```

For the `logical_test` portion, we'll test whether the `Close Date` field has a value—if it does, the position obviously must be closed. We'll test for this with a third built-in function: `ISBLANK()`. `ISBLANK()` takes a single field and returns true if it does not contain a value and false if it does. So now our formula looks like:

```
IF( ISBLANK( Close_Date__c ) ,
        value_if_true,
        value_if_false)
```

By replacing `value_if_true` and `value_if_false` with the other formulas we talked about, we've now figured out our whole formula.

```
IF( ISBLANK( Close_Date__c ) ,
        TODAY()   -   Open_Date__c ,
        Close_Date__c   -   Open_Date__c )
```

Great! Our formula calculates the number of days a position has been open, regardless of whether it's currently open or closed. Now, let's go define a field for it on our Position object.

Try It Out: Define a "Days Open" Custom Formula Field

We'll begin building the formula field the same way we created our other custom fields.

1.
   From the Positions tab, click [icon] to open the quick access menu (if it isn't open already).

2. Hover over **View Fields** and click **New**.

Opening the New Custom Field Wizard from the Quick Access Menu

3. Select the `Formula` data type, and click **Next**.

Step 2 of the New Custom Field wizard appears.

Custom Formula Field Wizard Step 2

Position
New Custom Field

Help for this Page

Step 2. Choose output type   **Step 2 of 5**

Previous Next Cancel

Field Label Days Open   Field Name Days_Open
                                             i

Indicates the formula's result is a number

Formula Return Type

Indicates number of digits to display to the right of the decimal place

○ None Selected   Select one of the data types below.

○ Currency   Calculate a dollar or other currency amount and automatically format the field
                       as a currency amount.
                       Example: Gross Margin = Amount - Cost__c

○ Date   Calculate a date, for example, by adding or subtracting days to other dates.
                       Example: Reminder Date = CloseDate - 7

○ Date/Time   Calculate a date/time, for example, by adding a number of hours or days to
                       another date/time.
                       Example: Next = NOW() + 1

⊙ Number   Calculate a numeric value.
                       Example: Fahrenheit = 1.8 * Celsius__c + 32

○ Percent   Calculate a percent and automatically add the percent sign to the number.
                       Example: Discount = (Amount - Discounted_Amount__c) / Amount

○ Text   Create a text string, for example, by concatenating other text fields.
                       Example: Full Name = LastName & ", " & FirstName

Options   Decimal Places 0 ⌄ Example: 999

Previous Next Cancel

4. In the `Field Label` field, enter *Days Open*. `Field Name` is populated automatically.

5. Select the `Number` formula return type.

In this case, even though we're subtracting Date fields, we want to end up with just a regular numeric value.

6. Change the `Decimal Places` value to *0*, and click **Next**.

Now it's time to enter the details of our formula.

7. Click the Advanced Formula tab, as shown in the following screenshot.

Custom Formula Field Editor

We want to use the Advanced Formula tab so we can access the platform's built-in functions through the Functions list on the right side.

8. From the `Functions` list, double-click `IF`.

Our formula now looks like this:

```
IF(logical_test, value_if_true, value_if_false)
```

Let's go ahead and define the logical test:

9. Delete *logical_test* from the formula, but leave your cursor there.

10. From the `Functions` list, double-click `ISBLANK`.

11. Delete *expression* from the `ISBLANK` function you just inserted, but leave your cursor there.

12. Click the **Insert Field** button. Two columns appear in an overlay.

13. In the left column, select Position.

14. In the right column, select Close Date.

15. Click **Insert**.

Did you notice that you didn't have to remember to use the API name of the Close Date field? The platform remembered for you when it inserted the value. Our formula now looks like this:

```
IF( ISBLANK( Close_Date__c ) , value_if_true, value_if_false)
```

Now, let's specify the value if our logical test evaluates to true:

16. Delete *value_if_true* from the formula, but leave your cursor there.

17. Press ENTER on your keyboard, and space over 10 spaces.

Adding the carriage return and spaces makes our formula more legible for others.

18. From the Functions list, double-click TODAY.

19. Click the **Insert Operator** button and choose Subtract.

20. Click the **Insert Field** button.

21. In the left column, select Position.

22. In the right column, select Open Date.

23. Click **Insert**.

We're getting closer—our formula now looks like this:

```
IF( ISBLANK( Close_Date__c ) ,
         TODAY()  -  Open_Date__c , value_if_false)
```

Finally, let's specify the value if our logical test evaluates to false:

24. Delete *value_if_false* from the formula, but leave your cursor there.

25. Press ENTER on your keyboard, and space over 10 spaces.

26. Click the **Insert Field** button.

27. In the left column, select Position.

28. In the right column, select Close Date and click **Insert**.

29. Click **Insert Operator** and choose Subtract.

30. Click the **Insert Field** button.

31. In the left column, select Position.

32. In the right column, select `Open Date` and click **Insert**.

Our formula now matches our original:

```
IF( ISBLANK( Close_Date__c ) ,
        TODAY()  -  Open_Date__c ,
        Close_Date__c  -  Open_Date__c )
```

Now that we've gone through those steps of the procedure, note that we could have just typed in the formula that we figured out in the last section. However, using the formula editor is a lot easier because you don't have to remember function syntax or API names of fields and objects. Let's keep going and finish up this field:

33. Click **Check Syntax** to check your formula for errors.

34. Select `Treat blank fields as blanks`, and click **Next**.

35. Accept all remaining field-level security and page layout defaults.

36. Click **Save**.

37. On the Positions Fields page, scroll down to the Positions Custom Fields & Relationships section.

38. Click **Edit** next to the new Days Open field.

39. In the `Description` text box, enter *The number of days a position has been (or was) open.*

40. Add an optional `Help Text` description if you wish.

41. Click **Save**.

Try It Out: Give Fields Dynamic Default Values

We can also use custom formulas to give our fields dynamic default values. Some fields like the `Travel Required` checkbox or the `Job Location` picklist have default values that apply in every situation. There are other fields with defaults that can't be so easily defined. For example, at Universal Containers, recruiters are expected to fill a position within 90 days of it being opened. We can't choose a single date that will always be 90 days after a position is opened. We *can* define a custom formula that adds 90 days to the date the position was created. Because Salesforce calculates default field values when you create a new position, we'll represent the date a position is created with the `TODAY()` function, and then add 90 days to it. The platform allows us to specify this formula as the `Hire By` field's default value:

1. From Setup, enter *Objects* in the `Quick Find` box, then select **Objects**.

2. Click **Position**.

3. In the Custom Fields & Relationships related list, click **Edit** next to the `Hire By` field.

4. Next to the `Default Value` text box, click **Show Formula Editor**.

Look familiar? This editor is similar to the one we used to define our `Days Open` custom formula field.

5. From the `Functions` list, double-click `TODAY`.

6. Click the **Insert Operator** button, and choose **Add**.

7. Type *90*.

Your default value formula is:

```
TODAY() + 90
```

8. Click **Save**.

It's that easy! Now to wrap up the fields on our Positions tab, let's set the default value of the `Open Date` field to the day that the record was created. Follow these steps again, but use `TODAY()` as the `Default Value`.

Look at What We've Done

Let's revisit the Positions tab to take a look at what we've just done.

1. Click the Positions tab.

2. Click **New**.

Our `Days Open` formula field doesn't show up on our Position edit page—that's because it's a formula field and doesn't require any user input to display. However, we can see that our `Open Date` and `Hire By` fields already have default values: `Open Date` should be today's date, and `Hire By` is 90 days later. We can change these values if we want, or we can just leave them as they are.

In order to see our `Days Open` field, we'll have to define our first position record. Let's do that now.

3. Enter any values you want to define for a new position. At the very least, you must enter a value for the required `Position Title` field.

4. Click **Save**.

The new position is now displayed in its own record detail page. At the bottom of the page, notice our `Days Open` formula field, just above the `Created By` field. It should show 0, since we just created the position. If you want to see the value change, edit the record and set the `Open Date` to a week earlier. Isn't that neat?

Introducing Validation Rules

Now that we've defined all the fields that we want on our Position object, let's see if we can articulate a couple of rules about the data that should be entered into those fields. Even though the recruiters and hiring managers at Universal Containers are bright people, everyone sometimes makes mistakes when filling out a form, and a good app should catch the obvious errors.

For example, does it ever make sense for the value of the `Min Pay` field to be more than the value of the `Max Pay` field? Or should `Close Date` ever be unspecified if the `Status` field is set to Closed - Filled or Closed - Not Approved? Clearly not. We can catch these sorts of errors in our app with yet another built-in feature of the platform: *validation rules*.

Validation rules verify that the data a user enters in your app meets the standards that you specify. If it doesn't, the validation rule prevents the record from being saved, and the user sees an error message that you define either next to the problematic field or at the top of the edit page. Let's build a couple of validation rules now for our Recruiting app.

> 💡 Tip: You can find many sample validation rules in the Salesforce Help.

Try It Out: Define a Validation Rule for Min and Max Pay

For our first validation rule, let's start off simple: `Min Pay` should never be greater than `Max Pay`.

1. From the Positions tab, click ▮ to open the quick access menu (if it isn't open already).
2. Hover over **View Validation Rules**, and click **New**.

Validation Rule Edit Page

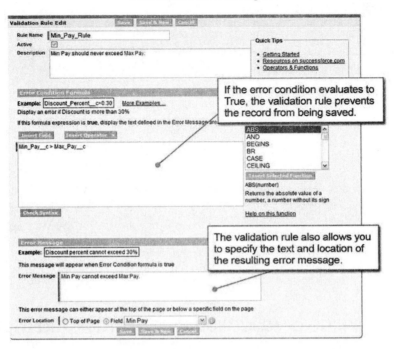

3. In the `Rule Name` text box, enter `Min_Pay_Rule`.

The name of a validation rule can't include any spaces, but if you forget, the platform helpfully changes them to underscores (_) for you.

4. Select the `Active` checkbox.

This checkbox specifies whether the validation rule should start working as soon as it's saved. Because this rule is pretty straightforward (and because we want to test it later!), it makes sense to turn it on right away.

5. In the `Description` text box, enter `Min Pay should never exceed Max Pay.`

Now it's time to define the meat of our validation rule: the *error condition*. If you have a sense of déjà vu when looking at the Error Condition Formula area of the page, don't be alarmed! Just like formula fields and default field values, a validation rule can leverage a number of built-in operators and functions to define a true-or-false error condition that determines whether data is valid. When this condition evaluates to true, an error message displays and the record can't be saved.

We want our error condition to be true whenever `Min Pay` is greater than `Max Pay`, so let's use our formula editor to specify that now:

6. Click the **Insert Field** button. Just like in the formula field editor, two columns appear in an overlay.

7. In the left column, select Position.

8. In the right column, select `Min Pay`.

9. Click **Insert**.

10. Click the **Insert Operator** button, and choose Greater Than.

11. Click the **Insert Field** button once again.

12. In the left column, select Position.

13. In the right column, select `Max Pay`.

14. Click **Insert**.

You should now have an error condition formula that looks like this:

```
Min_Pay__c  >  Max_Pay__c
```

Now the only thing that remains is to specify the error message when our error condition evaluates to true.

15. In the `Error Message` text box, enter *Min Pay cannot exceed Max Pay.*

16. Next to the `Error Location` field, select `Field` and choose `Min Pay`.

17. Click **Save**.

Easy! Now that we've familiarized ourselves with a simple validation rule, let's define one that's a little trickier.

Try It Out: Define a Validation Rule for Close Date

For our next validation rule, let's ensure that `Close Date` has a value whenever the `Status` field is set to Closed - Filled or Closed - Not Approved.

The hardest part of this validation rule is defining the error condition formula. When defining a condition like this, it's sometimes easiest to think about it in logical terms first, and then translate that logic to the functions and operators that are provided in the formula editor. In this case, our error condition is true whenever:

```
Close Date is Not Specified

AND

(Status is "Closed - Filled" OR
          "Closed - Not Approved")
```

Let's start with the first piece: "Close Date is Not Specified." To translate this into terms the formula editor understands, we'll need to use the `ISBLANK()` function again. As you might remember from defining the `Days Open` custom formula field, `ISBLANK()` takes a single field or expression and returns true if it doesn't contain a value. So, remembering that we have to use the internal field name of the `Close Date` field in our formula, `Close Date is Not Specified` translates to:

```
ISBLANK( Close_Date__c )
```

Next, let's figure out how to translate "Status is 'Closed - Filled'." To test for picklist values, we'll need to use another function: `ISPICKVAL()`. `ISPICKVAL()` takes a picklist field name and value, and returns true whenever that value is selected. So "Status is 'Closed - Filled'" translates to:

```
ISPICKVAL( Status__c , "Closed - Filled")
```

> 💡 **Tip:** When working with picklists in formulas, convert them to text using either the `ISPICKVAL()` function or the `TEXT()` function. For example, to check the value of a picklist using the `TEXT()` function, use `TEXT(Status__c) = "Closed - Filled"`.

Now we just have to combine these translations, which we can do using a mix of the `&&` and `||` functions. Both functions evaluate an unlimited number of expressions, but `&&` returns true if **all** of the expressions are true while `||` returns true if **any** of the expressions are true. For example:

```
exp1 && exp2 && exp3
```

returns true when *exp1*, *exp2*, and *exp3* are all true. Likewise,

```
exp1 || exp2 || exp3
```

returns true when any one of *exp1*, *exp2*, or *exp3* are true.

Put these functions all together with our other expression translations, and we get our completed error condition formula:

```
ISBLANK(Close_Date__c) &&
    (ISPICKVAL(Status__c , "Closed - Filled") ||
     ISPICKVAL(Status__c , "Closed - Not Approved"))
```

Phew! Now we can quickly define our second validation rule using this formula:

1. From Setup, enter *Objects* in the `Quick Find` box, then select **Objects**.

2. Click **Position**.

3. In the Validation Rules related list, click **New**.

4. In the `Rule Name` text box, enter *Close_Date_Rule*.

5. Select the `Active` checkbox.

6. In the `Description` text box, enter *Close Date must be specified when Status is set to 'Closed - Filled' or 'Closed - Not Approved.'*

7. In the Error Condition Formula area, enter the following formula:

```
ISBLANK(Close_Date__c) &&
    (ISPICKVAL(Status__c , "Closed - Filled") ||
     ISPICKVAL(Status__c , "Closed - Not Approved"))
```

8. Click **Check Syntax** to make sure the format of the formula is correct.

9. In the `Error Message` text box, enter *Close Date must be specified when Status is set to 'Closed.'*

10. Next to the `Error Location` field, select the `Field` radio button, and then choose `Close Date` from the drop-down list.

11. Click **Save**.

Look at What We've Done

Let's revisit the Positions tab to test the validation rules that we've just made.

1. Click the Positions tab.

2. Click **New**.

First let's try defining a new position with a value for `Min Pay` that's larger than `Max Pay`.

3. Specify any value for the required `Position Title` field.

4. In the `Min Pay` field, enter *80,000*.

5. In the `Max Pay` field, enter *40,000*.

6. Click **Save**.

Did you see what happened? Your custom error message popped exactly like any other error message in the app!

Error Message from a Validation Rule

Now let's test our other validation rule:

7. In the `Min Pay` field, enter *40,000*.

8. In the `Max Pay` field, enter *80,000*.

9. From the `Status` drop-down list, choose Closed - Not Approved.

10. Click **Save**.

Our second validation rule is triggered, this time because we didn't specify a value for `Close Date`. Once we do, the record saves normally.

Check It Out in Mobile

Before we move on, let's take a look at how our new fields appear on a mobile device.

1. Launch Salesforce1 on your mobile device. If prompted, log in.

2. Tap ☰ to open the navigation menu, and then tap **Positions**. If you don't see Positions in the list of items, remember to tap **Show More**.

3. Tap **New** to create a position record.

Just like when we first created fields for the Position object, all of our advanced fields appear in Salesforce1 automatically. Verify that all of our advanced fields work as expected.

Dependent Picklists and Validation Rules in Salesforce1

All of our advanced fields are in order if:

*   We can only update `Job Level` once we've selected a value for `Functional Area`

- We don't see the `Days Open` formula field
- `Open Date` has already been populated with today's date
- `Hire By` has already been populated with 90 days from today
- A position's `Min Pay` can't be more than its `Max Pay`
- A position's `Status` can't be Closed – Filled or Closed – Not Approved if `Close Date` is empty

We also want to check that the `Days Open` field is working according to plan, but since we created a position when we checked our fields in the full site, we can look at that existing record.

4. Tap **Cancel** to return to the list of recent position records.

5. Tap the position record we just created.

6. Scroll down until you see `Days Open`.

We see that, just like in the full site, `Days Open` shows the number of days that have passed since `Open Date`: 0.

The Positions tab is now fully functional, with a couple of validation rules to ensure that users don't make certain mistakes. But are the fields where we want them? Are the fields that must have values marked as required? In the next section, we'll fine-tune our Position custom object by modifying its page layout.

Introducing Page Layouts

After defining all those fields and validation rules, we now have a fully functional Position custom object. However, it doesn't look all that nice—all of the long text areas appear at the top, and it's hard to scan in our desktop browser. Just imagine how hard it would be to scan in a mobile device! Let's move some things around to make this page easier for our users. We can do that by customizing the Position object's page layout.

A *page layout* controls the position and organization of the fields and related lists that are visible to users when viewing a record. Page layouts also help us control the visibility and editability of the fields on a record. We can set fields as read-only or hidden, and we can also control which fields require users to enter a value and which don't.

Page layouts are powerful tools for creating a good experience for our users, but it's crucial that we remember one important rule: *page layouts should never be used to restrict access to sensitive data that a user shouldn't view or edit*. Although we can hide a field from a page layout, users can still access that field through other parts of the app, such as in reports or via the API. (We'll learn more about security that covers all parts of the app in Securing and Sharing Data on page 145.)

Now let's see if we can organize the fields on our Position object in a way that's more user friendly.

Becoming Familiar with the Page Layout Editor

The Force.com platform has two drag-and-drop tools for editing page layouts: the original page layout editor and the enhanced page layout editor.

The enhanced page layout editor provides all of the same functionality as the original editor, but with additional enhancements, including an intuitive WYSIWYG interface and the ability to customize the space between fields in your layouts. Since the enhanced page layout editor is enabled by default, it's the one we'll use to edit page layouts in this book.

> Note: The enhanced page layout editor doesn't work with some older browsers. If you don't want to upgrade your browser, you can always switch to the original page layout editor from Setup by entering *User Interface* in the Quick Find box, then selecting **User Interface** and deselecting Enable Enhanced Page Layout Editor; however, if you use the original page layout editor, what you see on your screen will not match the procedures in this book, and you won't be able to customize the space between fields in your layouts.

Let's try using the page layout editor to edit the page layout of the Position object:

1. From Setup, enter *Objects* in the Quick Find box, then select **Objects**.

2. Click **Position**.

3. In the Page Layouts related list, click **Edit** next to Position Layout.

Welcome to the page layout editor! As you can see, this editor is different from the ones that we've already used in other areas of the platform. That's because we're designing a user interface and need to see how our page will look as we're working. Before going any further, let's give ourselves a quick orientation to how this page is set up.

Page Layout Editor

The page layout editor consists of a palette at the top of the screen and the page layout below it. The palette contains the user interface elements that are available for you to add to the page layout, including fields, buttons, links, and related lists. To add one of these user interface elements to the page layout, simply select the category to which the element belongs on the left column of the palette and drag the element from the palette to the page layout. To remove a user interface element from the page layout, drag the element from the page layout to the right side of the palette, or hover over the element you want to remove and click ⊖ . A toolbar above the palette provides various functions, such as saving and previewing your changes.

Now that we know what we're looking at, let's rearrange the fields in the way a user might want to see them.

Try It Out: Group Fields into a New Section

Let's start modifying our page layout by first defining a new section for salary information. On a page layout, a section is simply an area where we can group similar fields under an appropriate heading. This makes it easy for our users to quickly identify and enter the information for a record, especially if our object has a large number of fields:

1. In the palette, select the Fields category.

2. Drag the Section user interface element from the palette to just above the System Information section on the page layout.

When you drag a new section on to the page layout, the Section Properties popup window appears.

3. In the `Section Name` text box, enter `Compensation`.

The `Section Name` field controls the text that's displayed as the heading for the section.

4. In the Display Section Header On area, select both `Detail Page` and `Edit Page`.

Displaying the header on both the detail and edit pages helps users understand the context of the information, regardless of whether they are editing the position or just viewing it.

5. In the `Layout` drop-down list, choose 2-Column.

This option allows us to choose whether we want the fields in our section to be arranged in two columns or one. The default is two columns and is the most common choice. However, if our section is going to contain text area fields, the one-column layout gives them more space on the page for display.

6. In the `Tab-key Order` drop-down list, choose Left-Right.

This setting controls the direction that a user's cursor will move when using the Tab key to navigate from field to field.

7. Click **OK**.

We have a new section for Compensation just above the System Information section! Let's add the `Min Pay` and `Max Pay` fields:

8. While pressing CTRL, click both the `Min Pay` and `Max Pay` fields in the Information section, and drag them to the new Compensation section as shown.

Adding Fields to the Compensation Section

Pressing CTRL allows you to select multiple individual user interface elements with your mouse. Alternatively, pressing the SHIFT key allows you to select a group of elements.

Now that we've gone through the process for building one section, let's build two more. As we do this, you might have to scroll up and down to view the entire layout, depending on the size of your screen. Rest assured that if you have to scroll, the palette will move with you, making it easy to add user interface elements even at the very bottom of the page layout.

9. Create a new one-column Description section below the Compensation section, and drag `Job Description`, `Responsibilities`, `Skills Required`, and `Educational Requirements` into it.

10. Create a new two-column Required Languages section below the Description section, and drag `Apex`, `C#`, `Java`, and `JavaScript` into it.

As you work, you may notice that the fields you add to the page layout are grayed-out in the palette, but the Section user interface element is never grayed-out. This is because fields can only appear one time on each page layout, but the Section user interface element can be reused to create as many sections as you want.

💡 Tip: If you make a mistake while editing the page layout, you can use CTRL+Z and CTRL+Y to undo and redo your recent moves, respectively. The toolbar contains **Redo** and **Undo** buttons as well.

While we're shuffling fields around, let's reorganize the Information section so it's more readable.

11. Arrange the first column of the Information section as follows:

- Position Name
- Status
- Type
- Functional Area
- Job Level
- Travel Required
- Created By

12. Arrange the second column of the Information section as follows:

- Owner
- Location
- Open Date
- Hire By
- Close Date
- Days Open
- Last Modified By

That's much better—our fields are organized and it's easy to locate all the information we need.

The Information section still looks a little dense, though. Fortunately, the page layout editor provides a way to add blank spaces that separate the fields within the section to improve its readability even further.

Try It Out: Add Spaces Between Fields

When designing a page layout, you'll often want to distinguish or "pop" certain fields within a section. An easy and effective way to do this is by inserting blank spaces between fields. For example, in the Information section, inserting blank spaces below the first row in each column draws a user's eye to the most important information in the section, the position name and owner. We can also use blank spaces above the bottom row in each column to separate the Created By and Last Modified By fields from the critical position information. Let's give it a try!

1. Select the Fields category.

2. Drag the Blank Space user interface element from the palette to the page layout right below the Position Title field.

Dragging and Dropping Blank Spaces in a Page Layout

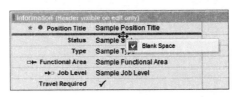

As with the Section user interface element, the Blank Space user interface element is never grayed-out in the palette when you drag it to the page layout because the element can be reused as many times as you want.

3. On the palette, select the Blank Space user interface element again and drag it below the `Owner` field.

4. Add two more blank spaces to the page layout, one above the `Created By` field and the other above the `Last Modified By` field.

Before we move on, you should be aware that if you accidentally navigate away from the page layout before saving your work, your changes will be lost. Rather than tempting fate, let's do a quick save of the work that we've done so far.

5. Click **Quick Save** in the toolbar above the palette, or press CTRL+S if you prefer using keyboard shortcuts.

The quick save feature allows you to save your changes and continue editing the page layout. Clicking **Save** in the toolbar also saves your work, but it takes you back to the page from which you accessed the page layout editor. We have a few more minor tweaks to make to our page layout, so we don't want to leave the page layout editor just yet.

Try It Out: Edit Field Properties

We just used the page layout editor to organize our Position page layout in a logical, easy-to-read fashion, but the page layout editor lets us do more than design the presentation of data—we can also use it to help determine which fields are required, and which fields are read-only:

*   If a field is required, a user won't be able to create a position record without specifying a value.

*   If a field is read-only, a user who views a position record edit page won't be able to change its value.

Required fields are denoted with a red asterisk (✹), while read-only fields are denoted with a lock icon (🔒).

> 🔺 Warning: Although we can make these changes on the page layout, don't forget our earlier warning! Page layouts should never be used as the sole means to restrict access to sensitive data that a user

shouldn't view or edit. That's because page layouts control only a record's edit and detail pages; they don't control access to those fields in any other part of the platform.

At this point, we don't have any fields that need to be read-only, but we do want to make sure that the salary range is always defined for each position, so let's make the `Min Pay` and `Max Pay` fields required. Once we do that, we'll be all done with our Position object!

To make the `Min Pay` and `Max Pay` fields required, we need to edit the properties of each field:

1. In the page layout editor, double-click the `Min Pay` field, or select the wrench icon (🔧) next to the field name.

This popup window allows us to edit the `Min Pay` field's properties. We can set the field to either read-only or required. If we didn't want a user to see the `Min Pay` field at all, we could simply drag it off the layout and onto the palette. We want to make sure it stays visible for right now, so let's leave it in its current spot.

2. Select the `Required` checkbox, and click **OK**.

3. Repeat these steps for the `Max Pay` field.

4. Click **Save** to finish customizing the page layout.

Hooray! We're all done with our Position object's page layout.

Look at What We've Done

Congratulations. We've just built ourselves a simple Recruiting app that tracks details about an organization's open positions. Let's check out what we've done by revisiting the Positions tab and clicking **New**. Because of the changes that we've made in our page layout, our Position edit page should now look like:

Final Version of the Position Layout

Let's take a look at our Position detail page before we move on. To do that, we have to create a position. Fill in the required fields, and click **Save**.

If we scroll to the bottom of the Position detail page, we'll notice a couple of related lists. Since we haven't customized the related lists that appear on positions, the platform displays the defaults: Open Activities, Activity History, and Notes & Attachments. Right now, there aren't any items in any of the lists. To see how one of those items would look, let's add a task.

1. In the Open Activities related list, click **New Task**.

Notice that some fields are already filled out for us. The platform made some educated guesses to determine who the task should be assigned to, what its status is, and how urgent it is. In addition, because we added the task through the related list on a position, the platform made the correct assumption that we want the task associated with that position. For now, let's leave the default values in those fields.

2. In Subject, enter *Post position online*.

3. In Due Date, select tomorrow's date.

4. Click **Save**.

Now, back on the detail page for our position, we see that the Open Activities related list contains the task we just created. From this list, we could dig in to the related task to see more details, make changes, or mark it complete.

Taking Your Page Layouts Mobile

Now that we've created a well-organized page layout and know that it works on the full Salesforce site, let's check how it looks on our mobile device.

1. Launch Salesforce1 on your mobile device, and log in.

2. From the navigation menu, tap **Show More** > **Positions**.

3. Tap **New**.

Compensation and Description Sections in Salesforce1

Just like when we tested out the advanced fields earlier in this chapter, our changes to better organize the fields are reflected in Salesforce1.

Now let's take a look at the position we just created in the full site to see how saved records look on a mobile device.

4. Tap **Cancel**.

5. Tap the position we just created.

In Salesforce1, we see two views, which we can toggle by swiping left and right. There's a third view, but we won't see that until we enable feed tracking in Collaborating with Chatter on page 207—so stay tuned!

Introducing the Record Detail Page

Our current view is the *record detail page*, which includes all the information that appears above a related list or mobile card in the page layout editor. Luckily, all the fields we've added are supported, but you should be aware that Salesforce1 doesn't support rich text area custom fields.

Record Detail Page for a Position Record

▓ Beyond the Basics

Because our page layout only includes a handful of fields, our layout should be okay for a mobile user. But, for future reference, always be aware of the different devices your users will be accessing these page layouts from. Having a large number of fields, such as more than 100, will make it difficult for your users to enter or find the information they need. It's best to either optimize all page layouts for mobile use or create page layouts specifically for mobile users. For more best practices, see the *Salesforce1 App Admin Guide*.

Introducing the Record Related Information Page

Swipe once to the left to see the record's *related information*.

Related Information Page for a Position Record

Unlike the full site, which show us the details of each related list, Salesforce1 displays just the names of the related lists. We can tap any of the related lists to see related records. Since we know the Open Activities related list has one item—the task we just created—let's check that related list out.

Tap **Open Activities** to drill in to that related list. In the Open Activities page, we see the task we created in the full site. For even more information about the task, we can tap the item to see the task record details.

Introducing Mobile Cards

That's not all! We can also add *mobile cards* to the record's related information page. You can add three types of elements to the related information page using mobile cards: *related lookup cards*, *components*, and *Visualforce page cards*.

Related lookup cards

Related lookup cards appear when you add a field from the Expanded Lookups category to the Mobile Cards section in the enhanced page layout editor. These fields all have a lookup relationship to another record.

Component cards

Component cards appear when you add an element from the Components category to the Mobile Cards section in the enhanced page layout editor.

Visualforce page cards

Visualforce page cards display Visualforce pages that have been enabled for Salesforce mobile apps. If you aren't familiar with Visualforce, don't worry. We'll talk about that in Moving Beyond Point-and-Click App Development on page 325.

We don't have any Visualforce pages or components to add to the related information page, but we do have some expanded lookups! Let's add one now.

1. In the full Salesforce site, open the page layout for Positions.

2. In the palette, select the Expanded Lookups category.

3. Drag `Last Modified By` to the Mobile Cards section.

4. Click **Save**.

An Expanded Lookup in the Mobile Cards Section

We only need to know the last user who modified our position record, but it's important to know that the mobile cards follow the order established in the page layout editor here, and the related lists always appear after the mobile cards. In addition, mobile cards will only show up in Salesforce1.

5. In Salesforce1, open our position record again.

The expanded lookup card we added now appears at the top of the related information page, identifying the user who last modified the record.

Related Information Page with an Expanded Lookup

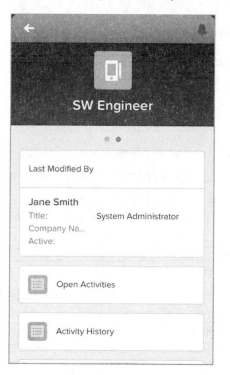

It looks like everything is in order! Just by doing a few things in Setup, we've created an object with a tab, we've added custom fields, and we've arranged them in a page layout. We've finished our simple app, and now we're well on our way to creating the more complex Recruiting app that we described earlier.

Introducing Compact Layouts

Now that we've seen how page layouts end up looking in Salesforce1, let's talk about another way we can customize how our Salesforce data appears on a mobile device. *Compact layouts* are used to display a record's key fields at a glance. Using compact layouts, we can indicate which fields should appear in a record's highlights area. These layouts were designed with touchscreen mobile devices in mind, where space is limited and users need to find important information quickly.

We can customize which fields appear in the highlights by customizing that object's compact layout. However, creating a custom compact layout isn't required. If we don't create one, Salesforce1 will use a read-only, predefined system default compact layout. For custom objects, this system default includes the record's name. In the case of our Position object, the system default compact layout displays `Position Title`.

Try It Out: Create a Compact Layout

Let's give our mobile users some more context in the highlights.

1. In the full Salesforce site, from Setup, enter `Objects` in the `Quick Find` box, then select **Objects**.

2. Click **Position**.

3. In the Compact Layouts related list, click **New**.

4. In `Label`, enter `Position`. Press TAB to automatically populate `Title`.

Now it's time to select the fields we want to include in the compact layout. We can include up to ten fields, but only four of those will appear in the record highlights on a mobile device. Notice that the list of available fields doesn't completely match the list of fields we created for the Position object. Only field types that are supported in compact layouts appear here. Compact layouts don't support text areas, long text areas, rich text areas, and multi-select picklists.

It's also important to know that if a user doesn't have the field-level security for a field that's included in a compact layout, the user will not see the field's value in the compact layout. For example, if we included `Min Pay` in this compact layout, and a user without access to that field was viewing a position record on her mobile phone, the compact layout would display a blank value for `Min Pay`.

Compact Layout Edit Page for Positions

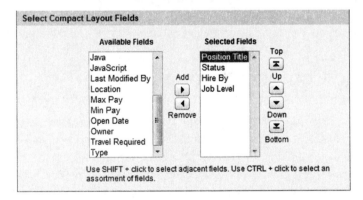

5. Select these fields for the compact layout, then click the **Add** button. You can select and add them individually or select them as a group using CTRL-click.

- Hire By
- Job Level
- Position Title
- Status

6. Using the **Up** or **Down** buttons, adjust the list so that the fields are in this order: `Position Title, Status, Hire By, Job Level`.

7. Click **Save**.

Try It Out: Assign the Primary Compact Layout

Before this compact layout will appear on our mobile device, we need to assign it to our users. Unlike with page layouts, where you can assign a different layout to each profile, one compact layout is applied to all users. Let's assign this new compact layout so our users will see more than just the position's title.

1. Click **Compact Layout Assignment**.

2. Click **Edit Assignment**.

3. In the `Primary Compact Layout` drop-down list, select Position.

4. Click **Save**.

Now let's test it out on our mobile device. The changes we just made should be reflected immediately in Salesforce1.

1. Launch Salesforce1, and log in if you haven't already.

2. From the navigation menu, tap **Show More** > **Positions**.

3. Tap a recent position to open it.

▦ Beyond the Basics

If you have record types associated with an object, you can override the primary compact layout assignment and assign specific compact layouts to different record types. If you don't set any record type overrides, all record types use the object's primary compact layout by default.

To find out more about compact layouts and record types, see "Assign Compact Layouts to Record Types" in the Salesforce Help.

Look at What We've Done

As you can see, now the record highlights displays the fields we selected in our custom compact layout. Now, instead of just the position title, we also see its status, when it must be filled, and what kind of job it is.

Notice that `Position Title` is more dominant than the other three. This is the *primary field*. When designing your own compact layouts, be aware that the first field in the Selected Fields list is the primary field in the highlights.

Record Detail Page with Customized Compact Layout

Things are going to get even more interesting in the next chapter. We'll add a few more custom objects to track things like candidates, job applications, and reviews, and then we'll enhance our Recruiting app even further by defining how our objects relate to one another. Before you know it, we're going to have an incredibly powerful Web application, all implemented with a few clicks in the platform.

CHAPTER 6 Expanding the Simple App Using Relationships

So far we've accomplished a fair amount—we've created the Recruiting app and built out a fully functional Position custom object with a tab and several types of fields. It's a good start, but there's more to do.

Having just one object in our Recruiting app is like having a party with just one guest—not all that interesting! We need to invite more "people" to the party by building custom objects to represent candidates, job applications, and reviews, and, even more importantly, we need to create *relationships* between them. Just like a party isn't all that fun if you don't know any of the other guests, an app isn't all that powerful unless its objects have links to other objects in the app. That's going to be the focus of this chapter, so let's get started!

Introducing Relationships

So what is a relationship, and why are they important for our app? Just as a personal relationship is a two-way association between two people, in terms of relational data, a relationship is a two-way association between two objects. Without relationships, we could build out as many custom objects as we could think of, but they'd have no way of linking to one another.

For example, after building a Position object and a Job Application object, we could have lots of information about a particular position and lots of information about a particular candidate who's submitted an application for it, but there would be no way of seeing information about the job application when looking at the position record, and no way of seeing information about the position when looking at the job application record. That's just not right!

With relationships, we can make that connection and display data about other related object records on a particular record's detail page. For example, once we define a relationship between the Position and Job Application objects we just talked about, our position record can have a related list of all the job applications for candidates who have applied for the position, while a job application record can have a link to the positions for which that candidate is applying. Suddenly the "people" at our Recruiting app "party" know some of the other guests, and the app just got a lot more interesting.

Relationships Allow Information about Other Object Records to be Displayed on a Record Detail Page

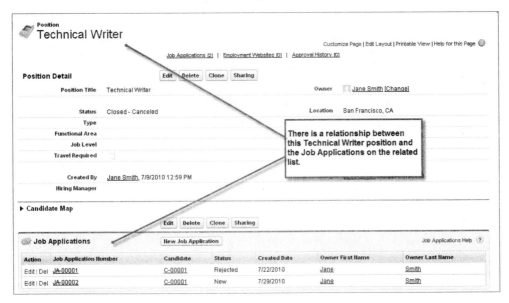

Introducing Relationship Custom Fields

As we learned in Reviewing Database Concepts on page 25, we can define a relationship between two objects through the use of common fields. On the platform, we can define relationships between objects by creating a *relationship* custom field that associates one object with another. A relationship field is a custom field on an object record that contains a link to another record. When we place a relationship custom field on an object, we're effectively creating a many-to-one relationship between the object on which the relationship field is placed and the other object.

There are different types of relationship fields, each with different implications. The simplest and most flexible type is a *lookup relationship* field, which creates a simple relationship between two objects. For example, if we place a lookup relationship field on a Job Application object that references position records, many job application records can be related to a single position record. This will be reflected both with a new `Position` field on the job application record and with a new Job Applications related list on the position record. You can also put multiple lookup relationship fields on a single object, which means that our Job Application object can also point to a Candidate object.

A second type of relationship field, *master-detail relationship*, is a bit more complex, but more powerful. Master-detail relationships create a special parent-child relationship between objects: the object on which you create the master-detail relationship field is the child or "detail," and the object referenced in the field is the parent or "master." In a master-detail relationship, the ownership and sharing of detail records are determined by the master record, and when you delete the master record, all of its detail records are automatically deleted along with it. Master-detail relationship fields are always required on detail records, and once you set a master-detail relationship field's value, you can't change it.

When do you use a master-detail relationship? If you have an object that derives its significance from another object. For example, say you have a Review custom object that contains an interviewer's feedback on a job application. If you delete a job application record, you will probably want all of its review records deleted as well, being that reviews of something that no longer exists aren't very useful. In this case, you want to create a master-detail relationship on the Review custom object with the Job Application object as the master object.

That's the sort of thing that we're going to do in this chapter. First, let's start with the really quick and easy example of putting a `Hiring Manager` field on our Position object—we'll create a many-to-one relationship between the Position object and the standard User object that comes with every organization, reflecting the fact that a hiring manager can be responsible for several positions at a time. Then we'll build out a few more objects and implement a more complex relationship involving positions, job applications, candidates, and reviews.

Try It Out: Relate Hiring Managers to Positions

For our first relationship, let's associate a hiring manager with a position by putting a lookup relationship field on the Position object. The lookup field will allow users to select the hiring manager for the position by selecting from all the users of the Recruiting app.

For example, if Mario Ruiz, our recruiter, wants to assign Phil Katz as the hiring manager for the Benefits Specialist position, he'll be able to do so by clicking the lookup icon (🔍) next to the lookup relationship field that we are going to create. His name will then appear on the Position detail page.

To create the lookup relationship field that accomplishes this, we'll need to go back to the now familiar Position object detail page.

1. From Setup, enter `Objects` in the `Quick Find` box, then select **Objects**.

2. Click **Position**.

3. In the Custom Fields & Relationships related list, click **New**.

4. Select `Lookup Relationship`, and click **Next**.

5. In the `Related To` drop-down list, choose User, and click **Next**.

As we've mentioned, User is a standard object that comes with all organizations on the platform. It contains information about everyone who uses the app in your organization.

6. In the `Field Label` text box, enter `Hiring Manager`. Once you move your cursor, the `Field Name` text box should be automatically populated with Hiring_Manager.

7. Click **Next**.

8. Accept the defaults in the remaining two steps of the wizard.

9. Click **Save**.

Look at What We've Done

Now return to the Positions tab, and click **New**. The Position edit page includes a new `Hiring Manager` lookup field! If you click the lookup icon next to this field (🔍), you can search through all of the users of the Recruiting app and select one as the hiring manager. That user's name now appears on the position record.

Hiring Manager Lookup Relationship

As you can see, it was easy to set up this simple relationship between positions and users. And as a general rule, you'll find that relationships are pretty easy to set up.

What gets a little tricky is when we start wanting to create relationships that don't represent a simple many-to-one relationship. We'll see an example of one of those in a little bit. Right now, let's build a custom object for candidates so we'll be able to create some more relationships in our Recruiting app.

Beyond the Basics

Did you know you can use Schema Builder to view the details of your schema and to quickly add and edit objects and relationship fields?

Say you're having a hard time visualizing how the Hiring Manager lookup is related to the Position and User objects. Schema Builder provides a dynamic environment that lets you see field details, such as whether the field is required, and shows how standard and custom objects are connected through lookup and master-detail relationships. You can zoom and pan in Schema Builder, edit an object's properties, and double-click any field to edit it.

To find out more, see "How Do I Access Schema Builder?" in the Salesforce Help.

Adding Candidates to the Mix

Let's add a Candidate custom object to our app so we can manage the information about our candidates. We'll also add fields to the object, modify the page layout properties, add a compact layout, and create a candidate record. The process for creating the Candidate custom object is almost identical to the one we followed to create the Position custom object, so we'll zip through this quickly.

Try It Out: Create the Candidate Object

To create our Candidate custom object, from Setup, enter `Objects` in the `Quick Find` box, then select **Objects**, click **New Custom Object**, and fill out the page according to the following table.

Table 8: Values for Defining the Candidate Object

Field	Value
Label	Candidate
Plural Label	Candidates
Object Name	Candidate
Description	Represents an applicant who might apply for one or more positions
Context-Sensitive Help Setting	Open the standard Salesforce Help & Training window
Record Name	Candidate Name
Data Type	Auto Number
Display Format	C-{00000}
Starting Number	00001
Allow Reports	Yes
Allow Activities	Yes
Track Field History	Yes
Allow Search	Yes
Deployment Status	Deployed
Add Notes & Attachments related list to default page layout	Yes
Launch New Custom Tab Wizard after saving this custom object	Yes

To create the Candidates tab, select a `Tab Style` in the first step of the wizard, and then accept all the defaults until you get to the Add to Custom Apps page. On this page, select only the Recruiting App and click **Save**.

The Recruiting app now has three tabs: Home, Positions, and Candidates. Now let's add some custom fields to the Candidate object.

Try It Out: Add Fields to the Candidate Object

To create custom fields on the Candidate object, from Setup, enter `Objects` in the `Quick Find` box, then select **Objects**, and click **Candidate** to view its detail page. In the Custom Fields & Relationships related list, use the **New** button to create custom fields according to the following table. Where necessary, we've indicated some additional values you'll need to fill in. Otherwise, you can simply accept all defaults.

One difference you'll see in the Candidate object fields is that three of them—`First Name`, `Last Name`, and `Email`—have the `External ID` option selected. This option allows the values in these fields to be indexed for search from the sidebar of the application. If we didn't select these values as external IDs, we'd only be able to search for records based on the `Candidate Number` field. Setting the `Email` field as an external ID is also going to help us with importing data a little later in this chapter.

Table 9: Candidate Object Custom Fields

Data Type	Field Label	Other Values
Text	First Name	Length: 50 External ID: Selected
Text	Last Name	Length: 50 External ID: Selected
Phone	Phone	
Email	Email	External ID: Selected
Text	Street	Length: 50
Text	City	Length: 50
Text	State/Province	Length: 50
Text	Zip/Postal Code	Length: 15
Text	Country	Length: 50

Data Type	Field Label	Other Values
Text	Current Employer	Length: 50
Number	Years of Experience	Length: 2
		Decimal Places: 0
Text	SSN	Length: 9
Picklist	Education	Picklist values:
		• HS Diploma
		• BA/BS
		• MA/MS/MBA
		• Ph.D.
		• Post Doc
Checkbox	Currently Employed	Default: Checked
Checkbox	US Citizen	Default: Checked
Checkbox	Visa Required	Default: Unchecked
Phone	Mobile	
Phone	Fax	

Try It Out: Modify the Candidate Page Layout Properties

Now let's organize all of our fields on the page layout and mark some fields as required. To do so, let's go to the Candidate page layout page.

1. From Setup, enter `Objects` in the `Quick Find` box, then select **Objects**.

2. Click **Candidate**.

3. In the Page Layouts related list, click **Edit** next to the Candidate Layout.

4. Create three new double-column sections below the Information section: Address, Employment, and Additional Details. Drag the appropriate fields into them, as shown in the Candidate Object Page Layout image, and don't forget to click **Quick Save** so you can save your work as you go.

5. Set the `First Name`, `Last Name`, and `Email` fields to required as follows:

   a. Use CTRL+click to select all three required fields.

    b. Double-click your selection.

    c. Select the `Required` checkbox in the Select All row, and click **OK**.

6. Click **Save**.

Your Candidate page layout should now look similar to the following screenshot.

Candidate Object Page Layout

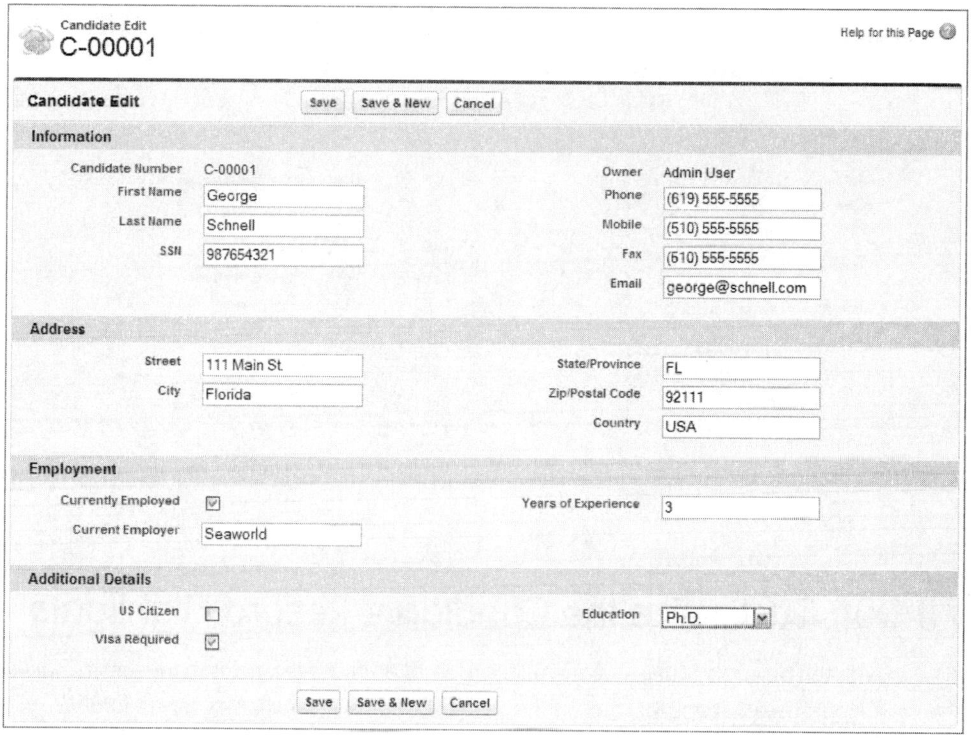

Look at What We've Done

Here's a quick way to verify that you did everything correctly.

1. Click the Candidates tab.

2. Click **New**.

3. Create a new record for a candidate named Ethan Tran in San Francisco.

4. Enter a value for each of the required fields. Salesforce will not verify the email address you enter in the `Email` field right now, so feel free to enter a fictitious one.

5. For the candidate's `City`, enter `San Francisco`.

6. Click **Save**.

How does the page layout look? Are the fields where you want them?

If your page layout doesn't look quite right and you need to make a few adjustments, click the **Edit Layout** link in the upper right corner.

Edit Layout Link

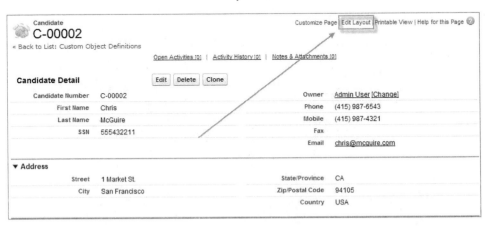

The **Edit Layout** link takes you directly to the page layout editor and lets you modify the page you are currently viewing.

Try It Out: Customize the Candidate Record Highlights

To finish up with this object, let's help out our mobile users by adding a few fields to the record highlights. Right now, the only field that appears there is the candidate number, which isn't very helpful. We want the highlights to give our mobile user the information they need about this candidate at a glance. Some useful data points might be the candidate's location or level of expertise.

1. From Setup, enter `Objects` in the `Quick Find` box, then select **Objects**.

2. Click **Candidate**.

3. In the Compact Layouts related list, click **New**.

4. Give the compact layout a name, and move fields to Available Fields so that they appear in the following order.

    •   `Last Name`

    •   `City`

- Education
- Years of Experience

5. Click **Save**.

Remember to quickly assign our new compact layout as the primary compact layout for candidates.

6. Click **Compact Layout Assignment**.

7. Click **Edit Assignment**.

8. From the drop-down list, select the compact layout you just created.

9. Click **Save**.

Look At What We've Done

Now let's check how a candidate record looks on our mobile device.

1. Launch Salesforce1, and log in if you're prompted.

2. From the navigation menu, tap **Show More** > **Candidates**

3. Tap **C-00001**.

Customized Record Highlights for C-00001

The record highlights includes some information, but two of the fields are blank. This is because when we created this record in the last section, we only filled in the required fields (First Name, Last Name, and Email) and City. Let's fill in those other fields so we can see the compact layout in all its glory!

4. Swipe left to the record details page.

5. Tap **Edit**.

6. Fill in some of the empty fields. You can add more, but at the least, make sure that Education and Years of Experience have values.

7. Tap **Save**.

Customized Record Highlights for C-00001 with All Fields Filled In

If you are able to successfully create a new candidate record and see the right values in the highlights, let's move on to the Job Application object!

Bringing Candidates and Positions Together with Job Applications

Our app can track candidates and open positions, but there's a crucial element that's missing: how do we know which candidates are interested in which positions? We can create lookup relationship fields on the Candidate object that let recruiters specify the positions in which the candidate is interested, but what if we want to track additional information, such as whether the candidate is currently scheduled to interview for one of those positions? And wouldn't it be helpful if the recruiter has a way of storing the cover letters that candidates tailor for each specific job to which they are applying?

We can satisfy these requirements with a Job Application custom object that stores data about an individual candidate's application to a single position. Each time a candidate wants to apply for a position, the recruiter can create a job application record that contains the candidate's name and the position to which he or she is applying, as well as any cover letter that the candidate may have submitted specifically for that position. Recruiters will also be able to indicate the status of the candidate's application, such as whether he or she is scheduled for an interview or if the application has been rejected. After we create the Job Application object and its fields, we'll make a few small modifications to the Position, Candidate, and Job Application objects so that each position record displays the names of the candidates who have applied to it, and each candidate record displays the name of the positions to which the candidate has applied.

Try It Out: Create the Job Application Object

You should be a pro at this by now! To create our Job Application custom object, from Setup, enter `Objects` in the `Quick Find` box, then select **Objects**, click **New Custom Object**, and fill out the page according to the following table.

Table 10: Values for Defining the Job Application Object

Field	Value
Label	Job Application
Plural Label	Job Applications
Object Name	Job_Application
Description	Represents a candidate's application to a position
Context-Sensitive Help Setting	Open the standard Salesforce Help & Training window
Record Name	Job Application Name
Data Type	Auto Number
Display Format	JA-{00000}
Starting Number	00001
Allow Search	Yes
Allow Reports	Yes
Allow Activities	Yes
Track Field History	Yes
Deployment Status	Deployed
Add Notes & Attachments related list to default page layout	Yes
Launch New Custom Tab Wizard after saving this custom object	Yes

To create the Job Applications tab, select a `Tab Style` in the first step of the wizard, and then accept all the defaults until you get to the Add to Custom Apps page. On this page, select only the Recruiting app, and then click **Save**.

We're now just a few custom fields away from linking the Job Application object with the Position and Candidate objects.

Try It Out: Add Fields to the Job Application Object

Here's another procedure that we've done several times before, but this time we only need to define four custom fields instead of the nearly twenty that we built for the Candidate object. We'll need to add a text field for the candidate's cover letter, a picklist field so that we can track the application's status, and two lookup relationship fields that will create relationships between the Job Application object and the Position and Candidate objects.

Although these fields are almost identical to the ones we created earlier, you'll notice when you're defining the lookup relationship fields that there's a new step in the custom field wizard *Step 6: Add Custom Related Lists*. This step of the wizard is where we can specify a heading for the Job Applications related list that will show up on both the Candidate and Position detail pages.

Why didn't we see this step earlier when we created our `Hiring Manager` lookup field? It turns out that User is a unique standard object: it doesn't have a tab, and you cannot add related lists to it. The platform knows this, so it leaves out the related list step whenever someone adds a lookup relationship field that references the User object.

Now that we're all squared away with that small difference, let's finish up these Job Application fields. From Setup, enter `Objects` in the `Quick Find` box, then select **Objects**, and then click **Job Application** to view its detail page. In the Custom Fields & Relationships related list, use the **New** button to create custom fields according to the following table. Where necessary, we've indicated some additional values you'll need to fill in. Otherwise you can simply accept all defaults.

Table 11: Add Custom Fields to the Job Application Object

Data Type	Field Label	Other Values
Lookup Relationship	Candidate	Related To: Candidate Related List Label: Job Applications
Lookup Relationship	Position	Related To: Position Related List Label: Job Applications
Text Area (Long)	Cover Letter	Length: 32,768 # of Visible Lines: 6
Picklist	Status	Picklist values: • New • Review Resume • Phone Screen

Data Type	Field Label	Other Values
		• Schedule Interviews
		• Extend an Offer
		• Hired
		• Rejected
		Use first value as default value: Selected

Try It Out: Customize the Job Application Record Highlights

Since there are only a few fields, we don't need to worry about customizing the page layout. It's a good time, however, to customize the compact layout.

1. From Setup, enter `Objects` in the `Quick Find` box, then select **Objects**.
2. Click **Job Application**.
3. In the Compact Layouts related list, use the **New** button to create a compact layout with the following fields. Enter a name in `Label`, and use the **Up** and **Down** buttons to match the order.

   • `Job Application Name`
   • `Status`
   • `Candidate`
   • `Position`

4. Click **Save**.

Remember to quickly assign our new compact layout as the primary compact layout for job applications.

5. Click **Compact Layout Assignment**.
6. Click **Edit Assignment**.
7. From the drop-down list, select the compact layout you just created.
8. Click **Save**.

Look at What We've Done

Tada! If you click on the new Job Applications tab and click **New**, you'll see the `Candidate` lookup field, a `Position` lookup field, the candidate's cover letter, and a `Status` picklist field.

Custom Fields on the Job Application Edit Page

Don't forget to launch Salesforce1 to see our new compact layout in action. Now mobile users will see important details without having to scroll through a list of fields.

Record Highlights for a Job Application Record

But there's more! Because we've built a couple of lookup relationships, our candidate and position record detail pages now each have a new Job Applications related list. And the Job Application detail page includes links to the candidate and position records that it references. All three objects are now related and linked to one another!

Job Application Links to Position and Candidate Data

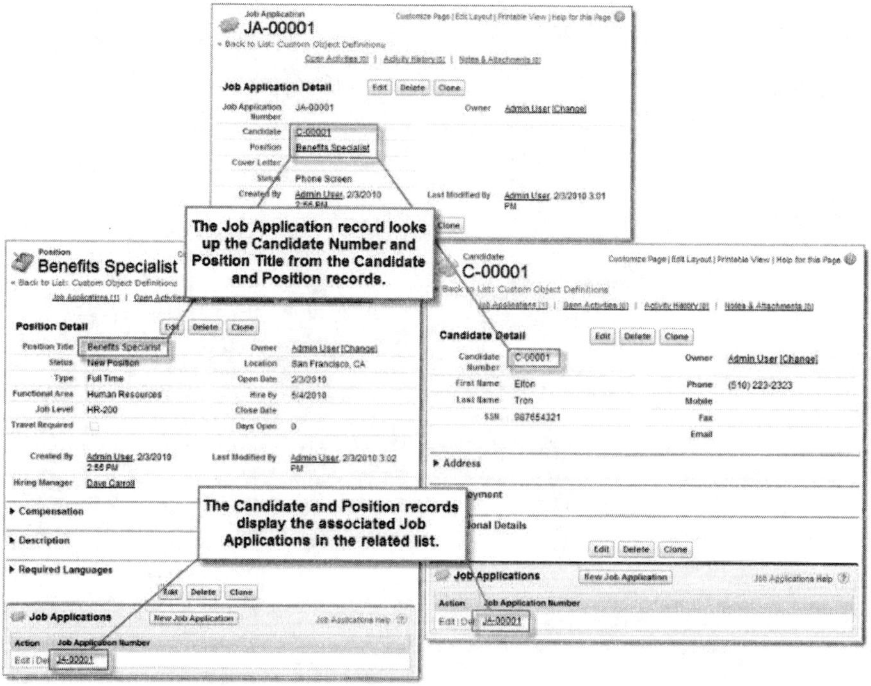

Before we move on, let's see if we can clean up the usability of our app a bit more so our users don't have to identify candidates and job applications by number when they click the lookup button in the Job Application edit page, or when they look at the Job Applications related list on the Candidate or Position detail pages.

Introducing Search Layouts

By default, all lookup dialogs and related lists that result from new relationships, such as the ones we've defined in this chapter, only display the record name or number. For example, if you go ahead and create a job application, you might find the Candidate lookup dialog a little cryptic because the only listed field is Candidate Number. You probably expected to see the First Name, Last Name, and additional fields, as shown in the following screenshot.

Default Candidate Lookup on the Job Application Object

Likewise, the Job Applications related lists on the Position and Candidate detail pages only display a job application number. It is much more useful if these related lists also include the associated candidate's name or position.

To fix these issues, we can add fields to the *search layouts* for the objects that we've defined. Search layouts are ordered groups of fields that are displayed when a record is presented in a particular context, such as in search results, a lookup dialog, or a related list. By adding fields, we can give users more information and help them locate records more quickly.

The Search Layouts related list on the custom object detail page is the place to modify these sets of fields. From Setup, enter `Objects` in the `Quick Find` box, then select **Objects** and select the Candidate object. You'll see that the available search layouts include:

Table 12: Available Search Layouts

Layout Name	Description
Search Results	The search results that originate from searching in the left sidebar search of the application or in advanced search.

Layout Name	Description
Lookup Dialogs	The lookup dialog results that originate from clicking 🔍 next to a lookup field on an edit page.
Lookup Phone Dialogs	The lookup dialog results that originate from clicking 🔍 next to a lookup field with a phone data type on an edit page.
Candidates Tab	The list of recent records that appears on the home page of a tab, and in related lists on other object detail pages.
Candidates List View	This layout isn't for specifying fields. Instead, use it to specify the buttons that appear on the list view page for an object.
Search Filter Fields	The filters that can be applied to search results.

Try It Out: Add Fields to the Candidate Lookup Dialog

Let's add fields to our Candidate lookup dialog:

1. From Setup, enter `Objects` in the `Quick Find` box, then select **Objects**.

2. Click **Candidate**.

3. In the Search Layouts related list, click **Edit** next to the Lookup Dialogs layout.

The Edit Search Layout page includes a list of available fields from the Candidate object. You can choose up to ten fields to include in the lookup dialog, and order them In any way you choose, except that the object's unique name or number field (such as `Candidate Name`) must be listed first.

4. Move the following fields into the Selected Fields box under `Candidate Name`:

   * `First Name`
   * `Last Name`
   * `City`
   * `State/Province`
   * `Phone`

5. Click **Save**.

That's it! To try it out, return to the Job Applications tab, and click **New**. When you click the lookup icon next to the `Candidate` field, the dialog is now much more useful.

Modified Candidate Lookup on the Job Application Object

Try It Out: Update Additional Search Layouts

Now that we've updated one search layout for lookups, the rest should be easy. Use the Search Layouts related list on the custom object detail page to modify the other search layouts as described in the following table.

Table 13: Additional Search Layouts

Object	Search Layout	Add These Fields
Candidate	• Search Results • Candidates Tab	• Candidate Name • First Name • Last Name • City • State/Province • Phone
Candidate	• Search Filter Fields	• Candidate Name • First Name • Last Name • Education • Years of Experience • City • State/Province

116

Object	Search Layout	Add These Fields
		• Country
		• Currently Employed
Position	• Search Results	• Position Name
	• Lookup Dialogs	• Location
	• Positions Tab	• Functional Area
	• Search Filter Fields	• Job Level
		• Type
		• Hiring Manager
		• Status
		• Open Date
		• Close Date
Job Application	• Search Results	• Job Application Name
	• Lookup Dialogs	• Candidate
	• Job Applications Tab	• Position
	• Search Filter Fields	• Status
		• Created Date
		• Owner First Name
		• Owner Last Name

Now let's create another custom object to provide our hiring managers and interviewers with a place to enter their comments about job applications.

Managing Review Assessments

Interviewers, recruiters, and hiring managers need to be able to create reviews so that they can record their comments about each candidate's job application, and rate the candidate's suitability for the position. They also need to see the reviews posted by other people. To allow our users to perform these tasks, we'll need to create a custom Review object and relate it to the Job Application object.

The Review object has a many-to-one relationship with the Job Application object because one job application can have one or more reviews associated with it. A related list on the job application record will show the associated reviews, representing the "many" side of the relationship.

Review Has a Many-to-One Relationship with Job Application

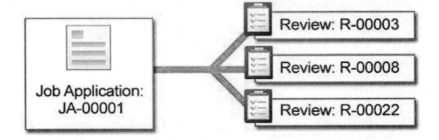

However, instead of creating this relationship with a lookup relationship field, this time we'll use a master-detail relationship field. A master-detail relationship field makes sense in this case because reviews lose their meaning when taken out of the context of a job application, so we'll want to automatically delete reviews when we delete the job application to which they're related.

Try It Out: Create the Review Object

To create the Review object, from Setup, enter `Objects` in the `Quick Find` box, then select **Objects**, click **New Custom Object**, and fill out the page according to the following table.

Table 14: Values for Defining the Review Object

Field	Value
Label	Review
Plural Label	Reviews
Object Name	Review
Description	Represents an interviewer's assessment of a particular candidate
Context-Sensitive Help Setting	Open the standard Salesforce Help & Training window
Record Name	Review Name

Field	Value
Data Type	Auto Number
Display Format	R-{000000}
Starting Number	000001
Allow Reports	Yes
Allow Activities	Yes
Track Field History	Yes
Allow Search	Yes
Deployment Status	Deployed
Add Notes & Attachments related list to default page layout	Yes
Launch New Custom Tab Wizard after saving this custom object	No

Notice that we didn't launch the tab wizard this time. Reviews don't need a tab of their own because they can be accessed via a related list on the Job Application detail page. When you create an object with a tab, the platform provides access to that object's records in various places other than just the tab, such as in search results and the Recent Items list in the sidebar area of every page. Because most Recruiting app users won't need to see reviews unless it's in the context of a Job application, we don't need to create a separate tab for them.

Now let's finish up the custom fields on the Review object.

Try It Out: Add Fields to the Review Object

Let's start by adding the master-detail relationship field, which will relate our Review object with the Job Application object. To create the master-detail relationship field, access the Review object detail page.

1. From Setup, enter *Objects* in the Quick Find box, then select **Objects**.
2. Click **Review**.
3. In the Custom Fields & Relationships related list, click **New**.
4. Select *Master-Detail Relationship*, and click **Next**.

5. In the `Related To` drop-down list, choose Job Application, and click **Next**.

6. Click in the `Field Name` text box to automatically populate it with the field name `Job_Application`.

7. Leave the `Read/Write` radio button selected.

This sharing setting prevents people from creating, editing, or deleting a review unless they can also create, edit, or delete the associated job application. We'll learn about sharing and security in the next chapter.

8. Click **Next**.

9. Accept the defaults in the remaining three steps of the wizard.

10. Click **Save**.

Your master-detail relationship is complete!

> ### Beyond the Basics
>
> Did you know you can create master-detail relationships with multiple levels? With multilevel master-detail relationships you can create reports that roll up data from all levels of the data model, and trigger cascading deletes when a master record is deleted.
>
> Say you want a candidate's applications and review records to be deleted when a hiring manager deletes a candidate. You can create a new master-detail relationship field that relates the Job Application object with the Candidate object. Because the Review and Job Application objects are already related to each other in a master-detail relationship, you've built a multilevel relationship where Candidate is the master, Job Application is the detail, and Review is the subdetail.

Now that your master-detail relationship is in place, let's think about the other types of fields that would be useful to people looking at a review record.

Most likely, users will want to see the name of the candidate and the position for which they are being reviewed. We could create a lookup relationship to the Position and Candidate objects, and then require reviewers to enter those fields when creating a review record, but what if they select the wrong value? Besides, wouldn't it be better if these fields were somehow automatically populated?

To solve this, we'll tap into the synergy of formulas and relationships to create *cross-object formulas*. Cross-object formulas are formulas that span two or more objects by referencing merge fields from related records. This means that formulas on our Review object can access fields on the Job Application object, and formulas on the Job Application object can access fields on both the Position and Candidate objects. We're going to take it even one step further by creating formula fields on our Review object that *span* the Job Application object to reference fields on the Candidate and Position objects. You'll quickly discover that using related data is much easier than it sounds!

Let's begin by building a formula field on the Review object that references the title of the position on the review's parent job application record.

1. From Setup, enter `Objects` in the `Quick Find` box, then select **Objects**.

2. Click **Review**.

3. In the Custom Fields & Relationships related list, click **New**.

4. Select the `Formula` data type, and click **Next**.

5. In the `Field Label` field, enter `Position`. Once you move your cursor, the `Field Name` text box automatically populates with Position.

6. Select the `Text` formula return type and click **Next**.

7. Click the **Insert Field** button.

The Insert Field overlay appears, as shown below.

Insert Field Overlay

8. Select Review in the first column.

When you choose Review, the second column displays all of the Review object's fields as well as its related objects, which are denoted by a greater-than sign (>). Notice that the `Created By` and `Last Modified By` fields also have greater-than signs. This is because these are lookup fields to the User object.

9. Select `Job Application` > in the second column. The third column displays the fields of the Job Application object.

10. Select `Position` > in the third column. The fourth column displays the fields of the Position object.

Be sure that you select `Position` > (with the greater than sign) and not `Position`. The one with the greater-than sign is the Position object, while the one without the greater than sign is the `Position` lookup field on the Job Application object. In most cases, formulas that access lookup fields return a cryptic record ID. Instead, we want our formula to return the position's title.

11. Choose `Position Name` in the fourth column.

12. Click **Insert**.

Your formula now looks like:

```
Job_Application__r.Position__r.Name
```

The formula spans to the review's related job application (`Job_Application__r`), then to the job application's related position (`Position__r`), and finally references the position's title (`Name`). Notice that each part of the formula is separated by a period, and that the relationship names consist of the related object followed by `__r`.

13. Click **Next**.

14. Accept all remaining field-level security and page layout defaults.

15. Click **Save**.

That wraps up our first cross-object formula field. Let's try another. This time, we'll add a cross-object formula field on our Review object that displays the first and last names of the candidate being reviewed. We'll also up the ante by using the `HYPERLINK` function so that users can access the candidate's record by clicking the field.

1. From Setup, enter `Objects` in the `Quick Find` box, then select **Objects**.

2. Click **Review**.

3. In the Custom Fields & Relationships related list, click **New**.

4. Select the `Formula` data type, and click **Next**.

5. In the `Field Label` field, enter `Candidate`. Once you move your cursor, the `Field Name` text box automatically populates with Candidate.

6. Select the `Text` formula return type and click **Next**.

7. From the `Functions` list, double-click `HYPERLINK`.

The `HYPERLINK` function lets you create a hyperlink to any URL or record in Salesforce. The text of the hyperlink can differ from the URL itself, which is useful here because we want our hyperlink to display the first and last names of the candidate while the URL points to the candidate record itself.

8. Delete `url` from the `HYPERLINK` function you just inserted, but leave your cursor there.

9. Click the **Insert Field** button, and select `Review >`, `Job Application >`, `Candidate >`, `Record ID`, and click **Insert**.

Salesforce generates a unique ID for every record. By inserting the record ID of the candidate in our `HYPERLINK` function, we're enabling our formula field to locate and link to the candidate's record.

10. Delete `friendly_name` from the `HYPERLINK` function, but leave your cursor there.

11. Click the **Insert Field** button, and select `Review >`, `Job Application >`, `Candidate >`, `First Name`, then click **Insert**.

12. Enter a space, then click the **Insert Operator** button and choose Concatenate.

The Concatenate operator inserts an ampersand (&) in your formula, and joins the values on either side of the ampersand. Here we're going to use the Concatenate operator to join the first and last names of the candidate in a single field, even though they are stored in separate fields on the Candidate object. The Concatenate operator also lets us insert a space between the two names, as you'll see in the next step.

13. Enter another space, then type a blank space enclosed in quotes, like this:

```
" "
```

This appends a blank space after the first name of the candidate.

14. Enter a space, then click the **Insert Operator** button and choose Concatenate once more to add a second ampersand in your formula.

15. Click the **Insert Field** button, and select `Review >`, `Job Application >`, `Candidate >`, `Last Name`, then click **Insert**.

16. Delete `[ target ]` from the `HYPERLINK` function. This is an optional parameter that isn't necessary for our formula field.

17. Click **Check Syntax** to check your formula for errors. Your finished formula should look like this:

```
HYPERLINK
      ( Job_Application__r.Candidate__r.Id ,
      Job_Application__r.Candidate__r.First_Name__c
      &
      " "
      &
      Job_Application__r.Candidate__r.Last_Name__c )
```

18. Click **Next**.

19. Accept all remaining field-level security and page layout defaults.

20. Click **Save**.

Whew! That one required a little more thought, but using a bit of brainpower here has tremendously improved the usability of our app, which you'll see in a moment when we test our changes to the Review object. Before we start testing, though, let's quickly add two more easy fields to finish our Review object. We need a text area field for the reviewer's assessment, and a number field in which the reviewer can give the candidate a numeric score.

From Setup, enter `Objects` in the `Quick Find` box, then select **Objects** and select the Review object. Use the **New** button in the Custom Fields & Relationships related list to create the remaining custom fields for the Review object according to the following table. Where necessary, we've indicated some additional values you'll need to fill in. Otherwise, accept all defaults.

Table 15: Add Custom Fields to the Review Object

Data Type	Field Label	Other Values
Text Area (Long)	Assessment	Length: 32,768
		# of Visible Lines: 6
Number	Rating	Length: 1
		Always require a value in this field in order to save a record
		Help text: *Enter a 1-5 rating of the candidate.*

When you're done, add a quick validation rule to ensure that the Ratings field only accepts the numbers 1 through 5. This will keep our review rating system consistent throughout our organization.

1. From Setup, enter `Objects` in the `Quick Find` box, then select **Objects**.
2. Click **Review**.
3. In the Validation Rules related list, click **New**.
4. In the `Rule Name` text box, enter `Rating_Scale_Rule`.
5. Select the `Active` checkbox.
6. In the `Description` text box, enter `Rating must be between 1 and 5.`
7. Enter the following error condition formula:

```
(Rating__c <1 || Rating__c > 5)
```

This formula prevents the record from being saved if the value of the `Rating` field is less than one or greater than five.

8. In the `Error Message` text box, enter *Invalid rating. Rating must be between 1 and 5.*

9. Next to the `Error Location` field, select the `Field` radio button, and then choose `Rating` from the drop-down list.

10. Click **Save**.

Our Review object is complete! We've added several features that will help users access the data they need in order to assess each job application. There's one more easy improvement we need to streamline our job application review process. It involves returning to our Job Application object and taking advantage of one of the benefits we gain by using a master-detail relationship.

Introducing Roll-Up Summary Fields

The rating system we created on the Review object lets users quickly see each reviewer's opinion of the candidate's suitability for the position. While each individual opinion is important, it would be even better to see these ratings compiled in a way that summarizes how the candidate did overall. For example, wouldn't it be great if we could have a `Total Rating` field on each Job Application record that shows the sum of all the job application's review ratings?

The good news is that we can! A simple roll-up summary field on the Job Application object can summarize data from a set of related detail records and automatically display the output on a master record. Use roll-up summary fields to display the sum, minimum, or maximum value of a field in a related list, or the record count of all records listed in a related list.

Try It Out: Create Roll-Up Summary Fields

Begin creating your roll-up summary just as you create any other custom field:

1. From Setup, enter *Objects* in the `Quick Find` box, then select **Objects**.

2. Click **Job Application**.

3. In the Custom Fields & Relationships related list, click **New**.

4. Select the `Roll-Up Summary` data type, and click **Next**.

When creating a field on an object that is not the master in a master-detail relationship, the `Roll-Up Summary` data type is not available. This is because roll-up summary fields are only available on the master object in a master-detail relationship.

125

5. In the `Field Label` field, enter *Total Rating.* Once you move your cursor, the `Field Name` text box automatically populates with Total_Rating.

6. Click **Next**.

7. In the `Summarized Object` drop-down list, choose Reviews.

8. Under Select Roll-Up Type, select `SUM`.

9. In the `Field to Aggregate` drop-down list, select `Rating`.

10. Leave `All records should be included in the calculation` selected, and click **Next**.

11. Accept all remaining field-level security and page layout defaults.

12. Click **Save**.

Now our job application records aggregate the ratings of their related reviews. This data could be a little deceptive, though, since some job applications might get reviewed more than others. It would be more helpful if we could see the average rating.

Roll-up summary fields themselves don't allow you to average values together, but you can use them in formulas that do. Let's create a second roll-up summary field on the Job Application object, and then build a simple formula field that uses both roll-up summary fields to find the average rating.

1. From Setup, enter *Objects* in the `Quick Find` box, then select **Objects**.

2. Click **Job Application**.

3. In the Custom Fields & Relationships related list, click **New**.

4. Select the `Roll-Up Summary` data type, and click **Next**.

5. In the `Field Label` field, enter *Number of Reviews.* Once you move your cursor, the `Field Name` text box automatically populates with `Number_of_Reviews`.

6. Click **Next**.

7. In the `Summarized Object` drop-down list, choose Reviews.

8. Under Select Roll-Up Type, select `COUNT`.

We don't need to specify a `Field to Aggregate` this time since we're just counting the number of related detail records and are not interested in any specific field.

9. Leave `All records should be included in the calculation` selected, and click **Next**.

10. Accept all remaining field-level security and page layout defaults.

11. Click **Save**.

Both roll-up summary fields are in place now. Let's build a formula field called `Average Rating` that divides the value of the first roll-up summary field by the value of the second.

1. From Setup, enter `Objects` in the `Quick Find` box, then select **Objects**.

2. Click **Job Application**.

3. In the Custom Fields & Relationships related list, click **New**.

4. Select the `Formula` data type, and click **Next**.

5. In the `Field Label` field, enter `Average Rating`. Once you move your cursor, the `Field Name` text box automatically populates with `Average_Rating`.

6. Select the `Number` formula return type and click **Next**.

7. Click the **Insert Field** button.

8. Select `Job Application >`, then `Total Rating`, and click **Insert**.

9. Click the **Insert Operator** button and choose `Divide`.

10. Click the **Insert Field** button again.

11. Choose `Job Application >`, then `Number of Reviews`, and click **Insert**. Your formula should look like this:

```
Total_Rating__c / Number_of_Reviews__c
```

12. Click **Next**.

13. Accept the defaults in the remaining steps of the wizard.

14. Click **Save**.

That wraps up all the fields and relationships we need to manage our reviews. Let's quickly organize the presentation of our fields and then test everything we've created.

Try It Out: Customize the Review Object's Page and Search Layouts

First, let's update the page layout of the Review object so that the `Assessment` text field is in a single column section of the same name.

1. From Setup, enter `Objects` in the `Quick Find` box, then select **Objects**.

2. Click **Review**.

3. In the Page Layouts related list, click **Edit** next to Review Layout.

4. Drag a new section just below the System Information section. The Section Properties dialog box opens.

5. Name the section *Assessment*, and configure it to contain one column.

6. Drag the Assessment and Rating fields into the Assessment section.

7. Click **Save**.

Now, let's configure our Review search layouts so that reviews are always displayed with the associated job application, position, and candidate.

1. In the Search Layouts related list on the Review object detail page, click **Edit** next to Lookup Dialogs and add the following fields:

   * Review Name
   * Rating
   * Job Application
   * Candidate
   * Position
   * Created Date

2. Repeat for the Search Filter Fields layout.

To update the Reviews related list that appears on the Job Application detail page, we'll have to edit the related list directly on the Job Application page layout. This is different from how we added fields to the Job Application related list on the position and candidate detail pages because the Review object doesn't have an associated tab, and therefore, doesn't have a tab search layout. Remember—the tab search layout is responsible for both the fields that appear in the list on the tab home page and the default fields that appear in related lists on other object detail pages.

 Note: The tab search layout is responsible for the fields in the related list layout only if the related list properties have not been modified on other objects' page layouts. For example, if you modify the properties of the Job Application related list on the Position page layout, those changes will always override the field specifications of the Job Application tab search layout.

Because the Review object doesn't have a tab search layout, we have to set those fields another way.

1. From Setup, enter *Objects* in the Quick Find box, then select **Objects**.

2. Click **Job Application**.

3. In the Page Layouts related list, click **Edit** next to Job Application Layout.

4. On the Job Application page layout, locate the Reviews related list and click the wrench icon ( ) to edit its properties.

5. On the Related List Properties dialog box, add the following fields to the Selected Fields box:

- Review Name
- Rating
- Candidate
- Position
- Created Date

6. From the Sort By drop-down list, choose Review Name.

7. Click **OK**.

8. Click **Save** on the page layout edit page.

Try It Out: Customize Record Highlights for Reviews

Now, let's create a custom compact layout to give mobile users more context when looking at review records.

1. From Setup, enter Objects in the Quick Find box, then select **Objects**.

2. Click **Review**.

3. In the Compact Layouts related list, use the **New** button to create a compact layout with the following fields. Enter a name in Label, and use the **Up** and **Down** buttons to match the order.

   - Review Name
   - Rating
   - Candidate
   - Created By

4. Click **Save**.

Remember to quickly assign our new compact layout as the primary compact layout for reviews.

5. Click **Compact Layout Assignment**.

6. Click **Edit Assignment**.

7. From the drop-down list, select the compact layout you just created.

8. Click **Save**.

Look at What We've Done

Terrific! Let's go see what we've made:

1. Click the Job Applications tab and select a record, or create one if you haven't already.

129

> **Tip:** When you use the Candidate and Position lookup dialogs as you're creating a job application record, note that, by default, they only display the most recently viewed records. You can locate additional records by using the search box, which returns records based on the `Candidate Number` or `Position Title` fields, respectively.
>
> Use the * wildcard with other characters to improve your search results. For example, searching on C* returns every candidate record. Likewise, searching on *e returns all position records that include the letter 'e' in the title.

After the job application is created, notice that the Reviews related list now appears on the Job Application detail page. That's because we related the Review object to the Job Application object with a master-detail relationship.

2. In the Reviews related list, click **New Review** to create a review.

Do you see how the platform automatically filled in the job application number in the review's edit page? That's one of the small, but important, benefits of using the platform to build an application like this—not only is it easy to create links and relationships between objects, but the platform anticipates what we're doing and helps us accomplish our task with as few clicks as possible.

3. Complete the fields on the review, and click **Save**.

Notice that the name of the candidate and the title of the position appear on the review detail page. If you click the candidate's name, his or her record displays.

Before we move on, let's check out how that review we created looks in Salesforce1 with our compact layout.

1. In Salesforce1, open the navigation menu and tap **Show More** > **Job Applications**.

2. Tap **JA-00001** to open the job application record we just created.

3. Swipe over the related information page.

4. Tap the Reviews preview card to see all the reviews associated with this application.

5. Tap **R-000001** to open the review record.

Go ahead and tap—or click, if you're back in the full site—around the rest of the app, creating a few more positions, job applications, candidates, and reviews. Pretty neat, huh? Our data is all interconnected, and our edits to the search layouts allow us to view details of several related objects all at once.

Creating a Many-to-Many Relationship

Our Recruiting app now has quite a few many-to-one relationships, but what if we needed to create a many-to-many relationship? For example, what if we have an object that stored information about various employment websites, and we wanted to track which open positions we posted to those sites? This would require a many-to-many relationship because:

- One position could be posted on many employment websites.
- One employment website could list many positions.

Here's where we get a little creative. Instead of creating a relationship field on the Position object that directly links to the Employment Website object, we can link them using a *junction object*. A junction object is a custom object with two master-detail relationships, and is the key to making a many-to-many relationship.

For our app, we're going to create a junction object called Job Posting. A job posting fits into the space between positions and employment websites—one position can be posted many times, and one employment website can have many job postings, but a job posting always represents a posting about a single position on a single employment website. In essence, the Job Posting object has a many-to-one relationship with both the Position and the Employment Website objects, and through those many-to-one relationships, we'll have a many-to-many relationship between the Position and Employment Website objects.

> 💡 Tip: In many apps, the sole purpose of a junction object is to simply relate two objects, so it often makes sense to give the junction object a name that indicates the association or relationship it creates. For example, if you wanted to use a junction object to create a many-to-many relationship between bugs and cases, you could name the junction object `BugCaseAssociation`.

Let's look at a typical scenario at Universal Containers. There are open positions for a Project Manager and a Sr. Developer. The Project Manager position is only posted on Monster.com, but the Sr. Developer position is more difficult to fill, so it's posted on both Monster.com and Dice. Every time a position is posted, a job posting record tracks the post. As you can see in the following diagram, one position can be posted many times, and both positions can be posted to the same employment website.

Using a Job Posting Object to Create a Many-to-Many Relationship Between Positions and Employment Websites

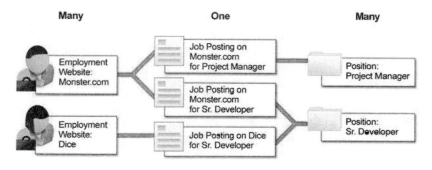

131

In relational database terms, each job posting record is a row in the Job Posting table consisting of a foreign key to a position record and a foreign key to an employment website record. The following entity relationship diagram shows this relationship.

Entity Relationship Diagram for the Position, Job Posting, and Employment Website Objects

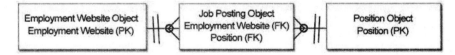

Consequently, in order to define a many-to-many relationship between the Position and Employment Website objects, we'll need to create a Job Posting object with the following fields:

- A Position master-detail relationship
- An Employment Website master-detail relationship

Let's get started.

Try It Out: Create the Employment Website Object

To create our Employment Website custom object, from Setup, enter `Objects` in the `Quick Find` box, then select **Objects**, click **New Custom Object**, and fill out the page according to the following table.

Table 16: Values for Defining the Employment Website Object

Field	Value
Label	Employment Website
Plural Label	Employment Websites
Starts with Vowel Sound	Checked
Object Name	Employment_Website
Description	Information about a particular employment website
Context-Sensitive Help Setting	Open the standard Salesforce Help & Training window
Record Name	Employment Website Name
Data Type	Text
Allow Reports	Yes

Field	Value
Allow Activities	Yes
Track Field History	Yes
Deployment Status	Deployed
Add Notes & Attachments related list to default page layout	Yes
Launch New Custom Tab Wizard after saving this custom object	Yes

To create the Employment Website tab, select a `Tab Style` in the first step of the wizard, and then accept all the defaults until you get to the Add to Custom Apps page. On this page, select only the Recruiting App, and then click **Save**.

Let's wrap up the Employment Website object by adding a few custom fields.

Try It Out: Add the URL Field to the Employment Website Object

Obviously, the Employment Website object needs to store the Web address of the employment website. We'll use the URL data type for this field. That way, when users click the field, the URL will open in a separate browser window. In addition to the URL, since most employment websites charge per posting, we'll want to keep track of how much it costs to post there, as well as our maximum budget for posting on the site.

From Setup, enter `Objects` in the `Quick Find` box, then select **Objects**, and then click **Employment Website** to view its detail page. In the Custom Fields & Relationships related list, use the **New** button to create three custom fields according to the following table. Where necessary, we've indicated some additional values you'll need to fill in when creating the fields. Otherwise you can simply accept all defaults.

Table 17: Add Three Custom Fields to the Employment Website Object

Data Type	Field Label	Other Values
URL	Web Address	Required
Currency	Price Per Post	Length: 5 Decimal Places: 2 Required

Data Type	Field Label	Other Values
Currency	Maximum Budget	Length: 6
		Decimal Places: 2
		Required

Try It Out: Create the Job Posting Object

Now it's time to create our Job Posting junction object! From Setup, enter `Objects` in the `Quick Find` box, then select **Objects**, click **New Custom Object**, and fill out the page according to the following table.

Table 18: Values for Defining the Job Posting Object

Field	Value
Label	Job Posting
Plural Label	Job Postings
Object Name	Job_Posting
Description	Represents the junction object between a position and an employment website
Context-Sensitive Help Setting	Open the standard Salesforce Help & Training window
Record Name	Job Posting Name
Data Type	Auto Number
Display Format	JP-{00000}
Starting Number	00001
Allow Reports	Yes
Allow Activities	Yes
Track Field History	Yes
Deployment Status	Deployed

Field	Value
Add Notes & Attachments related list to default page layout	Yes
Launch New Custom Tab Wizard after saving this custom object	No

That was simple enough, but we're not quite done. We need to create the master-detail relationship fields that relate the Job Posting object with the Position and Employment Website objects.

Try It Out: Add Fields to the Job Posting Object

To turn the Job Posting object into the junction object that relates the Position and Employment Website objects, we'll need to add two master-detail relationship fields. The first master-detail relationship will be the *primary relationship*. The detail and edit pages of our junction object (Job Posting) will use the color and any associated icon of the primary master object (Position). In addition, the junction object records will inherit the value of the Owner field and sharing settings from their associated primary master record.

1. From Setup, enter `Objects` in the `Quick Find` box, then select **Objects**.

2. Click **Job Posting**.

3. In the Custom Fields & Relationships related list, click **New**.

4. Select `Master-Detail Relationship`, and click **Next**.

5. In the `Related To` drop-down list, choose Position, and click **Next**.

6. In the `Field Label` text box, enter `Position`. When you move your cursor, the `Field Name` text box should be automatically populated with Position as well.

7. Accept the remaining defaults, and click **Next** until you reach the final step of the wizard.

Here, we are given the chance to add the Job Postings related list to the Position object page layout. Instead of displaying information about related job postings, we want this list to show all the employment websites where this position is posted. So let's add the Job Posting related list, but rename it `Employment Websites`.

8. In the `Related List Label` text box, enter `Employment Websites`.

9. Accept the other defaults and click **Save & New**.

We're halfway through the creation of our many-to-many relationship. The next step is to create a second master-detail relationship on the Job Posting object to link it with the Employment Website object.

The second master-detail relationship creates a *secondary relationship*. Unlike the primary relationship, the secondary relationship has no affect on the look and feel of the junction object. However, just as in the primary relationship, the sharing settings of the master record in the secondary relationship also affect who can access the junction record, and deleting a record of the secondary master object will automatically delete its associated junction object records. So in our app, if you delete an employment website record, all of its associated job posting records are deleted as well, even if the position is open.

10. Select `Master-Detail Relationship`, and click **Next**.

11. In the `Related To` drop-down list, choose Employment Website, and click **Next**.

12. In the `Field Label` text box, enter `Employment Website`. When you move your cursor, the `Field Name` text box should be automatically populated with Employment_Website as well.

13. Click **Next**. Because we are creating a master-detail relationship, these settings cannot be changed.

14. Click **Next**. These settings cannot be changed as well.

15. Click **Next** to view the final step of the wizard.

This time we are given the chance to add the Job Postings related list to Employment Website object page layout. We'll eventually configure this related list to show all the positions that are posted on this website, so let's add the Job Postings related list but rename it `Positions`.

16. In the `Related List Label` text box, enter `Positions`.

17. Accept the other defaults and click **Save**.

Now our many-to-many relationship is complete! Or is it?

While we have an Employment Websites related list on the Position object and a Positions related list on the Employment Websites object, both related lists still display job posting records. This won't do.

In order to achieve our goal of listing multiple positions on an employment website record and multiple employment websites on a position record, we need to customize the fields in these related lists.

Customizing Related Lists in a Many-to-Many Relationship

The capability to customize related lists in a many-to-many relationship is more robust than the capability to customize related lists in a lookup relationship. When you have a lookup relationship between two objects (like the one we created between the Job Application and Candidate objects), the related list on one object can only display fields from the object to which it is directly related; it cannot span to other objects the way formulas can. For example, the Job Applications related list on a candidate record can display any job application field, but it can't display any fields from the Position object, even though the Job Application object has lookup relationships with both the Candidate and Position objects.

Fortunately for us, many-to-many relationships allow for greater flexibility. When working with a many-to-many relationship, the junction object's related list on one master object can display the other master object's fields. We're going to take advantage of this by configuring the Positions related list on each employment website record to display fields from the Position object and vice versa, thus allowing these two objects to span to each other. It's all coming together now!

Try It Out: Customize the Positions and Employment Websites Related Lists

Let's start by modifying the Employment Websites related list on the Position object.

1. From Setup, enter `Objects` in the `Quick Find` box, then select **Objects**.
2. Click **Position**.
3. In the Page Layouts related list, click **Edit** next to the Position Layout.
4. Locate the Employment Websites related list and click its wrench ( ) icon.

In the popup window that appears, you'll notice the `Available Fields` column lists fields from both the Job Posting object and the Employment Website object. If there wasn't a master-detail relationship between job postings and employment websites, the `Available Fields` column list would only list job posting fields.

5. Move the `Employment Website: Employment Website Name` and `Employment Website: Web Address` fields to the `Selected Fields` column, and use the up and down arrows to arrange the fields in the following order:

   - `Employment Website: Employment Website Name`
   - `Employment Website: Web Address`
   - `Job Posting: Job Number`

6. Click **OK**.
7. Click **Save** on the page layout.

Now do the same for the Positions related list on the Employment Website object as follows:

1. From Setup, enter `Objects` in the `Quick Find` box, then select **Objects**.
2. Click **Employment Website**.
3. In the Page Layouts related list, click **Edit** next to the Employment Website Layout.
4. Locate the Positions related list and click its wrench icon ( ).
5. Move the following fields to the `Selected Fields` column, and use the up and down arrows to arrange them in the following order:

- Position: Position Name
- Job Posting: Job Posting Name
- Position: Functional Area
- Position: Location
- Position: Open Date

6. Click **OK**.

7. Click **Save** on the page layout.

Try It Out: Customize Record Highlights for Employment Websites and Job Postings

Like with our other custom objects, we need to customize the record highlights by creating a new compact layout for each object.

1. From Setup, enter *Objects* in the Quick Find box, then select **Objects**.

2. Click **Employment Website**.

3. In the Compact Layouts related list, use the **New** button to create a compact layout with the following fields. Enter a name in Label, and use the **Up** and **Down** buttons to match the order.

- Employment Website Name
- Price Per Post
- Web Address
- Maximum Budget

4. Click **Save**, and then assign our new compact layout as the primary compact layout for employment websites.

Now let's do the same thing for job posting.

1. From Setup, enter *Objects* in the Quick Find box, then select **Objects**.

2. Click **Job Posting**.

3. In the Compact Layouts related list, use the **New** button to create a compact layout with the following fields. Enter a name in Label, and use the **Up** and **Down** buttons to match the order.

- Job Posting Name
- Employment Website
- Position

4. Click **Save**.

Remember to quickly assign our new compact layout as the primary compact layout for job postings.

5. Click **Compact Layout Assignment**.

6. Click **Edit Assignment**.

7. From the drop-down list, select the compact layout you just created.

8. Click **Save**.

Look at What We've Done

Our many-to-many relationship is complete! Let's see it in action.

1. Create a few sample position and employment website records.

2. Scroll down to the Employment Websites related list at the bottom of any position record, and click **New Job Posting**. The Job Posting edit page appears.

3. Use the lookup icon to select the employment website where you want to post the position, and click **Save**.

4. Launch Salesforce1 and open your sample position and employment website records.

The Employment Websites related list on that position now shows the name and Web address of the website to which you just posted, as well as the job posting number. Click the name of the employment website in the related list and scroll down to view the Positions related list, which shows all the positions posted to that website.

Now you know how easy it is to make related information just a click away!

Putting it All Together

We just created several objects and a lot of relationships. The following simple diagram shows us what we've accomplished so far.

Recruiting App Relationships

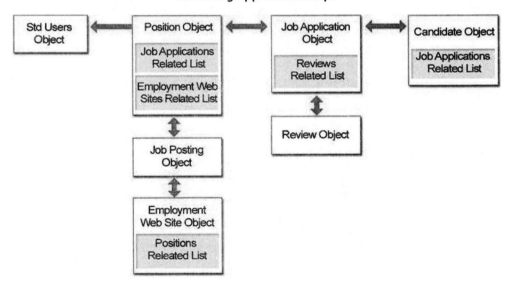

All of these relationships, objects, and fields are shown below in an entity relationship diagram. An entity relationship diagram (ERD) is a conceptual representation of structured data, and is especially useful for planning and understanding an app.

Recruiting App Entity Relationship Diagram

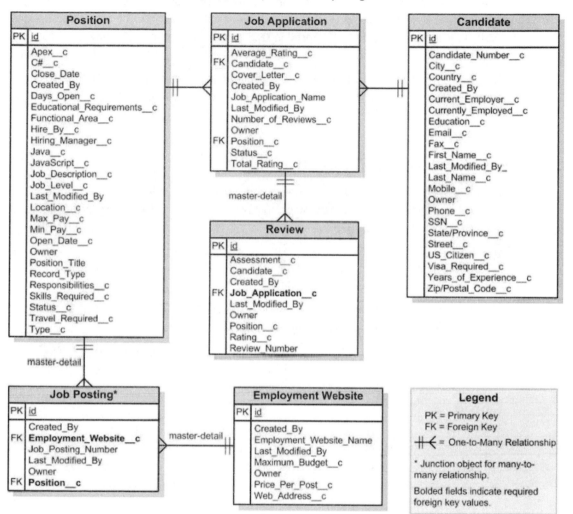

We've now built all of our Recruiting app objects and tabs, and we've defined lots of custom fields—everything from text fields and picklists to more complex formula fields and lookup relationship fields. We've created a robust user interface so that our recruiters and hiring managers can enter and retrieve data about positions and related candidates, job applications, and reviews, and we did all of this without writing a single line of code!

Remember when we assigned Phil Katz as the hiring manager for the Benefits Specialist position? Let's look at what Phil can do now: He can create and update his positions, and track which websites he's posted them on. He can look at details about any candidates who have applied for the Benefits Specialist job, and he can review their related job applications. He can also check the status of the job applications. He no longer has to go to Human Resources to search through Microsoft Word documents and spreadsheets to manage his tasks in the hiring process. The Recruiting app is well on its way to becoming a fully-functional and useful application!

However, before we leave this chapter behind, let's get ourselves prepared for the rest of this book by creating and importing some real data. It'll help us when we get to our next chapter on security and sharing if we have some records that we can work with.

Try It Out: Download Sample Data

In addition to entering data via our tabbed pages, we can also use the handy Import Wizard to import multiple records at a time. The ability to easily import data into your custom objects is one of the Force.com platform's key benefits. Let's download some sample data so we can add more records to our custom objects without tons of typing.

1. Download the `RecruitingApp-9_0.zip` file containing the sample CSV (comma-separated values) import files from `developer.salesforce.com/page/Force_Platform_Fundamentals`.

2. Extract the zip file to any directory on your computer.

3. Go to the directory to which you extracted the zip file. This directory contains three CSV files: `Positions.csv`, `Candidates.csv`, and `Job_Applications.csv`. (The directory also contains other files that you'll use later in Moving Beyond Point-and-Click App Development on page 325.)

Before we import anything, we need to make a modification to the import file for positions. The sample `Positions.csv` you downloaded contains fictional users in the Hiring Manager column. The names of these users most likely won't match any user in your organization, and if you import the file "as is," the Import Wizard won't be able to find any matching users, and the `Hiring Manager` field on each position record will be left blank. So let's go ahead and make that change.

4. Go to the directory to which you extracted the zip file and open `Positions.csv` in Excel, a text editor, or any other program that can read CSV files.

5. In the Hiring Manager column, replace the fictional users with the first and last name of a user in your organization.

6. Save the file, making sure to maintain the CSV format.

> **Note:** If your locale isn't English (United States), the date and field values in `Positions.csv` are also invalid. You'll need to change them before you import.

Try It Out: Use the Import Wizard

Now, let's walk through the process of importing position records using the Import Wizard and the `Positions.csv` file you downloaded.

1. From Setup, enter *Import Custom Objects* in the `Quick Find` box, then select **Import Custom Objects**.

2. Click **Start the Import Wizard!** The Import Wizard appears.

3. Select `Position` for the type of record you're importing, and click **Next**.

4. Choose `Yes` to prevent duplicate position records from being created as a result of this import. Leave the other options as their defaults.

5. Select `None` for the record owner field. We didn't include a User field in the CSV file to designate record owners. The Import Wizard assigns you as the owner of all new records.

6. Choose the `Hiring Manager` lookup relationship field so you can link position records with existing User records in the Recruiting app, and click **Next**.

7. Click **Browse** and find `C:\recruiting\Positions.csv`. Click **Next**.

8. Use the drop-down lists to specify the Salesforce fields that correspond to the columns in your import file. For your convenience, identically matching labels are automatically selected. Click **Next**.

9. Click **Import Now!**

10. Click **Finish**.

Use the following table to repeat the import process for candidate records. You'll notice the wizard skips the two steps about lookup relationship field matching—because the Candidate object doesn't have any lookup relationship fields, the Import Wizard automatically leaves those steps out.

Table 19: Importing the `Candidates.csv` File

For this wizard step...	Select these options...
Choose Record	Candidate
Prevent Duplicates	No—insert all records in my import file
Specify Relationships	None
File Upload	Browse to `C:\recruiting\Candidates.csv`
Field Mapping	Accept all defaults
Verify Import Settings	Click **Import Now!**

Finally let's do it one more time for job application records. In this iteration, we're going to make use of the `Email` field, an external ID on the Candidate object, to match up job applications with the correct candidate records.

Table 20: Importing the `Job_Applications.csv` File

For this wizard step...	Select these options...
Choose Record	Job Application
Prevent Duplicates	No—insert all records in my import file
Specify Relationships	`Which user field...?` None
	`Which lookup fields...?` Candidate, Position
Define Lookup Matching	`Which field on Candidate...?` Email (External ID)
	`Which field on Position...?` Position Title
File Upload	Browse to `C:\recruiting\Job_Applications.csv`
Field Mapping	`Email (col 0):` Candidate
	`Position Title (col 1):` Position
Verify Import Settings	Click **Import Now!**

Great! While the files are importing, you can from Setup, click **Imports** or **Monitor** > **Imports** to check on their status.

Once the import operations have completed, return to the Positions, Candidates, or Job Applications tab and click **Go!** next to the `View` drop-down list. You'll see a list of all the new records you just imported.

We've just added a bunch of data to our app without a lot of work. In the next chapter, we'll take a look at all the ways we can control access to this data using the built-in tools of the platform. We'll get into the nitty-gritty about security, sharing rules, permissions, roles, and profiles.

CHAPTER 7   Securing and Sharing Data

In the last chapter, we expanded the Recruiting app to include advanced fields and complex object relationships. The new Candidate object tracks information about prospective employees, recruiters can relate candidates to positions through the new Job Application object, and interviewers can add assessments and ratings of the candidates on the new Review object. That's a pretty robust app! The enhanced data model also lays the groundwork for adding powerful functionality like workflow and approvals and reporting, which we'll cover in later chapters.

Now that we've got all of our object relationships in place, it's time to start thinking about who's actually going to be using the app and how much access they should have to its data. As with many apps, our Recruiting app exposes sensitive information, like social security numbers, salary amounts, and applicant reviews that could really come back to haunt us if the wrong people saw them. We need to provide security without making it harder for our recruiters, hiring managers, and interviewers to do their jobs.

Here we're going to see another one of the huge benefits that the Force.com platform has to offer. You get simple-to-configure security controls that easily allow us to restrict access to data that users shouldn't see, without a lot of headaches. Similar to Access Control Lists or Windows folder permissions, the Force.com platform allows us to specify who can view, create, edit, or delete any record or field in the app. In this chapter, we'll see how we can use the Force.com platform to implement those rules.

> Note: Although Developer Edition orgs include all the features in Salesforce, these orgs are more limited than sandbox orgs. Developer Edition orgs, for example, are limited to two registered users. If you're using a Developer Edition version of Salesforce, you might not be able to complete some of the exercises in this chapter.

Controlling Access to Data in Our App

As we've already seen, there are three types of users who will need to access the data in our Recruiting app: recruiters, hiring managers, and interviewers. To these three, let's add a fourth type of user—a standard employee who doesn't perform any interviews and who never needs to hire anyone. (This employee will help us determine the default permissions that should apply to all of the new recruiting objects in our app.)

One by one, let's take a look at the kinds of access that each one of these users needs and, more importantly, the kinds of access they *don't* need to do their jobs. Once we've compiled a set of required permissions, we'll figure out how to implement them in the rest of the chapter.

Required Permissions for the Recruiter

For our first set of required permissions, let's take a look at Mario Ruiz, a recruiter at Universal Containers. To do his job, Mario needs to be able to create, view, and modify any position, candidate, job application, or review that's in the system, and have full control over job postings on employment websites. Likewise, Mario needs to view and modify the recruiting records that all of the other recruiters own, since all of the recruiters at Universal Containers work together to fill every position, regardless of who created it.

Although Mario has the most powerful role in our Recruiting app, we still can't give him complete free reign. While it's OK for job posting and employment website data to be permanently deleted at any time, state and federal public records laws require that all other recruitment-related records be saved for a number of years so that if a hiring decision is questioned, it can be defended in court. Consequently, we need to make sure that Mario will never accidentally delete a record that needs to be saved to fulfill the law.

But how will he keep the number of positions, candidates, job applications, and reviews in check if he can't delete them? Won't the app become swamped with old data? Not if we're smart about it—instead of having Mario delete old records, we can use the `Status` field on a record as an indication of whether it's current. We'll filter out all of the old records by using a simple list view.

Here's a summary of the required permissions that we need to implement for a recruiter:

Table 21: Summary of Required Permissions: Recruiter

	Read	Create	Edit	Delete
Position	✓	✓	✓	
Candidate	✓	✓	✓	
Job Application	✓	✓	✓	

	Read	Create	Edit	Delete
Review	☑	☑	☑	
Job Posting	☑	☑	☑	☑
Employment Website	☑	☑	☑	☑

Required Permissions for the Hiring Manager

Our next set of required permissions is more challenging. Ben Stuart, our hiring manager, needs to be able to access the recruiting records related to his open positions, but he shouldn't be mucking around with other recruiting records (unless they're owned by other hiring managers who report to him). Also, there are certain sensitive fields that he has no need to see, like the social security number field. Let's go object by object to really drill down on what Ben does and doesn't need to access in order to perform his job.

Position

First of all, Ben likes to post his own positions so that he can publicize them as fast as possible, but in our app, Mario the recruiter ultimately needs to take ownership of the record to make sure the position gets filled. As a result, Ben needs the ability to create positions, but then we'll need to find a mechanism to make sure that they ultimately get transferred to Mario for ownership. (Hint: as you'll see In Automating Business Processes on page 235, we'll tackle that problem with a workflow rule that transfers position ownership to a recruiter when a new position is created by a hiring manager. For now just assume that this already works.)

Ben should also be able to update and view all fields for positions for which he's the hiring manager, but he should only be able to view other managers' positions.

Candidate

Ben sometimes wants to poach a prime candidate who's applying for a position under another manager, but this is a practice that Universal Containers frowns upon. As a result, Ben should only be able to view those candidates who have applied for a position on which he's the hiring manager. Also, since Ben has no reason to see a candidate's social security number, this field should be restricted from his view.

Job Application

As the hiring manager, Ben needs to be able to update the status of those job applications to specify which candidates should be selected or rejected. However, he should not be able to change the candidate listed on the job application, nor the position to which the candidate is applying, so we'll have to find a way of preventing Ben from updating the lookup fields on job applications.

Review

To make a decision about the candidates who are applying, Ben needs to see the reviews posted by the interviewers, as well as make comments on them if he thinks the interviewer was being too biased in his or her review. Likewise, Ben needs to be able to create reviews so that he can remember his own impressions of the candidates he interviews.

Job Posting

Ben wants to make sure his harder-to-fill positions are visible to the most talented people in the field. The most efficient way to do this is by posting open positions on various employment websites. Given that employment websites have different types of users with varying skill sets, we should give Ben the power to unilaterally create job postings on employment websites, since Ben is the best person to ascertain which skill sets are necessary for his open positions.

Employment Website

If Ben had his way, he would usurp all of the company's budget for posting his open positions on employment websites; therefore, Ben shouldn't be allowed to modify employment website records, as that would let him redefine the company's budget for posting jobs and could lead to an accounting fiasco. Still, we need to make sure that Ben can view employment website records to get an idea of the employment websites with which Universal Containers has accounts, and how much of the budget for that employment website is available.

Here's a summary of the required permissions we need to implement for a hiring manager:

Table 22: Summary of Required Permissions: Hiring Manager

	Read	Create	Edit	Delete
Position	✓	✓	✓*	
Candidate	✓* (No SSN)			
Job Application	✓		✓ (No lookup fields)	
Review	✓	✓	✓	
Job Posting	✓*	✓*	✓*	
Employment Website	✓			

* Only for those records that are associated with a position to which the hiring manager has been assigned

Required Permissions for the Interviewer

For our third set of required permissions, let's take a look at Melissa Lee's role as an interviewer. Ben, her manager, likes Melissa to interview candidates for highly technical positions, but doesn't want her speaking with folks who are applying for roles on the user interface team. As a result, Melissa should be able to view only the candidates and job applications to which she's assigned as an interviewer. No such restriction needs to exist on the positions that are out there, but she shouldn't be able to view the minimum and maximum salary values for any of them. Likewise, she shouldn't see the social security number of any candidate, since it's sensitive information that has nothing to do with her job.

Melissa must be able to create and edit her reviews so that she can record her comments about each candidate, but she shouldn't be able to see the reviews of other interviewers—reading them might sway her opinion one way or the other. As with hiring managers and recruiters, Melissa also shouldn't be allowed to delete any records to ensure that public records laws are fulfilled.

Finally, the posting of jobs to employment websites has no bearing on Melissa's responsibilities, so both the employment website and job posting records should be completely off-limits to her.

Here's a summary of the required permissions we need to implement for an interviewer:

Table 23: Summary of Required Permissions: Interviewer

	Read	Create	Edit	Delete
Position	☑ (No min/max pay)			
Candidate	☑* (No SSN)			
Job Application	☑*			
Review	☑**	☑	☑**	
Job Posting				
Employment Website				

* Only for those records that are associated with a position to which the interviewer has been assigned

** Only for those records that the interviewer owns

Required Permissions for the Standard Employee

Employees, such as Manny Damon on the Western Sales Team, are often the best resources for recruiting new hires, even if they are not active hiring managers or interviewers. For this reason, we need to make sure that employees like Manny can view open positions, but that they can't see the values for the positions' minimum and maximum salary fields—otherwise they might tip off friends to negotiate for a position's maximum salary value! Manny also shouldn't be able to view any other records in our Recruiting app.

Here's a summary of the required permissions we need to implement for a standard employee:

Table 24: Summary of Required Permissions: Standard Employee

	Read	Create	Edit	Delete
Position	☑ (No min/max pay)			
Candidate				
Job Application				
Review				
Job Posting				
Employment Website				

So Where Are We Now?

Now that we've gone through the required permissions for each of our four users, let's organize our thoughts by summarizing them in the following table. In the rest of this chapter, we'll figure out how we can use the platform to implement these rules in our Recruiting app.

Table 25: Summary of Required Permissions

	Recruiter	Hiring Manager	Interviewer	Standard Employee
Position	Read Create Edit	Read Create Edit*	Read (No min/max pay)	Read (No min/max pay)
Candidate	Read Create Edit	Read* (No SSN)	Read * (No SSN)	

	Recruiter	**Hiring Manager**	**Interviewer**	**Standard Employee**
Job Application	Read Create Edit	Read Edit (No lookup fields)	Read *	
Review	Read Create Edit	Read Create Edit	Read ** Create Edit **	
Job Posting	Read Create Edit Delete	Read *Create *Edit *		
Employment Website	Read Create Edit Delete	Read		

* Only for those records that are associated with a position to which the hiring manager/interviewer has been assigned

** Only for those records that the interviewer owns

🔹 Tip: When implementing the security and sharing rules for your own organization, it's often useful to create a required permissions table like this to organize your thoughts and make sure you don't forget to restrict or grant access to a particular user. You'll see that we're going to refer back to this table again and again as we go through this chapter.

Data Access Concepts

Before we get started implementing our security and sharing rules, let's quickly take a look at all the ways that we can control data on the platform:

Object-Level Security

The bluntest way that we can control data is by preventing a user from seeing, creating, editing, or deleting any instance of a particular type of object, like a position or review. Object-level access allows us to hide whole tabs and objects from particular users, so they don't even know that type of data exists.

On the platform, we set object-level access with object permissions in user profiles and permission sets. We'll learn more about them in a little bit.

Field-Level Security

A variation on object-level access is field-level access, in which a user can be prevented from seeing, editing, or deleting the value for a particular field on an object. Field-level access allows us to hide sensitive information like the maximum salary for a position or a candidate's social security number without having to hide the whole object.

On the platform, we set field-level access with field permissions, also in profiles and permission sets. We'll also learn more about them shortly.

Record-Level Security

To control data with a little more finesse, we can allow particular users to view an object, but then restrict the individual object records that they're allowed to see. For example, record-level access allows an interviewer like Melissa Lee to see and edit her own reviews, without exposing the reviews of everyone else on her team.

On the platform, we actually have several ways of setting record-level access rules:

- *Organization-wide defaults* allow us to specify the baseline level of access that a user has in your organization. For example, we can make it so that any user can see any record of a particular object to which their object permissions give them access, but so that they'll need extra permissions to actually edit one.

- *Role hierarchies* allow us to make sure that a manager will always have access to the same records as his or her subordinates.

- *Sharing rules* allow us to make automatic exceptions to organization-wide defaults for particular groups of users.

- *Manual sharing* allows record owners to give read and edit permissions to folks who might not have access to the record any other way.

Controlling Data with the Force.com Platform

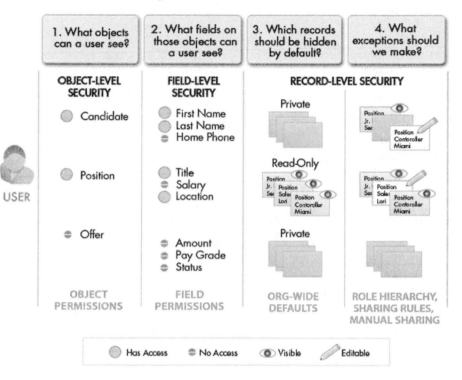

The combination of all of these sharing and security settings in the platform means that we can easily specify user permissions for an organization of thousands of users without having to manually configure the permissions for each individual. Pretty neat! Now let's get started learning more about each of these methods for controlling data, and actually implementing the security and sharing rules for our app.

Controlling Access to Objects

First let's configure access to our Recruiting app custom objects. As we mentioned previously, we can control whether a user knows that a particular object exists in the app by setting permissions in his or her profile and permission sets. But exactly what are profiles and permission sets, and what do they control?

Introducing Profiles

A *profile* is a collection of settings and permissions that determine what a user can do in the platform, kind of like a group in a Windows network, where all of the members of the group have the same folder permissions and access to the same software. Profiles control:

- **Object permissions**—The objects the user can view, create, edit, and delete
- **Field permissions (also known as "field-level security")**—The object fields the user can view and edit
- **User permissions**—The specific functions that users can perform, like viewing the Setup menu and customizing applications
- **Tab settings**—The tabs the user can view in the app
- **App settings**—The standard and custom apps the user can access
- **Apex class access**—The Apex classes a user can execute
- **Visualforce page access**—The Visualforce pages a user can execute
- **Page layouts**—The page layouts a user sees
- **Record types**—The record types available to the user
- **Login hours**—The hours during which the user can log in to the app
- **Login IP ranges**—The IP addresses from which the user can log in to the app

Profiles are typically defined by a user's job function (for example, system administrator or sales representative), but you can have profiles for anything that makes sense for your organization. A profile can be assigned to many users, but a user can be assigned to only one profile at a time.

Standard Profiles

The platform provides the following set of standard profiles in every Salesforce org.

- Read Only
- Standard User
- Marketing User
- Contract Manager
- Solution Manager
- System Administrator

Each of these standard profiles includes a default set of permissions for all of the standard objects available on the platform.

When a custom object is created, most profiles (except those with "Modify All Data") don't give access to the object. You can find more detailed descriptions of all the standard profiles in the Salesforce Help, but the important thing to know is that you can never edit the object permissions on a standard profile. If you have access to the Professional, Enterprise, Unlimited, Performance, or Developer Editions of the platform, it's a good idea to make copies of the standard profiles and then customize the copies to fit the needs of your org. You can also use permission sets to grant additional permissions.

For our Recruiting app, we'll make a copy of the standard profile and customize it (and as a result, Enterprise, Unlimited, Performance, and Developer Editions will be the only editions that the Recruiting app will support). We'll also use permission sets to grant additional permissions to a smaller set of users.

Introducing Permission Sets

Like a profile, a *permission set* is a collection of settings and permissions that determine what a user can do. Permission sets include some of the same permissions and settings you'll find in profiles.

- Object permissions
- Field permissions (also known as "field-level security")
- User permissions
- Tab settings
- App settings
- Apex class access
- Visualforce page access

So why profiles *and* permission sets?

The most significant difference between the two is that users can have only one profile, but they can have many permission sets. This means you can use profiles to grant the minimum permissions and settings that every type of user needs, then use permission sets to grant additional permissions, without changing anyone's profiles.

There are a couple of ways to use permission sets to your advantage.

- **To grant access to custom objects or entire apps.**

  Let's say you have many users in your organization with the same fundamental job functions. You can assign them all one profile that grants them all the access they need to do their job. But suppose a few of those users are working on a special project and they need access to an app that no one else uses. And suppose a few other users need access to that app, as well as *another* app that the first group doesn't need. If we only had profiles, you'd have to create more profiles that were customized to those few users' needs, or take your chances and add more access to the original profile, making the apps available to users that don't need it. Neither of these options is ideal, especially if your organization is growing and your users' needs change regularly. Permission sets make it easy to grant access to the various apps and custom objects in your organization, and to take away access when it's no longer needed.

- **To grant permissions—temporarily or long term—to specific fields.**

    For example, let's say you have a user, Dana, who needs temporary edit access to a field while her co-worker is on vacation. You can create a permission set that grants access to the field and assign the permission set to Dana. When Dana's co-worker returns from vacation and Dana no longer needs access to the field, you just remove the permission set assignment from Dana's user record.

Profiles and Permission Sets in Our Recruiting App

We've talked about four types of users: recruiters, hiring managers, standard employees, and interviewers. Let's take a closer look.

Recruiters are pretty straightforward—they definitely represent a particular job function, and they need access to different types of data than other users. They need their own profile.

A hiring manager, however, is not exactly a single type of position. For most organizations, a hiring manager in the Sales department will almost certainly need access to a different type of data than a hiring manager in Engineering. However, for our app, sales managers and software managers still need the same types of access to recruiting data—reviews, candidates, positions, job applications, job postings, and employment websites. If we incorporated our app into an organization with other CRM functionality, the hiring manager permissions for recruiting-related data might need to be shared by several types of users who may have different profiles. In this case, we'll make a hiring manager permission set that can be assigned to various types of users.

Standard employees are pretty generic, and they don't reflect a particular job function. Standard employees can start with a profile that gives access to a small set of data, and then depending on what their specialties are, we can create and assign permission sets to give them more access as needed.

Finally, let's look at interviewers. When you think about it, just about anyone in an organization might be called upon to perform an interview. Furthermore, a company may have a peak recruiting season, when many employees will be interviewers for a limited amount of time. Ideally, permissions for interviewers could be easily granted and revoked as needed. It's easy to define permission sets based on a particular task—and even easier to assign and unassign them, so let's define a permission set for interviewers.

Try It Out: Create the Recruiter Profile

All right—we're finally ready to dig into the app and create our first profile! Let's start with the Recruiter profile.

1. From Setup, enter *Profiles* in the Quick Find box, then select **Profiles**.

Standard Profiles

User Profiles

Below is a list of the profiles for your organization. clicking on the profile link.

For custom profiles, you can edit any of the attributes. For standard profiles, you have to accept the permissions settings as they are.

Profile			New	
Action	Profile Name		User License	Custom
Edit	Authenticated Website		Authenticated Website	☐
Edit	Chatter Moderator		Chatter	☐
Edit	Chatter User		Chatter	☐

Here you should see the list of standard profiles that we talked about earlier. After we create our custom profiles, they'll also show up in this list.

First, we can quickly tell which profiles we can play with by looking at the Custom column—if it's checked, that means it's a custom profile and we can edit anything about it. If that column is not checked, we can still click the **Edit** link; we just can't modify any of the permission settings. (What does that leave for us to edit on a standard profile? Well, we can choose which tabs should appear at the top of a user's page, and we can also select the apps that are available in the Force.com app menu in the top-right corner of the page.)

2. Create a new profile named Recruiter based on the Standard User profile.

There are actually two ways of doing this—we can either click **New Profile**, select an existing profile to clone, name it, and click **Save**, or we can simply click **Clone** in the detail page of the profile that we want to copy, name it, and click **Save**. Ultimately, it's the same number of clicks, so choose the method you like best. Standard User is the profile that most closely resembles what we want our new Recruiter profile to look like, so it's a good starting point.

3. In the new Recruiter profile's detail page, click **Edit**.

The Recruiter edit page should look and function exactly like the Standard User profile edit page except with one important difference: you have the ability to modify any of the permission settings.

4. In the Custom App Settings area, make the Recruiting app visible to users assigned to the Recruiter profile, as shown in the following screenshot.

Profile Custom App Settings Area

Custom App Settings						= Required Information
	Visible	Default			Visible	Default
Sales	☑	○		Service & Support	☑	○
Marketing	☑	○		Recruiting	☑	◉

 Tip: You can also give this profile access to any of the other available apps as well. Every profile needs to have at least one visible app.

When an app is visible, a user can select it from the Force.com app menu at the top-right corner of the page. Be aware, however, that even if an app is visible, the app's tabs won't show up unless a profile has permissions to view the tabs and permission to view the associated object. (We'll set both of those permissions lower down in the Profile edit page.)

 5. Select **Default** next to the Recruiting app.

Making this selection means that the Recruiting app will be displayed when a user logs in. You'll notice that when you select an app as the default, its `Visible` checkbox is automatically selected, because it doesn't make sense for an app to be the default if it's not visible to the user.

 6. In the Object Settings area, select Default On for the Candidates, Employment Websites, Job Applications, and Positions tabs.

 Tip: You can choose whether you want other tabs to be displayed based on the additional apps that you made visible in the last step.

For the purposes of our Recruiting app, all of our custom recruiting tabs are on by default. For any other tabs that you select, you can choose which should be displayed on top of the user's page (Default On), hidden from the user's page but available when he or she clicks the All Tabs tab on the far right (Default Off), or completely hidden from the user (Tab Hidden).

Realize that even if you completely hide a tab, users can still see the records that would have appeared in that tab in search results and in related lists. (To prevent a user from accessing data, we have to set the proper restrictions in the Standard and Custom Object Permissions areas lower down in the Profile edit page—we'll get there shortly!)

The `Overwrite users' personal tab customizations` setting appears if you have an organization that's currently in use and you want to make sure your existing users are viewing the tabs that you've selected. You don't need to select this for our app because we're defining a brand-new profile and no one has personalized his or her tab visibility settings yet. However, if you do want to select this option at some point in the future, just make sure you're not going to annoy your users by deleting all of their customizations!

Profile Tab Settings Area

Just below the Tab Settings area, the Administrative and General User Permissions areas of the profile allow you to grant special access to features and functionality that don't map directly to particular objects. None of these permissions affects our Recruiting app, but you can learn more about them in the Salesforce Help.

It's time to move on to the object-level permissions.

7. In the Custom Object Permissions area, specify the object-level permissions for our Recruiter profile according to the following table.

Table 26: Summary of Required Permissions: Recruiter

	Read	Create	Edit	Delete	View All	Modify All
Candidate	✓	✓	✓			
Employment Website	✓	✓	✓	✓	✓	✓
Job Application	✓	✓	✓			
Job Posting	✓	✓	✓	✓	✓	✓
Position	✓	✓	✓		✓	
Review	✓	✓	✓			

Tip: Depending on the apps that you made visible previously, you can also set additional object permissions on standard or other custom objects.

Since there are no instances when a recruiter should be allowed to delete positions, candidates, job applications, and reviews, we should make sure that the object-level permissions for deletion are turned off for these objects. Also, make sure the "View All" permission is only selected for Employment Websites, Positions, and Job Postings, and the "Modify All" permission is only selected for Job Postings and Employment Websites. These are special kinds of object permissions that we'll discuss later in this chapter.

By restricting the power to delete recruiting-related objects here, recruiters will *never* be able to delete these objects. However, the fact that we're granting recruiters permission to create, read, or edit our recruiting objects does not necessarily mean that recruiters will be allowed to read or edit *every* recruiting object record. Why?

Here we see the result of two really important concepts in the platform:

- The permissions on a record are always evaluated according to a combination of object-, field-, and record-level permissions.
- When object- versus record-level permissions conflict, the most restrictive settings win.

What this means is that even though we are granting this profile create, read, and edit permissions on the recruiting objects, if the record-level permissions for an individual recruiting record prove to be more restrictive, those will be the rules that will define what a recruiter can access.

For example, our new profile gives a recruiter permission to create, edit, and view reviews. However, if we set organization-wide defaults for reviews to Private (a record-level permission), our recruiter will be allowed to edit and view only his own reviews, and not the reviews owned by other users. We'll learn more about record-level permissions later and go through more examples of how they work with the object-level ones, but for now, just understand that object-level permissions are only one piece of the puzzle.

8. Click **Save** to create your profile and return to the profile detail page.

Congratulations! We're done with our first profile. As you can see, it really wasn't that hard, because we'd already analyzed our required permissions and knew what objects recruiters will need access to. In the next section, let's quickly finish up our other two profiles and then move on to field-level security.

Beyond the Basics

Did you know that you can use an improved user interface to manage profiles?

Say you manage a lot of profiles and you'd like a more a streamlined experience. With the enhanced profile user interface, you can easily navigate, search, and modify profile settings.

To find out more, see "Enhanced Profile User Interface Overview" in the Salesforce Help.

Try It Out: Create the Standard Employee Profile

Now that we've created our Recruiter profile, let's finish up with a profile for standard employees. As we mentioned earlier, in your own company, you may want to create additional profiles with basic access settings for the various core job functions, but for our purposes, these will work just fine for now.

To refresh our memories, let's take a look at our required permissions summary table:

Table 27: Summary of Required Permissions: Standard Employee

	Positions	Candidates	Job Applications	Reviews	Job Postings	Employment Websites
Standard Employee	• Read (No min/max pay)	-	-	-	-	-

Standard employees don't need much access, but we do want them to be able to view all the open positions so they can help recruit new employees. Creating this profile will be easy. Go ahead and follow the steps that we outlined in the previous section and specify the following.

- Name the profile *Standard Employee*, and base it on the Standard User profile.
- Enable the "Read" permission on the Positions object.

Fantastic! We've just finished defining profiles for all the users in our Recruiting app. Next we'll create permission sets to grant additional permissions to the people that need them.

Try It Out: Create the Hiring Manager Permission Set

We've created two profiles for our easy-to-define job functions. Now we need to grant additional access for functions that may not be specific to any given job title.

1. From Setup, enter *Permission Sets* in the Quick Find box, then select **Permission Sets**.
2. On the Permission Sets page, click **New**.
3. In the Label field, enter *Hiring Manager*.
4. The API Name field is defaulted to *Hiring_Manager*. Let's leave it as is.

When you assign permission sets to a user, you can only assign permission sets that have the same user license as the user or permission sets with no associated license. You can't change the license later, so it's important to choose the correct user license when you create a permission set.

5. In the `User License` field, select *Salesforce*.

6. Click **Save**.

Permission Set Overview Page

We've taken the initial step of creating a permission set. While you can clone permission sets, you can also create one completely from scratch, and that's what we did when we created this one. At the moment, this permission set has no enabled settings or permissions—it's a blank slate. So let's enable some permissions and settings. Since this permission set is for hiring managers, we'll start by making the Recruiting app visible.

7. Click **Assigned Apps**.

8. In the Assigned Apps page, click **Edit**.

9. Under Available Apps, select `Recruiting` and click **Add** to add it to the Enabled Apps list.

Assigning the Recruiting App in the Hiring Manager Permission Set

10. Click **Save**.

Next we want to enable tab settings and permissions for our custom objects. Where are those enabled and how do we get there? In permission sets, you have a few easy ways to move from one page to another. Let's take a look.

11. Next to Assigned Apps, click the down arrow to open the navigation menu, and select Object Settings.

Permission Set Navigation Menu

The Object Settings page shows an overview for all objects and tabs in your organization. It includes a summary of tab settings, object permissions, and field permissions for every object and tab. Let's drill down to the Positions object.

12. In the list of objects, click **Positions**.

13. On the Positions page, click **Edit**.

You may notice that tab settings labels in permission sets are different from the labels in profiles. They are configured a bit differently, but you'll get the same results.

Table 28: Comparing Tab Settings in Permission Sets and Profiles

Enabled Settings in Permission Sets	Enabled Setting in Profiles	Description
`Available`	`Default Off`	The tab is available on the All Tabs page. Individual users can customize their display to make the tab visible in any app.
`Available and Visible`	`Default On`	The tab is available on the All Tabs page and appears in the visible tabs for its associated app. Individual users can customize their display to hide the tab or make it visible in other apps.
None	`Tab Hidden`	The tab isn't available on the All Tabs page or visible in any apps.

14. Under Tab Settings, select **Available** and **Visible**.

15. Under Object Permissions, enable **Read**, **Create**, and **Edit**.

Now we'll grant access to the fields in position records. We'll learn lots more about field permissions in Introducing Field-Level Security on page 168, but for now, we'll enable the field permissions we need.

16. Under Field Permissions, enable the **Edit** checkboxes for all the fields.

 Tip: When you enable **Edit** for a field, **Read** is automatically enabled as well.

You'll probably notice that you can't change the settings for some of the fields. These fields have preset access because they are required or their data is automatically calculated. For example, because Days Open is a formula field, it's never editable, but you should make it readable.

17. Enable **Read** for Days Open.

18. Click **Save**.

Now we need to specify access for our remaining objects. As we saw previously, you can use the navigation menu to quickly jump from one page to another. On the Positions page, notice that there are now two down arrows: one next to Object Settings, and another one next to Positions. Whenever you're in a specific object page, this second navigation menu is available. Click the second down arrow and you'll see all of the objects and tabs in your organization.

Object Navigation Menu

But that's not the only way to jump around in a permission set. Another option is the **Find Settings...** box, which is available on every page in a permission set. Here you can enter three or more consecutive letters of an object, setting, or permission name, then select the item you want from the list that appears. Let's try it.

19. Click in the 🔍 **Find Settings...** box and type *job*.

There are two objects with the string "job" and they both appear in the list.

20. Select **Job Applications**.

Using the Find Settings Box

Now that we know how to move around easily in a permission set, go ahead and add the rest of the permissions and settings, according to this table.

Table 29: Tab Settings and Object Permissions for Hiring Managers

Object Name	Tab Settings	Object Permissions	Field Permissions
Job Applications	• Available • Visible	• Read • Edit	• **Read** on all • **Edit** on Cover Letter and Status
Candidates	• Available • Visible	• Read	• No access on SSN • **Read** on all others
Reviews	-	• Read • Create • Edit	• **Read** on Candidate and Position • **Read** and **Edit** on Assessment
Job Postings	-	• Read • Create • Edit	-
Employment Websites	-	• Read	-

Great! We've created our first permission set and added the settings we need for hiring managers. Now we'll create another permission set for a different job function, interviewing candidates.

Try It Out: Create the Interviewer Permission Set

Now we're ready to create the Interviewer permission set.

Using the steps that we discussed in the last section, create a permission set with the following settings:

- Name this permission set *Interviewer* and assign the *Salesforce* user license.
- Under Assigned Apps, make the Recruiting app visible.
- Enable the following tab settings and object permissions:

Table 30: Tab Settings and Object Permissions for Interviewers

Object Name	Tab Settings	Object Permissions	Field Permissions
Positions	– Available – Visible	– Read	– No access on Min Pay and Max Pay – **Read** on all others
Candidates	– Available – Visible	– Read	– No access on SSN – **Read** on all others
Job Applications	– Available – Visible	– Read	– **Read** on all
Reviews	-	– Read – Create – Edit	– **Read** on Candidate and Position – **Read** and **Edit** on Assessment

Let's review the required permissions for hiring managers, interviewers, and standard employees.

Table 31: Summary of Required Permissions: Hiring Manager, Interviewer, and Standard Employee

	Positions	Candidates	Job Applications	Reviews	Job Postings	Employment Websites
Hiring Manager	• Read • Create • Edit*	• Read* (No SSN)	• Read • Edit (No lookup fields)	• Read • Create • Edit	• Read* • Create* • Edit*	• Read
Interviewer	• Read (No min/max pay)	• Read* (No SSN)	• Read*	• Read** • Create • Edit**	-	-

	Positions	Candidates	Job Applications	Reviews	Job Postings	Employment Websites
Standard Employee	• Read (No min/max pay)	-	-	-	-	-

* Only for those records that are associated with a position to which the hiring manager/interviewer has been assigned

** Only for those records that the interviewer owns

Great, but what about those asterisks? Do we need to take those into account when we set our object permissions?

Not at all. Those asterisks represent record-level security settings that we're going to specify shortly. The only things we need to care about here are the permissions that these users will need to have access to at least *some* of the time—that's the whole point of object permissions.

However, we do need to make sure that sensitive data on these objects is protected from users who don't need access, and then we need to drill down on the actual records that each user should be allowed to view and edit.

Controlling Access to Fields

Now that we've restricted access to objects as a whole, it's time to use a finer-toothed comb to manage the security of individual object fields. These are the settings that allow us to protect sensitive fields such as a candidate's social security number without having to hide the fact that the candidate object even exists.

Introducing Field-Level Security

In the platform, we control access to individual fields with *field-level security*. Field-level security controls whether a user can see, edit, and delete the value for a particular field on an object.

Unlike page layouts, which only control the visibility of fields on detail and edit pages, field-level security controls the visibility of fields in any part of the app, including related lists, list views, reports, and search results. Indeed, in order to be absolutely sure that a user can't access a particular field, it's important to use the field-level security page for a given object to restrict access to the field. There are simply no other shortcuts that will provide the same level of protection for a particular field.

Field-Level Security in Our Recruiting App

Just to refresh our memories about what field-level security settings we need for our Recruiting app, let's take another look at our required permissions in the following table. We'll keep them organized by recruiter, hiring manager, and standard employee, because it turns out that (surprise!) field-level security settings are closely related to profiles and permission sets:

Table 32: Revised Summary of Required Permissions

	Recruiter	**Hiring Manager**	**Standard Employee**
Position	Read Create Edit	Read Create Edit*	Read (No min/max pay)
Candidate	Read Create Edit	Read* (No SSN)	Read* (No SSN)
Job Application	Read Create Edit	Read Edit (No lookup fields)	Read*
Review	Read Create Edit	Read Create Edit	Read** Create Edit**
Job Posting	Read Create Edit Delete	Read*Create*Edit*	
Employment Website	Read Create Edit Delete	Read	

* Only for those records that are associated with a position to which the hiring manager/interviewer has been assigned

** Only for those records that the interviewer owns

For field-level security settings, we'll first zero in on those rules that include field restrictions in parentheses, specifically:

- On the Position object, hide minimum and maximum pay from standard employees and interviewers
- On the Candidate object, hide social security numbers from hiring managers and interviewers
- On the Job Application object, make the `Position` and `Candidate` lookup fields read-only for hiring managers

So let's get down to it!

Try It Out: Limit Access to Fields in the Standard Employee Profile

Let's review our field-level security rules.

- *On Positions, hide minimum and maximum pay from standard employees and interviewers*
- *On Candidates, hide social security numbers from interviewers and hiring managers*
- *On Job Applications, make Candidate and Position lookup fields read only for hiring managers.*

To define these rules, we'll access field-level security settings in the Standard Employee profile.

You may be wondering: the last two rules are about interviewers and hiring managers, but those functions are defined by permission sets. Why are we concerned with them right now?

Permissions are additive: you can never remove a user's existing permissions by assigning a permission set; you can only add permissions. If we want to limit access, we need to make sure that the base profile for our users—as well as any of their permission sets—limits this type of access. In the case of our organization, we know we're going to assign the Interviewer and Hiring Manager permission sets to users with the Standard Employee profile, so we need to restrict field permissions in this profile as well as in the permission sets.

So let's set up field-level security in the Standard Employee profile, and later we'll check the field-level security for our permissions sets.

1. From Setup, enter `Profiles` in the `Quick Find` box, then select **Profiles**, and select the Standard Employee profile.

Standard Employee Profile Detail Page

The first thing you'll notice about the Standard Employee profile's detail page is that it includes several more areas than the edit page that we originally used to define the profile. These additional areas include Page Layouts (which we learned about earlier), Field-Level Security, Record Type Settings, Login Hours, and Login IP Ranges. Although we won't go into detail in this book about how to use any areas other than Field-Level Security (and record types later on), they're part of what makes a profile so powerful in our application. You can learn more about them in the Salesforce Help.

2. In the Field-Level Security area, click **View** next to the Position object.

3. Click **Edit**.

Field-Level Security Edit Page

Position Field-Level Security for profile

Standard Employee

Help for this Page

Field Name	Field Type	Visible	Read-Only
Apex	Checkbox	☑	☐
C#	Checkbox	☑	☐
Close Date		☑	☐
Created By		✓	✓
Days Open	Number	☑	✓
Educational Requirements	Long Text Area	☑	☐
Functional Area		☑	☐
Hire By		☑	☐
Hiring Manager	Lookup	☑	☐
Java	Checkbox	☑	☐
JavaScript	Checkbox	☑	☐
Job Desciption	Long Text Area	☑	☐
Job Level	Picklist	☑	☐
Last Modified By	Lookup	✓	✓
Location		☑	☐
Max Pay		☐	☐
Min Pay		☐	☐
Open Date	Date	☑	☐

Annotations:
- If both boxes are selected, the field is Read-Only.
- If only the Visible box is selected, the field is editable.
- If neither box is selected, the field is hidden from the user.

Here we see security settings for all of the fields on the Position object, including `Min Pay` and `Max Pay`, the two fields that we want to restrict. You'll notice that some field-level security settings on some fields cannot be modified—this is because either they are system-generated fields or they act as lookup relationship fields (foreign keys) to other records.

Since the security settings checkboxes can be a little bit confusing, let's do a quick exercise to map their values (`Visible` and `Read-Only`) to the three logical permission settings for a field: "Hidden," "Read Only," and "Editable":

Table 33: Field-Level Permission Mappings

Permission	Visible	Read-Only
Hidden		
Read Only	X	X
Editable	X	

After doing this exercise, it's easy to see that most fields are editable, because their `Visible` checkbox is the only one selected. To restrict a field from ever being viewed by a user, all we have to do is deselect both checkboxes.

4. Next to the `Max Pay` field, deselect `Visible`.

5. Next to the `Min Pay` field, deselect `Visible`.

6. Click **Save**.

Now let's take care of the remaining field-level security rules. Again, since we know that our interviewers and hiring managers will be assigned the Standard Employee profile, we'll ensure that its field permissions are set correctly.

7. Click **Back to Profile**.

8. In the Field-Level Security area, click **View** next to the Candidate object.

9. Click **Edit**.

10. Next to the `SSN` field, deselect `Visible`.

11. Click **Save**.

12. Click **Back to Profile**.

13. In the Field-Level Security area, click **View** next to the Job Application object.

14. Click **Edit**.

15. Next to the `Candidate` and `Position` fields, select `Read Only`.

16. Click **Save**.

We're done setting field-level security for the Standard Employee profile. We didn't have to change anything in the Recruiter profile because, as we already determined in the planning stage, recruiters can access all the fields we created in our objects.

Try It Out: Check Field-Level Security in Permission Sets

But what about the permission sets we created?

Remember how we specified field permissions when we created the Hiring Manager and Interview permission sets? Now that we know more about field-level security, let's double-check the most sensitive fields in our permission sets to make sure they are correct.

If any of these settings are incorrect, go ahead and edit them. Be sure to click **Save** each time you go to a different page. First, let's check field permissions in the Interviewer permission set.

1. From Setup, enter `Permission Sets` in the `Quick Find` box, then select **Permission Sets**, and select the Interviewer permission set.

2. In the 🔍 **Find Settings...** box, type *pos*, then select Positions.

3. Next to the `Max Pay` and `Min Pay` fields, both **Read** and **Edit** should be disabled.

Now let's check the Hiring Manager permission set.

4. Open the Hiring Manager permission set and navigate to the Positions object.

5. Next to the `Max Pay` and `Min Pay` fields, both **Read** and **Edit** should be enabled.

Finally, we want to make sure hiring managers can see which candidate and position are associated with each job application, but prevent them from changing those lookup fields.

6. In the 🔍 **Find Settings...** box, type *job*, then select Job Applications.

7. Next to the `Candidate` and `Position` fields, **Read** should be enabled and **Edit** should be disabled.

All done! We've just finished the second piece of our security and sharing puzzle by defining field-level security for the sensitive fields in our Recruiting app. Now, for the final piece of the puzzle, we need to specify the individual records to which each user needs access. We need to protect our data without compromising any employee's ability to perform his or her job.

Controlling Access to Records

By setting object and field-level access permissions in our profiles and permission sets, we have effectively defined all of the objects and fields that any one of our Recruiting app users can access. In this section, we'll focus on setting permissions for the actual records themselves. Should our users have open access to every record, or just a subset? If it's a subset, what rules should determine whether the user can access them? We'll use a variety of platform security and sharing tools to address these questions and make sure we get it right.

Introducing Organization-Wide Defaults

When dealing with record-level access settings, the first thing we need to do is to determine the organization-wide defaults (commonly called "org-wide defaults") for each object in our Recruiting app. Also called a sharing model, org-wide defaults specify the baseline level of access that the most restricted user should have. We'll use org-wide defaults to lock down our data to this most restrictive level, and then we'll use our other record-level security and sharing tools (role hierarchies, sharing rules, and manual sharing) to open up the data to other users who need to access it.

Org-Wide Defaults in Our Recruiting App

To determine the org-wide defaults that we'll need in our Recruiting app, we need to answer the following questions for each object:

1. Who is the most restricted user of this object?

2. Is there ever going to be an instance of this object that this user shouldn't be allowed to see?

3. Is there ever going to be an instance of this object that this user shouldn't be allowed to edit?

Based on our answers to these questions, we can determine the sharing model that we need for that object as illustrated in the following diagram.

Determining the Sharing Model for an Object

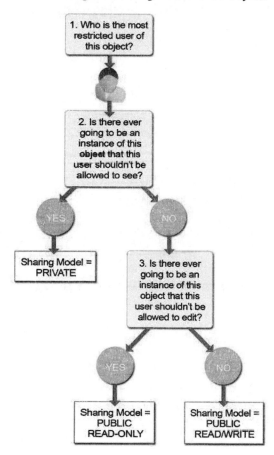

For example, let's consider the Position object in our recruiting app. To refresh our memories, here's our table of required permissions:

Table 34: Revised Summary of Required Permissions

	Recruiter	**Hiring Manager**	**Standard Employee**
Position	Read Create Edit	Read Create Edit*	Read (No min/max pay)
Candidate	Read Create Edit	Read* (No SSN)	Read* (No SSN)
Job Application	Read Create Edit	Read Edit (No lookup fields)	Read*
Review	Read Create Edit	Read Create Edit	Read** Create Edit**
Job Posting	Read Create Edit Delete	Read*Create*Edit*	
Employment Website	Read Create Edit Delete	Read	

* Only for those records that are associated with a position to which the hiring manager/interviewer has been assigned

** Only for those records that the interviewer owns

Now let's go through and answer our list of questions for the Position object:

1. Who is the most restricted user of this object?

A member of the Standard Employee profile. All that they're allowed to do is view a position.

2. Is there ever going to be an instance of this object that this user shouldn't be allowed to see?

No. Although the values for the minimum and maximum pay are hidden from standard employees, they're still allowed to view all position records.

3. Is there ever going to be an instance of this object that this user shouldn't be allowed to edit?

Yes. Standard employees aren't allowed to edit any position record.

According to our flowchart, answering "Yes" to question #3 means that the sharing model for the Position object should be set to Public Read-Only.

The same is true for the Employment Website and Job Posting objects, except hiring managers are the most restricted users instead of standard employees. (Standard employees have no permissions on these objects, but of the users that *do* have permissions, hiring managers are most restricted.) We want to allow hiring managers to view all employment website and job posting records without being able to edit them, so the answer to the second question is "No" while the answer to the third question is "Yes;" therefore, the sharing model for the Employment Website and Job Posting objects should be Public Read-Only.

Going through the rest of our recruiting objects required permissions, we can easily figure out their sharing models, too. The Standard Employee profile is the most restricted user for each object, and there are going to be candidate, job application, and review records that particular employees won't be able to view. Consequently, the sharing model for the Candidate, Job Application, and Review objects should all be set to Private.

Try It Out: Set Org-Wide Defaults

Now that we've figured out the org-wide defaults for each of our recruiting objects, let's go ahead and implement them in our Recruiting app.

1. From Setup, enter `Sharing Settings` in the `Quick Find` box, then select **Sharing Settings**. If you see an introductory splash page, click **Set Up Sharing** at the bottom of the page to skip to the actual tool.

The Sharing Settings page is where we control both org-wide defaults and sharing rules. We'll talk more about this page when we talk about sharing rules a little further down. For now, let's just edit our org-wide default settings.

2. In the Organization Wide Defaults area, click **Edit**.

This page controls the org-wide defaults for every object in our organization. You'll notice that some standard objects (like leads and calendars) use a different set of org-wide default values than we have available for our custom recruiting objects. You can learn more about them in the Salesforce Help. For now, let's just set our recruiting objects to the org-wide defaults that we decided on in the last section.

Org-Wide Defaults Edit Page

3. Next to `Candidate` and `Job Application`, select Private.

4. Next to `Employment Website` and `Position`, select Public Read Only.

Right about now, you're probably wondering why you can't set the org-wide defaults for the Review and Job Posting objects. The reason is that those objects are on the detail side of master-detail relationships, and, as mentioned in the last chapter, a detail record automatically inherits the sharing setting of its parent. So in our app, the Review object is automatically set to Private, and the Job Posting object is automatically set to Public Read Only.

You also might be wondering about the `Grant Access Using Hierarchies` column of checkboxes. Leave these selected for now. We'll discuss hierarchies in the next section.

5. Click **Save**.

Easy! Now that we've locked down our data with org-wide defaults, users are currently allowed to work on only candidate, job application, and review records that they own, and are allowed to view position, employment website, and job posting records that anyone owns. Because those settings are way too restrictive for any user to get any benefit out of our app, now we need to use role hierarchies, sharing rules, and manual sharing to open up candidate, job application, and review record access to those employees who'll need it.

Introducing Role Hierarchies

The first way that we can share access to records is by defining a role hierarchy. Similar to an org chart, a role hierarchy represents a level of data access that a user or group of users needs. Users assigned to roles near the top of the hierarchy (normally the CEO, executives, and other management) get to access the data of all the users who fall directly below them in the hierarchy. The role hierarchy enables these behaviors:

* A manager will always have access to the same data as his or her employees, regardless of the org-wide default settings. For custom objects, you can override this behavior by deselecting the `Grant Access Using Hierarchies` checkbox. However, we want our role hierarchy to apply to all of our custom objects, so leave the checkboxes selected.

* Users who tend to need access to the same types of records can be grouped together—we'll use these groups later when we talk about sharing rules.

To illustrate, let's take a look at a portion of the role hierarchy for Universal Containers:

Universal Containers Role Hierarchy

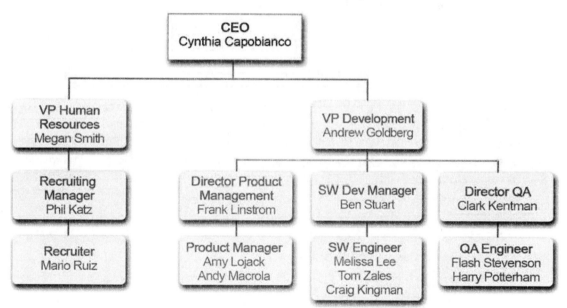

Role hierarchies don't necessarily need to match your org chart exactly. Instead, each role in the hierarchy should just represent a level of data access that a user or group of users needs. For example, suppose your organization employs a corporate lawyer who needs to access all of the records in the app. One easy way to accomplish this is by assigning the lawyer to the CEO role in your organization's role hierarchy. Since the CEO role is placed at the top of the hierarchy, anyone assigned to that role automatically gets full access to any record in the organization. It doesn't matter that technically the lawyer appears below the CEO in the regular org chart.

Comparing Roles, Profiles, and Permission Sets

Although it's easy to confuse profiles and permission sets with roles, they actually control two very different things.

As we learned earlier in this chapter, profiles and permission sets control a user's object- and field-level access permissions. Indeed, a user can't be defined without being assigned to a particular profile, since the profile specifies the most basic access for users.

Roles, on the other hand, primarily control a user's record-level access permissions through role hierarchy and sharing rules. Although a role assignment isn't exactly required when we define a user, it would be foolish of us *not* to assign a role since it makes it so much easier to define our record-level permissions. Indeed, trying to define record-level permissions without assigning a role to a user would be a lot like trying to travel from New York to San Francisco by car when there's an airplane available—there's just a much more efficient way of doing it!

To help you remember which controls what, remember: **R**oles control **R**ecords.

Role Hierarchies in Our Recruiting App

Given the Universal Containers role hierarchy that's pictured in the Universal Containers Role Hierarchy image, let's think about how implementing this hierarchy will open up certain kinds of record-level permissions to various users of our Recruiting app. Remember, since defining our org-wide defaults, our hiring managers are currently allowed to only view all position, job posting, and employment website records, and to view and update other recruiting records that they own. That doesn't make our app all that useful. However, once we implement our role hierarchy, we'll automatically grant several kinds of record-level permissions to various users. For example:

- The CEO, Cynthia Capobianco, will be able to view and update every record that anyone else in the organization can view and update.
- The VP of Development, Andrew Goldberg, will be able to view and update any record that his managers or his managers' employees can view or update.
- The VP of Human Resources, Megan Smith, will be able to view and update any record that Phil Katz, her recruiting manager, or Mario Ruiz, Phil's recruiter, can view and update.
- The Recruiting Manager, Phil Katz, will be able to view and update any record that is owned by Mario Ruiz, his recruiter.
- The Software Development manager, Ben Stuart, will be able to view and update any record that is owned by Melissa Lee, Tom Zales, or Craig Kingman, his software engineers.

- The director of QA, Clark Kentman, will be able to view and update any record that is owned by Flash Stevenson or Harry Potterham, his QA Engineers.

- The director of Product Management, Frank Linstrom, will be able to view and update any record that is owned by Amy Lojack or Andy Macrola, his product managers.

As we can see, the role hierarchy is very powerful in opening up data for people high up in the role hierarchy tree! However, let's look at some of the gaps that we still have in our record-level permissions:

- Megan Smith (and her whole recruiting team) won't be able to view any reviews that are owned by members of Andrew Goldberg's Development team because she doesn't have a direct line down to any Development roles in the role hierarchy.

- Ben Stuart, the software development manager, also won't be able to see any reviews that were written by members of the QA or Product Management groups, even if QA engineers or product managers interviewed candidates for a software engineering position in his group.

- Melissa Lee, a software engineer, won't be able to see the records for candidates that she's supposed to interview.

Clearly we'll need to use other record-level sharing methods to open up data between peers in the same group, and also between groups that appear in different branches of the role hierarchy (we'll get to those later in this chapter). However, the role hierarchy does give us a good start toward opening up record access, so let's take a look now at how to define it.

Try It Out: Create a User

Before we set up the role hierarchy, we're going to need some users to assign the roles to. First let's create the CEO of Universal Containers: Cynthia Capobianco.

1. From Setup, enter `Users` in the `Quick Find` box, then select **Users**.

2. Click **New User**.

3. In `First Name`, enter `Cynthia`.

4. In `Last Name`, enter `Capobianco`.

5. Enter your email address in the `Email` field, and a fake email in `Username`.

Each user must have a unique username across all Salesforce organizations. The value in `Email` must be a valid email address, though. We can use the "fake" value in the `Username` field to log in to the app as Cynthia, but we'll get her automatically generated password at the real email account specified in `Email`. Without that password, we'd never be able to log in!

New User Edit Page

New User

User Edit   Save

General Information

First Name   [   ]
                              Enter your real email address
Last Name   [   ] here so you can receive an
                              automatically-generated
Alias   [   ] password for your test user.

Email   [   ]
                              Use a fake email
Username   [   ] address here to
                              define your test
Nickname   [   ] user's login.
                  [i]

Title   [   ]
                              Enter a nickname for
Company   [   ] identifying the user in user
                              communities.
Department   [   ]

Division   [   ]

> **Tip:** When creating a new user, you're also required to create the user's nickname. The nickname is used to identify the user in the Ideas app, which is a community of users who post, vote for, and comment on ideas. Consider it an online suggestion box that includes discussions and popularity rankings for any subject. The nickname can contain up to 40 alphanumeric characters. For more information, see the Salesforce Help.

6. Leave `Role` unspecified. We'll assign this when we create our role hierarchy.

7. In `User License`, select Salesforce.

8. In `Profile`, select Standard Employee.

9. Fill in any remaining fields that you want to.

10. Click **Save**.

Try It Out: Define a Role Hierarchy

Implementing a role hierarchy in the platform is easy once you have an idea of what the hierarchy should look like. It's best to start with your company's org chart and then consolidate different job titles into single roles wherever possible. For example, if Ben Stuart's software development group has a staff software engineer and a junior software engineer, these positions can be consolidated into a single Software Engineer role in the hierarchy.

Once that's squared away, we can get started defining the role hierarchy itself. For our exercise, we'll use the role hierarchy we talked about previously.

1. From Setup, enter `Roles` in the `Quick Find` box, then select **Roles**. If you see an introductory splash page called Understanding Roles, click **Set Up Roles** at the bottom of the page to skip to the actual tool.

Empty Role Hierarchy Page in Tree View Mode

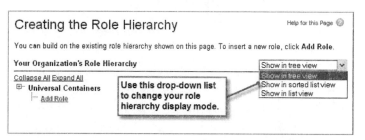

The default view for this page is the tree view, as indicated in the drop-down list on the far right side of the Role Hierarchy title bar. When creating a role hierarchy, it's probably easiest to stick with this or the list view, because they both make it easy to see how the roles all fit together in the hierarchy. The sorted list view is best if you know the name of a role that you want to find but aren't sure where it fits in the hierarchy, or if you don't want to click open all the tree nodes. For our purposes, we'll stick with the tree view.

When you first start defining a role hierarchy, the tree view displays a single placeholder node with the name of your organization. From this point, we need to add the name of the role that is highest up in the hierarchy—in our case, the CEO.

 Note: If you're building your Recruiting app with a free Developer Edition organization, you may have a role hierarchy predefined as a sample. That's alright. You can still follow along and create some more roles.

2. Just under the name of your organization—in this case, Universal Containers—click **Add Role**.

    Note: If the CEO role already exists, click **Edit**.

3. In the `Label` text box, enter `CEO`. The `Role Name` text box autopopulates with CEO.

4. In the `This role reports to` text box, click the lookup icon and click **Select** next to the name of your organization.

By choosing the name of the organization in the `This role reports to` text box, we're indicating that the CEO role is a top-level position in our role hierarchy and doesn't report to anyone.

5. In the `Role Name as displayed on reports` text box, enter `CEO`. This text is used in reports to indicate the name of a role. Since you may not want a long role name, like Vice President of Product Development, taking up too much space in your report columns, it's advisable to use a shortened, yet easily identifiable, abbreviation.

6. Leave any other options, such as `Opportunity Access`, set to their defaults. These access options don't have anything to do with our Recruiting app, and only appear if you have the org-wide defaults for a standard object set to a level more restrictive than Public Read/Write.

7. Click **Save**.

CEO Role Detail Page

Now that we've created our first role, we can assign the appropriate user to it.

8. Click **CEO** to open the CEO role detail page.

9. In the CEO role detail page, click **Assign Users to Role**.

10. In the `Available Users` drop-down list, select All Unassigned.

11. Choose a user from the list (in our case, Cynthia Capobianco), and click **Add** to move her to the `Selected Users for CEO` list.

12. Click **Save**.

If we return to the main Roles page from Setup by entering `Roles` in the `Quick Find` box, then selecting **Roles**, we can now see our new CEO role in the hierarchy.

> Note: If you see the Sample Role Hierarchy image, click **Set Up Roles**.

13. Define the rest of the roles according to the Universal Containers Role Hierarchy diagram.

There's no need to assign users to every role at this point—we'll do that later when we create the rest of our users and test out our app.

Universal Containers Role Hierarchy

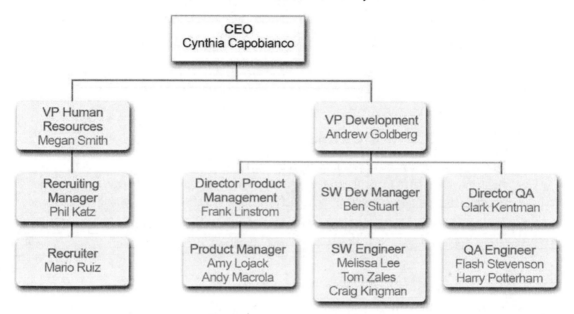

Tip: To speed up the process of adding a new role, click **Add Role** directly under the name of the role to which the new role should report. When you do this, the `This role reports to` text box is automatically filled in with the name of the appropriate role.

Not too hard, right? With org-wide defaults and a role hierarchy in place, we're actually pretty close to finishing up our record-level access permissions. All we have left to do is share recruiting-related records between groups that appear in separate branches of the role hierarchy, and between peers in a single group. Fortunately, we can accomplish both of those tasks with a combination of sharing rules and manual sharing. We just need to figure out what's left that needs to be shared, and with whom.

What's Left to be Shared?

So what *is* left to be shared? After reviewing our table of required permissions, it turns out it's just a few more things (remember, since users always have access to the records that they own, we need to worry only about the read and update permissions for our record-level access settings):

- Recruiters need read and update access on every position, candidate, job application, and review record that exists in the app.
- Hiring managers need:
  - Read and update access on position and job posting records on which they're the hiring manager

- Read access on candidate records for which they're the hiring manager
- Read and update access on every job application and review record

- Interviewers need read access on the candidate and job application records for people they're interviewing, and the ability to update their reviews.

That shouldn't be too hard! Let's go do it.

Introducing Sharing Rules

First let's see what we can do with sharing rules. Sharing rules let us make automatic exceptions to organization-wide defaults for particular groups of users. We've already defined several specific groups with the roles that we created in the previous section, but we can also make up other groups as needed.

The thing to remember with sharing rules is that, like role hierarchies, we can use them only to open up record access to more users. Sharing rules and role hierarchies can never be stricter than our org-wide default settings.

Sharing Rules in Our Recruiting App

Sharing rules work best when they're defined for a particular group of users that we can determine or predict in advance, rather than a set of users that is frequently changing. For example, in our Recruiting app, we need to share every position, candidate, job application, and review with every recruiter. Since recruiters all belong to either the Recruiting Manager or Recruiter roles in the role hierarchy, we can easily use a sharing rule to share those objects with the Recruiting Manager role and its subordinates.

Alternatively, consider another use case from our Recruiting app: interviewers need read access on the candidates and job applications for people they're interviewing. In this case, the set of interviewers is a lot harder to predict in advance—hiring managers might use different sets of interviewers depending on the position for which they're hiring, and the interviewers might come from different groups in the role hierarchy. As a result, this use case probably shouldn't be handled with sharing rules—the team of interviewers for any given manager is just too hard to predict.

Let's go through the set of required permissions we still need to implement and pick out the ones that would work best with sharing rules:

Use Case	Should we use a sharing rule?
Recruiters need read and update access on every position, candidate, job application, and review record that exists in the app.	**Yes.** As we discussed previously, it's easy to pick out the group of recruiters in our role hierarchy.

Use Case	Should we use a sharing rule?
Hiring managers need read and update access on position and job posting records on which they're the hiring manager.	**No**. It's too hard to predict which positions will be assigned to which hiring manager. We'll need to handle this use case some other way.
Hiring managers need read access on candidate records on which they're the hiring manager.	**No**. Again, it's too hard to predict which positions will be assigned to which hiring manager.
Hiring managers need read and update access on every job application and review record.	**Yes**. Since we're not restricting which job applications and reviews a hiring manager gets to read and update, we can easily pick out all of the hiring managers from our role hierarchy and define a sharing rule for them.
Interviewers need read access on the candidate and job application records for people they're interviewing.	**No**. As we discussed previously, it's hard to predict who will be a member of an interview team for a particular position.

Great! Now that we know the required permissions we want to implement with sharing rules, let's go ahead and define them.

Try It Out: Define a Public Group

Before we dive head first into creating our sharing rules, we need to make sure that we have the appropriate public groups set up. A *public group* is a collection of individual users, other groups, individual roles, and/or roles with their subordinates that all have a function in common. For example, users with the Recruiter profile as well as users in the SW Dev Manager role both review job applications. Using a public group when defining a sharing rule makes the rule easier to create and, more important, easier to understand later, especially if it's one of many sharing rules that you're trying to maintain in a large organization. You'll need to create a public group if you ever want to define a sharing rule that encompasses more than one or two groups or roles, or any individual.

Looking at the required permissions that we want to implement, there are just two objects that need a public group for their sharing rules: Job Application and Review. The good news is that we can cover these objects in a single group because the Review object is on the detail side of a master-detail relationship, so it inherits the sharing settings we apply to the Job Application object. Since both recruiters and hiring managers need read and update access to job applications and reviews, let's go ahead and make a public group called Reviewers that encompasses recruiters and hiring managers.

1. From Setup, enter `Public Groups` in the `Quick Find` box, then select **Public Groups**.

2.   Click **New**.

New Public Group Page

The New Public Group page allows you to choose other public groups, individual roles, individual roles including the roles' subordinates, or individual users.

3.   In the `Label` text box, enter *Reviewers*. Click in the `Group Name` text box to populate it automatically. `Group Name` refers to the unique name used by the API and managed packages.

4.   In the `Search` drop-down list, choose Roles.

5.   In the `Available Members` list, select SW Dev Manager, Director Product Management, and Director QA, then click **Add**.

6.   Go back up to the `Search` drop-down list, and this time choose Role and Subordinates.

7.   In the `Available Members` list, select Recruiting Manager, and click **Add**.

8.   Click **Save**.

Easy! Now we're ready to define our sharing rules.

Try It Out: Define Sharing Rules

Since we just defined our Reviewers public group, let's use it to define our sharing rule for review records.

1. From Setup, enter *Sharing Settings* in the `Quick Find` box, then select **Sharing Settings**.

Remember this page? We were last here when we defined our org-wide defaults.

2. In the `Manage sharing settings for` drop-down list, choose Job Application.

Choosing an object in this drop-down list allows us to focus in on the org-wide defaults and sharing rules for a single object at a time rather than looking at all of them in a long page—a really useful thing if you've got a large organization with several custom objects.

If you had chosen Review instead of Job Application, you wouldn't have the option of creating sharing rules, since you can't create sharing rules for a detail record in a master-detail relationship. However, since you chose Job Application, a Sharing Rules related list appears. We'll use that to create the sharing rules that will apply to both the Job Application and the Review objects.

3. In the Job Application Sharing Rules area, click **New**.

4. In the `Label` text box, enter *Review Records*.

5. Click the `Rule Name` text box to populate it automatically.

6. For the rule type, make sure `Based on record owner` is selected.

7. In the `Job Application: owned by members of` drop-down list, select Public Groups.

8. Next to that drop-down list, choose All Internal Users.

Just as we talked about already, you can define a sharing rule only for a single public group, role, or role with all of its subordinates. By default, the platform includes a default public group that encompasses every user in your organization.

9. In the `Share with` drop-down list, select Public Groups.

10. Next to that drop-down list choose Reviewers.

11. In the `Access Level` drop-down list, select Read/Write.

12. Click **Save**.

13. Click **OK** in the dialog box that says this operation could take significant time.

And that's it! We just created a rule that shares reviews written and owned by any member of the organization with all recruiters and hiring managers. Since reviewers and hiring managers all need the power to read and update reviews, we handled everyone with a single sharing rule and a public group.

To finish up, create the following owner-based sharing rules:

Table 35: Additional Sharing Rules

Object	Rule Label	Owned by...	Should be shared with...	Access Level
Candidate	Edit Candidates	All Internal Users	The role and subordinates of the Recruiting Manager	Read/Write
Employment Website	Edit Employment Websites	The role and subordinates of the Recruiting Manager	Reviewers	Read/Write
Position	Edit Positions	The role and subordinates of the Recruiting Manager	The role and subordinates of the Recruiting Manager	Read/Write

The sharing rule for the Employment Website object is necessary to let hiring managers post jobs, even though they will never update employment website records directly (the org-wide defaults prevent that). Without the rule, hiring managers can see employment website records but can't create job postings. This is because the Job Posting object is a junction object (as you may recall from the last chapter), and the Employment Website object is one of the Job Posting object's two master-detail relationships. Sharing access to a junction object record is determined by a user's sharing access to both associated master records (in this case, the associated position and employment website records) and the Sharing Setting option on the relationship field. For example, if the sharing setting on both parents is Read/Write, then the user must have Read/Write access to both parents in order to have Read/Write access to the junction object.

In the sharing rule for the Employment Website object, we opted to use the existing Reviewers public group. Doing this saved us a few clicks without granting access to any users who shouldn't be looking at employment website records.

Beyond the Basics

Did you know you can use criteria-based sharing rules to open up record access to users?

Say you want to share records based on field values in records instead of record owners. You can set up sharing rules based on field value criteria and apply filter logic to open up specific record access to users.

To find out more, see "Criteria-Based Sharing Rules" in the Salesforce Help.

Introducing Manual Sharing

Now let's talk about what we have left to do to finish defining our sharing model. After implementing our sharing rules, the following required permissions remain:

- *Hiring managers need read and update access on position records on which they're the hiring manager.*

- *Hiring managers need read access on candidate records on which they're the hiring manager.*

- *Interviewers need read access on the candidate and job application records for people they're interviewing.*

We didn't implement those required permissions with sharing rules because it was too hard for us to come up with a consistent group of users who would need access to a particular set of records. Really, this is where the job of the recruiter comes into play. A recruiter like Mario Ruiz owns the position, candidate, and job application records for jobs that he's trying to fill, and he also knows the hiring manager and interviewers who should be assigned to them.

Fortunately, we have one final type of record-access setting that allows Mario to share specific records with other specific users: manual sharing. With manual sharing, Mario can grant read or read/write access on records that he owns to any other user, role, or public group. Although it isn't automated like organization-wide defaults, role hierarchies, or sharing rules, manual sharing gives Mario the flexibility to share particular records with the ever-changing groups of interviewers and hiring managers with whom he has to deal every day.

Try It Out: Define a Manual Sharing Rule

Let's pretend that we're a recruiter like Mario and we need to share a particular candidate record that we own with another role, group, or user:

1. On the detail page for the candidate, click **Sharing**.

Sharing Detail Page

Since we own this candidate record, we get to see details about who else can see the record and why. If we didn't own this record, there would be a message about not having sufficient privileges.

> 💡 Tip: If we wanted to view the names of each user who has access to the record rather than just the names of the roles and public groups, we could click **Expand List** in this page. Although the operation can take some time depending on the number of users in our organization, it's helpful to determine whether we need to define a manual sharing rule for a particular user or if he or she already has access.

2. Click **Add**.

3. In the `Search` drop-down list, choose whether we want to manually share the record with a user, public group, role, or role and subordinates.

4. In the `Available` list, select the user, public group, or role that should have access to the record, and click **Add**.

5. In the `Access Level` drop-down list, specify whether the user, public group, or role should have read or read/write access to the record.

6. Click **Save**.

Not too hard! When we roll out our Recruiting app to users, we'll have to train our recruiters to take these steps for the position, candidate, and job application records that their hiring managers and interviewers need to access. Once this training is complete, we will have implemented all of the required sharing and security settings that we discussed at the beginning of the chapter—well done!

> 📝 Note: Make sure you are logged in as the candidate record owner, Mario Ruiz, to share the candidate via the **Sharing** button. You might not see the button if you're not logged in as the candidate record owner or system administrator. The button is available when your organization-wide default for candidates is set to Private or Public Read Only.

Displaying Field Values and Page Layouts According to Profiles

Before we give our security and sharing model a thorough testing, let's leverage the work we've done to further enhance our app's usability and, at the same time, give our data integrity a little boost.

Both usability and data integrity are adversely affected by irrelevant data. The less irrelevant data we display to users, the better off everyone will be. Not only can irrelevant data be confusing and impede a user's efficiency, but it also makes he or she more prone to entering incorrect values. By taking away unnecessary choices, we reduce the risk of making avoidable mistakes.

Although we've already put plenty of thought into our app's usability, there's always room for improvement. We won't go into a detailed usability analysis here, but let's make minor modifications to get a feel for some of the ways you can improve the usability and data integrity of your apps in the future.

The modifications we're going to make involve position records. Currently, each position record displays the same data, even though there are a few items on the position record that are of no use to recruiters who create positions for departments other than Development. For example, a recruiter who is creating a position for a Sr. Financial Analyst would have no use for the Required Programming Languages section.

By the same token, there are some options on position records that have nothing to do with technical positions, such as the Human Resources and Warehousing values in the `Functional Area` picklist. Wouldn't it be nice if we could create two types of position records: one with IT-related data for IT positions, and another for non-IT personnel?

Fortunately, we can with *record types*! Record types allow you to specify categories of records that display different picklist values and page layouts. You can also associate record types with profiles, so you can specify the picklist values and page layouts that different types of users can see in record detail pages.

To address the issues discussed above, we'll create two position record types. The first position record type will be for IT positions and will include the Required Programming Languages section of the page layout. Additionally, it will exclude all of the options in the `Functional Area` picklist except for Information Technology and Miscellaneous. The second position record type will be for all non-IT positions and will include all of the `Functional Area` picklist values except for Information Technology, but will omit the Required Programming Languages section.

Try It Out: Create a Record Type

Let's start by creating the position record type for standard, non-IT positions.

1. From Setup, enter *Objects* in the `Quick Find` box, then select **Objects**.

2. Click **Position**.

3. In the Record Types related list, click **New**.

4. In the `Record Type Label` field, enter *Standard Position*. When you move your cursor, the value of the `Record Type Name` field changes to *Standard_Position*.

5. In the `Description` field, enter *Record type for all non-IT positions*.

6. Select the `Active` checkbox.

The bottom of the screen lists all your profiles. Here is where we can determine which profiles have access to this record type. All of them are selected by default.

7. Click **Next**.

8. Leave the `Apply one layout to all profiles` radio button selected, and select Position Layout in the adjacent drop-down list.

9. Click **Save**.

The Standard Position record type detail page appears. The page lists the picklist fields found on the record type's associated page layout, the Position Layout.

10. Click **Edit** next to the `Functional Area` field.

Since this is the record type for all non-IT positions, let's remove Information Technology from the `Functional Area` picklist.

11. In the Selected Values box, select Information Technology and use the arrows to move it to the Available Values box.

12. Leave the `Default` drop-down list set to None, and click **Save**.

You're done creating your first record type, but it's not quite configured the way we want it. While it omits the Information Technology value in the `Functional Area` picklist, it still displays the Required Programming Languages section. We'll fix this later when we modify the page layouts for our record types, but first we have to create one more record type.

1. From Setup, enter `Objects` in the `Quick Find` box, then select **Objects**.

2. Click **Position**.

3. In the Record Types related list, click **New**.

4. In the `Record Type Label` field, enter `IT Position`. When you move your cursor, the value of the `Record Type Name` field changes to `IT_Position`.

5. In the `Description` field, enter `Record type for all IT positions`.

6. Select the `Active` checkbox.

Once again, the bottom of the screen lists your org's profiles, although this time they are deselected by default.

7. Next to the Recruiter and Standard Employee profiles, select the `Enable for Profile` checkbox.

8. Click **Next**.

We are again given the option to apply different layouts to different profiles. We still need to create the page layout for this record type, though, so we'll have to apply the page layouts later.

9. Leave the `Apply one layout to all profiles` radio button selected, and select Position Layout in the adjacent drop-down list.

10. Click **Save**.

The IT Position record type detail page appears.

11. Click **Edit** next to the `Functional Area` field.

Since this is the record type for all IT positions, let's remove all the options from the `Functional Area` picklist except for Information Technology and Miscellaneous.

12. Use the arrows to move the values until the Selected Values box only contains Information Technology and Miscellaneous.

13. In the `Default` drop-down list, select Information Technology.

14. Click **Save**.

Both record types are now in place, and both are omitting the picklist values they're supposed to omit. It's time to configure the page layouts for these record types.

We'll need a separate page layout for each record type. Lucky for us, we already have one page layout for the Position object (Position Layout), so we just need to create one more.

1. From Setup, enter `Objects` in the `Quick Find` box, then select **Objects**.

2. Click **Position**.

3. In the Page Layouts related list, click **New**.

4. In the `Existing Page Layout` drop-down list, select Position Layout.

Selecting the existing page layout creates a copy on which we can base our new page layout. This saves us from having to create the layout from scratch.

5. In the `Page Layout Name` field, enter `IT Position Layout`, and click **Save**.

We're done creating our new IT position page layout. Now, let's edit both our new and original page layouts so they display relevant data. Since we're on the IT Position page layout, we'll start with that one.

This page layout already includes the Required Programming Languages section, so we don't need to add that; however, we do want to add the `Record Type` field to the page layout so users will instantly be able to tell what type of position record they're editing.

6. Select the Fields category in the palette, then drag the `Record Type` field to just below the `Last Modified By` field.

7. Click **Save**.

Now, let's edit the Position Layout page layout. This is the layout we'll use for our Standard Position record type, so we'll want to remove the Required Languages section.

1. From Setup, enter `Objects` in the `Quick Find` box, then select **Objects**.

2. Click **Position**.

3. In the Page Layouts related list, click **Edit** next to Position Layout.

4. Click ⊖ in the upper right corner of the Required Languages section.

We'll want to add the `Record Type` field to this page layout as well.

5. Select the Fields category in the palette, then drag the `Record Type` field to just below the `Last Modified By` field.

6. Click **Save**.

We're on the verge of finishing! There's just one more easy task to complete: assigning our Position page layouts to our new record types.

Assigning page layouts is easy because you can make all of the assignments for an object on a single page.

1. From Setup, enter *Objects* in the `Quick Find` box, then select **Objects**.

2. Click **Position**.

3. In either the Page Layouts related list or Record Types related list, click **Page Layout Assignment**.

4. Click **Edit Assignment**.

A table shows the Position page layout assignments for all of the different profile and position record type combinations. In the table, select the profile and position record type combinations you want to change. Use SHIFT+click to select a range of cells or CTRL+click to select multiple cells at once. Use the drop-down list above the table to indicate the page layout to which you want to reassign your selections.

5. Click the IT Position column heading. This selects all of the values in the IT Position record type column.

6. Select IT Position Layout in the `Page Layout To Use` drop-down list.

7. Click **Save**.

Your record types are good to go!

Putting It All Together

Congratulations! We've just implemented all of our required security and sharing settings, first by defining object-level access with profiles and permission sets, then by securing field-level access with field-level security, and finally by defining record-level access using org-wide defaults, role hierarchies, sharing rules, and manual sharing.

We learned about the difference between object-, field-, and record-level security, and how profiles, permission sets, and roles work together to first determine the objects and tabs that a user can possibly use, and then the specific records that the user can actually access and edit. We also learned ways to set up other profile-based features like record types to improve both our data integrity and our app's usability.

Let's now try it out for ourselves. To do so, we'll first have to define a number of users, and then we can play around with creating records and seeing who has access to what.

Try It Out: Create More Users

To really put our Recruiting app through its paces, we'll first need to define the rest of our users and assign a couple of them to some of the recruiting records that we imported earlier.

 Note: If you're implementing the Recruiting app in a Developer Edition organization, you'll have only a few additional users to play with besides the System Administrator user. You can still try out all of the use cases that we describe here, but you'll have to update the user's profile, permission sets, and role for whatever use case you're working on.

Table 36: Summary of Required Permissions: Recruiter and Standard Employee Profiles

	Recruiter	**Standard Employee**
Position	Read Create Edit	Read (No min/max pay)
Candidate	Read Create Edit	
Job Application	Read Create Edit	
Review	Read Create Edit	
Job Posting	Read Create Edit Delete	
Employment Website	Read Create Edit Delete	

Let's walk through the creation of our recruiter: Mario Ruiz. Then you can finish the other users on your own.

1. From Setup, enter `Users` in the `Quick Find` box, then select **Users**.
2. Click **New User**.
3. Fill out the required fields in the User edit page.

Just as you did with Cynthia Capobianco, in the `Email` field enter a real email address that you have access to, and in the `Username` field enter a "fake" email address (for example, mario.ruiz@recruiting.com).

4. From the `Profile` drop-down list, select Recruiter.
5. Click **Save**.

Now that we've created the Mario Ruiz user, let's give him ownership of the DBA position and its associated job application and candidate records.

6. Click the Positions tab.
7. From the `View` drop-down list, select All and click **Go**.

Tip: If you want to see more than just the `Position Title` field in this view, click **Edit** next to the `View` drop-down list and add additional fields in the Select Fields to Display section.

8. Click **DBA**.

9. Next to the `Owner` field, click **Change**.

10. Click the lookup icon 🔍 and choose Mario Ruiz.

11. Click **Save**.

12. In the Job Applications related list, click the name of the listed job application and repeat Steps 8-11.

13. Click the ID of the associated candidate on the Job Application detail page and repeat Steps 8-11.

 Note: When you imported records from Candidate, Job Application, and Position CSV files, you were probably logged in as a user other than a Recruiting Manager or subordinate. We created sharing rules that share the records that are owned by the role and subordinates of the Recruiting Manager, so now you should transfer ownership of the rest of these records to a Recruiting Manager or subordinate (Phil Katz or Mario Ruiz).

Now create the other users in Summary of User Profile Assignments on page 198 and assign them the profiles listed in the table. Since Mario is our only recruiter, he's the only user we'll assign the Recruiter profile to. Everyone else should have the Standard Employee profile.

Table 37: Summary of User Profile Assignments

User	Profile
Phil Katz	Standard Employee
Megan Smith	Standard Employee
Craig Kingman	Standard Employee
Tom Zales	Standard Employee
Melissa Lee	Standard Employee
Ben Stuart	Standard Employee
Andy Macrola	Standard Employee
Amy Lojack	Standard Employee
Frank Linstrom	Standard Employee
Andrew Goldberg	Standard Employee

User	Profile
Harry Potterham	Standard Employee
Flash Stevenson	Standard Employee
Clark Kentman	Standard Employee
Cynthia Capobianco	Standard Employee

Notice that most of our users have the same profile. With the Standard Employee profile, the only thing these users can do in our recruiting app is look at positions (not including certain fields). But what about the users who need to access more information, such as hiring manager Ben Stuart? Well, this is where our permission sets come in, which we created in Introducing Permission Sets on page 155. Here's a recap of the permissions we gave the Hiring Manager and Interviewer permission sets.

Table 38: Summary of Required Permissions: Hiring Manager and Interviewer Permission Sets

	Hiring Manager	**Interviewer**
Position	Read Create Edit*	Read (No min/max pay)
Candidate	Read* (No SSN)	Read * (No SSN)
Job Application	Read Edit (No lookup fields)	Read *
Review	Read Create Edit	Read ** Create Edit **
Job Posting	Read *Create *Edit *	
Employment Website	Read	

* Only for those records that are associated with a position to which the hiring manager/interviewer has been assigned

** Only for those records that the interviewer owns

Since Ben is a hiring manager for software development, he needs to be able to do things like creating new positions or looking at a candidate and her application. Let's assign the Hiring Manager permission set to Ben so he can accomplish those tasks.

1. From Setup, enter *Users* in the Quick Find box, then select **Users**.

2. Click Ben Stuart's name.

3. In the user detail page, scroll to the Permission Set Assignments related list and click **Edit Assignments**.

4. In the Available Permission Sets box, select Hiring Manager and use the arrows to move it to the Enabled Permission Sets box.

5. Click **Save**.

Repeat these steps for the other hiring managers: Andy Macrola, Amy Lojack, and Clark Kentman.

Now that we've assigned all of our hiring managers the right permission set, let's focus on our interviewers. Mario has scheduled a candidate for an interview next week, and Ben has asked two of his developers to interview the candidate. Assign the Interviewer permission set to Melissa Lee and Craig Kingman, so that they can check out the position and application, as well as leave their reviews of the interview.

Beyond the Basics

Did you know you can control who sees whom in the organization?

Say you want to let recruiters, hiring managers, and interviewers see and collaborate with each other, but not with standard employees. You can set the organization-wide default for the user object to Private, and create sharing rules to enable recruiters, hiring managers, and interviewers to see and collaborate with each other in the Recruiting App, while preventing standard employees from viewing those users and vice versa.

To find out more, see "User Sharing" in the Salesforce Help.

Try It Out: Verify that Everything Works

Now that we've got data assigned to actual users, let's go through our Recruiting app and see how the security and sharing permissions that we defined in this chapter play out:

1. First log in as Mario Ruiz—verify that he can see and edit all positions, all candidates, and all job applications. Verify that the **New** buttons are there for all objects in the Recruiting app. Verify that he can create positions using either position record type.

2. Log in as Melissa Lee—verify that she can view positions but that there's no **New** button. Verify that she can't see any candidates, job applications, reviews, or employment websites.

3. Log in as Ben Stuart—verify that he can view positions and that there's a **New** button. Verify that he can view but not edit employment websites. Verify that he can't see any candidates. Verify that he can view job applications, but not edit their lookup fields. Verify that he can view reviews and that there's a **New** button. (What do reviews look like? Can he see the names of the candidates and job applications on them?)

4. Log in again as Mario Ruiz—have him manually share read/write access on the DBA position with Ben. Have him manually share read access on the candidate with Melissa and Ben. Have him manually share read/write access on the job application with Melissa and Ben.

5. Log in again as Melissa Lee—verify that she can now see the candidate and job application that Mario just shared with her but that she can't see the candidate's social security number. Have her create a review for that candidate.

6. Log in again as Ben Stuart—verify that he can edit the DBA position. Verify that he can read and update Melissa's review. Verify that he can update the job application `Status` to *Extend an Offer*.

How did we do? If all of these use cases worked correctly, you've just successfully set up security and sharing for our Recruiting app! If a use case didn't work, check the role, profile, permission set, and sharing rules of each user against the information in the Summary of Required Permissions: Recruiter and Standard Employee Profiles table.

There is one critical security-related issue that we have yet to address: who will be responsible for overseeing the operation of the Recruiting app and its related data when the app goes live?

Delegating Data Administration

As with nearly all Force.com apps, our Recruiting app doesn't require tedious ongoing administration or a watchful eye monitoring its daily operation. Once the app is deployed, it just works! But from time to time, a decision or issue arises that requires human intervention, and some basic manual administration is required, like:

- A hiring manager is retiring and has forty open positions that need to be transferred to another manager
- A current Recruiting app user needs immediate access to private data owned by another user who happens to be on vacation
- Duplicate records have piled up in the Recruiting app and need to be removed
- A new employee just got hired and needs access to the Recruiting app

To handle these situations, someone might need to override the security and sharing configurations we just created. Who should have such powers within our app, and how can these powers be granted?

Obviously, your company's primary Salesforce administrator can handle just about any issue that users may encounter in Salesforce. Primary administrators are assigned to the System Administrator profile, which automatically grants several global administrative permissions, including:

- "View All Data"—View all data owned by other users in your organization
- "Modify All Data"—Modify all data owned by other users in your organization, mass update and mass delete records, and undelete records that other users deleted

- "Customize Application"—Customize just about anything in Salesforce, from page layouts to the data model
- "Manage Users"—Add and remove users, reset passwords, grant permissions, and more

For smaller companies, it makes sense to have a single administrator be the "go-to" person for all Salesforce issues. But for medium to large companies, assigning all Salesforce responsibilities to one person is not practical, especially when you consider that a company can run its entire business in the cloud using a different Force.com app to suit each of its business needs. This could add up to dozens of apps and hundreds or thousands of users! Your primary Salesforce administrator will likely go insane unless other folks can help with the administration. At the same time, every administrative privilege you grant increases the risk of exposing your company's sensitive data, so you need precise control over the amount of access you enable.

To preserve both your administrator's sanity and your company's security, the Force.com platform provides two ways to quickly delegate restricted data administration access: object-level permissions and delegated administration groups.

Overriding Sharing with Object Permissions

Believe it or not, we already delegated a few administrative responsibilities a few pages ago when we created the Recruiter permission set. If you go back to that section, you'll see that we selected the "View All" and "Modify All' object permissions for job postings and employment websites. As you might expect, "View All" lets users view all of the records of that object, while "Modify All" lets users read, edit, and delete all of the records of that object. So how does selecting these permissions differ from just selecting the "Create," "Read," "Edit," and "Delete" permissions individually? And how do "View All" and "Modify All" help you delegate administration?

The keyword here is "all." When you grant "View All" or "Modify All" for an object on a profile or permission set, you grant any associated users access to *all* records of that object regardless of the sharing and security settings. In essence, the "View All" and "Modify All" permissions ignore the sharing model, role hierarchy, and sharing rules that the "Create," "Read," "Edit," and "Delete" permissions respect. Furthermore, "Modify All" also gives a user the ability to mass transfer, mass update, and mass delete records of that specific object, and approve such records even if the user is not a designated approver. These tasks are typically reserved for administrators, but because "View All" and "Modify All" let us selectively override the system, responsibilities that are usually reserved for the administrator can be delegated to other users in a highly controlled fashion.

 Note: We'll learn more about approving records in the next chapter. Other administrative actions, such as mass updates, are covered in the Salesforce online help.

You may wonder if the "View All" and "Modify All" object permissions are similar to the "View All Data" and "Modify All Data" global permissions. It's true that they all ignore the sharing model, hierarchy, and sharing rules, but bear in mind that object permissions only apply to records of a specific object, whereas global permissions apply to records of every object in your organization. As a rule of thumb, when global administration permissions are too permissive for a particular user, use the object permissions instead to control data access on an object-by-object basis.

Because we already applied object permissions when we created the Recruiter permission set, there's no need to walk through the process again here; however, you can probably imagine other ways in which the "View All" and "Modify All" permissions might be useful for this app. For example, as we discussed before, certain laws may require your company to keep all position, candidate, and job application records for a specific amount of time. This law is why we opted not to give recruiters the ability to delete those records. When that legal time limit expires, though, your company may want to hire a contractor who specializes in data cleansing to remove old recruiting data from the system. By creating a permission set with the "Modify All" object permission on positions, candidates, and job applications, you can quickly give the contractor the permissions needed to get the job done without exposing the rest of your company's data.

Delegated Administration Groups

We just saw how the "View All" and "Modify All" object permissions can be used to take a considerable load off of the primary administrator's shoulders; however, there are still a few other administrative responsibilities that you might want to delegate but can't with object permissions. For example, you might not want to burden the primary administrator with the tasks of manually adding every new employee to Salesforce or resetting a user's password every time it's forgotten. Also, as time passes, your company may need a new field or two added to review records, or a new record type for positions. Sometimes, it's more efficient to delegate basic administrative tasks like these to members of a group so the primary administrator can focus on other things.

A *delegated administration group* is a group of non-administrator users with limited administrative privileges. These privileges can include:

- Creating and editing users and resetting passwords for users in specified roles and all subordinate roles
- Assigning users to specified profiles
- Logging in as a user who has granted login access to an administrator
- Managing custom objects created by the primary administrator

Let's define a delegated administration group in our Recruiting app that enables its members to manage our Recruiting app's users and make adjustments to the app's custom objects without having access to all of the other data in Salesforce.

Try It Out: Define the Recruiting Manager Administration Group

We'll start by creating the delegated administration group:

1. From Setup, enter *Delegated Administration* in the Quick Find box, then select **Delegated Administration**.

2. Click **New**.

3. In the Delegated Group Name text box, enter *Recruiting App Admins*.

4. In the Delegated Group detail page, click **Edit**.

5. Select the Enable Group for Login Access checkbox.

The Enable Group for Login Access option allows the delegated administrators in this group to log in as a user who has explicitly granted login access to administrators for a specific period of time. This can be useful for troubleshooting problems that might arise for the user.

6. Click **Save**.

In the Delegated Group detail page, we can use the Delegated Administrators related list to specify the users to include in this group.

7. Click **Add** in the Delegated Administrators related list.

8. In the first empty text box, enter *Phil Katz*, the Recruiting Manager at Universal Containers.

    Note: Members of delegated administrator groups must have the "View Setup and Configuration" permission.

Each delegated administration group can have up to five members, but we're only going to include our Recruiting Manager in this group, due to the focus of our app.

9. Click **Save**.

We're back on the Delegated Group detail page. The User Administration related list lets us specify the kinds of users this group can manage.

10. Click **Add** in the User Administration related list.

Instead of selecting individual users to manage, we'll select them by their roles. For each role we select, its subordinate roles are automatically selected too. (Flip back to the Universal Containers role hierarchy on page 179 if you can't remember which roles are subordinate.) We don't want to let members of this group administer the Salesforce accounts of executives at Universal Containers, but the group should be able to administer the Recruiting app for recruiters, directors, managers, and their subordinates.

11. In the Roles and Subordinates boxes, enter:

- *Recruiter*
- *Director Product Management*
- *Director QA*
- *SW Dev Manager*

12. Click **Save**.

The Assignable Profiles related list lets us specify the profiles this group can assign to the users they manage. Note that delegated administrators can't modify these profiles; they can only assign users to them.

13. Click **Add** in the Assignable Profiles related list.

14. In the Assignable Profiles boxes, enter *Recruiter* and *Standard Employee*.

15. Click **Save**.

The Custom Object Administration related list lets us specify the custom objects that delegated administrators of this group can administer. The delegated administrators can manage just about every aspect of the custom object, such as modifying page layouts, adding fields, and even deleting the object; however, they can't set permissions for the custom object, manage workflow and sharing for the object, and modify relationships to other objects.

16. Click **Add** in the Custom Object Administration related list.

Let's give the members of this delegated administrator group (in this case, Phil) the ability to modify the Position object. That way, if position records need another field or hiring managers request another record type in the future, Phil can handle it. (Of course, we'll also want to warn Phil that he should be careful not to delete the Position object altogether—custom object administrative rights give him that power as well!)

17. In the first empty text box, enter *Position*.

18. Click **Save**.

That wraps up the configuration of our delegated administration group! Our Recruiting app now has a delegated administrator who can provide our primary Salesforce administrator with some relief.

Try It Out: Verify that Delegated Administration Works

To see what a delegated Recruiting App administrator can and can't do, log in as Phil Katz.

1. From Setup, enter *Users* in the Quick Find box, then select **Users**.

Notice that the **Edit** link appears next to any user assigned to a role or subordinate role for which our delegate administrator group can manage users. The **Edit** link does not appear to users assigned to other roles, such as Cynthia Capobianco, the CEO.

You'll also see the **New User**, **Reset Password(s)**, and **Add Multiple Users** buttons are now available to Phil. Let's see what happens if Phil adds a new user.

2. Click **New User**.

The User Edit page appears. At first glance, this page looks just like the User Edit page we saw when we added users while logged in as the system administrator. If you look closely at the options available in the `Role` and `Profile` drop-down lists, though, you'll notice a difference—the options are limited to what we specified when we created our delegated administration group. For example, Phil can't create a user with an executive role, nor can he assign a user to any profile other than Recruiter or Standard Employee.

We don't need to create any more users right now, so just click **Cancel**.

The last thing to verify is Phil's ability to modify the Position object.

3. From Setup, enter `Objects` in the `Quick Find` box, then select **Objects**.

We see that the **Edit** and **Del** links are available next to the Position object. This means that Phil now has the ability to both edit and delete the Position object. Our testing is complete!

Beyond the Basics

Did you know that you can set up single sign-on between your organization and other authorized Web resources?

Say you want your employees to only have to remember one password when they sign on to the recruiting app, as well as your company website. You can work with an identity provider, exchange information with them, then configure Salesforce for single sign-on.

To find out more, see "Single Sign-On" in the Salesforce Help.

Summing Up

This chapter has covered quite a bit of ground! We discussed the differences between object-, field-, and record-level security. We learned how profiles and roles work together to first determine the objects and tabs that a user can possibly use, and then the specific records that the user can actually access and edit. We also discovered ways to set up other profile-based features like record types to improve both our data integrity and our app's usability. Finally, we tested everything, and delegated the administration of our Recruiting app in an efficient and secure way. Now that we've got security squared away, let's go incorporate some business logic into our app with workflow rules.

CHAPTER 8   Collaborating with Chatter

In this chapter ...

- Introducing Chatter
- Tracking Fields on Your Objects
- Following Records
- Starting a Group or Two
- Introducing Notifications
- Introducing Actions
- Summing Up

In the last chapter, we established a security and sharing model to determine who gets to see which data in the expanded Recruiting app. We've seen how easy it is to restrict access to fields and records using the Force.com platform. Now that our application is secure, let's make it easier for recruiters, interviewers, and hiring managers to collaborate on the hiring process. With Chatter, we provide them a fun, fast, and effective way to get and share information.

In this chapter, we'll introduce some of Chatter's basic features—like feed tracking and following records—and show how Chatter makes collaboration a piece of cake.

Introducing Chatter

Chatter makes your app collaborative like never before. Once you enable Chatter for your organization, you can turn on feeds for most standard objects and all custom objects, allowing you to see real-time updates whenever anything changes. Users can post to feeds, comment on other posts, share files and links, work together on documents, follow people and records, and more. With feed tracking, users can even follow specific fields on a record; when a value for one of those fields changes, Chatter posts an update to the feed, instantly alerting everyone who follows that record. With mentions, users can mention someone to make sure that person sees their update. And with hashtags, users can add topics to posts and comments so other people can find their updates more easily.

Chatter users have their own personal profile feeds, where they can post updates and see updates from the people and records they're following. Users can also form public or private groups for more focused collaboration. Each group has its own feed, where the group members can share information, ask questions, and upload files for collaboration. Chatter makes it easy to connect with the people and information you care about most.

For more information, see "Chatter Overview" in the Salesforce Help.

Tracking Fields on Your Objects

Chatter can track field changes for most of your records and objects, including your custom objects, and automatically push that information to the record's feed. Tracking fields keeps you up to date with the latest changes on objects and records that interest you. Simply enable feed tracking on the object, then choose the fields to track.

Try It Out: Enable Feed Tracking on Positions and Job Applications

The recruiters at Universal Containers want to know when a position's status or location changes. Hiring managers want to know when a job application is submitted. Let's track these fields for them in Chatter.

To enable Chatter for your organization:

1. From Setup, enter `Chatter Settings` in the `Quick Find` box, then select **Chatter Settings**.
2. Click **Edit**.
3. Select `Enable`.
4. Click **Save**.

Chatter Settings

Chatter Settings

Help for this Page ⊙

Chatter is a corporate network that lets your users work together, talk to each other, and share information, all in real time.

[Save] [Cancel]

Chatter Settings
       | = Required Information

Turn on Chatter and Global Search features. We have given you a head start - your users may auto-follow a few people or records by default and your search box is in the header. Learn More...

   Enable ☑

Email Notifications

Allow users to receive personal Chatter email notifications.

   Allow Emails ☑

Now, let's track changes to the `Status` and `Location` fields for positions:

1. From Setup, enter `Feed Tracking` in the `Quick Find` box, then select **Feed Tracking**.

2. Select the Position object.

3. Select the `Enable Feed Tracking` checkbox.

4. Select the `Status` and `Location` fields. If either of these fields changes for a position, that position's feed is updated, alerting the recruiters following it.

5. Click **Save**.

Feed Tracking for Positions

Similarly, the hiring manager wants to be notified when a Job Application's `Status` changes. Let's track that field:

1. From Setup, enter `Feed Tracking` in the `Quick Find` box, then select **Feed Tracking**.

2. Select the Job Application object.

3. Select `Enable Feed Tracking`.

4. Select the `Status` field. When the value changes—for instance, from New to Review Resume—the Job Application feed is updated, and hiring managers following that application are notified.

5. Click **Save**.

While we're at it, let's enable the rest of our custom objects for feed tracking. Repeat the steps you did for the Position and Job Application objects to enable Candidate, Employment Website, Job Posting, and Review for feed tracking.

Look At What We've Done

We chose to track updates to the `Status` and `Location` fields on the Position object. If people want to see field updates for a position, they can view the feed on that record's detail page. For example, when the recruiter helping to staff the Technical Publications department looks at the Documentation Writer record, she'll see that the location has changed to San Francisco, CA.

Location Field Update in a Position Record Feed in the Full Site

Launch Salesforce1 to see how field updates look on position records in a mobile device. From the navigation menu, tap **Show More** > **Positions**, and then tap **Documentation Writer**.

There are now three views, rather than the two we have seen in previous chapters. The new view, which appears first when you open a record, is the *record feed*. Record feeds appear only if feeds are enabled for the record's object type. The record feed displays any Chatter field updates for this record—for the fields that we selected when we enabled feeds on the Position object.

Location Field Update in a Position Record Feed in Salesforce1

Feed tracking is great, but who wants to keep going to the record detail page to see updates? Next, we'll show how easy it is to follow records, which brings the updates to you.

Following Records

Chatter lets you follow the users, groups, documents, and records that you're interested in. Updates on the people and information you care about are posted to your personal feed. You can also enable email alerts for actions, like someone commenting on your post, as well as get daily or weekly digests with posts and comments from your personal feed and groups you belong to.

Try It Out: Follow a Job Application Record

For our Recruiting app, we know that hiring managers want to keep track of job applications for their open positions. All they have to do is follow those records.

To try it yourself, just open the detail page for a job application and click **Follow**. It's that simple!

Following a Job Application Record

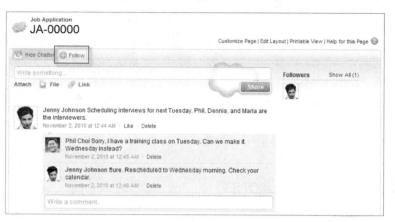

All tracked field updates, as well as other users' posts and comments on the records you're following, are posted to your personal feed. Use Chatter to connect the right people to the right records, and start collaborating in real time on the hiring process.

Beyond the Basics

Did you know you can use Chatter to collaborate outside of your browser?

Say you want to keep an eye on Chatter updates, but you can't log in through a browser. For example, you're creating a slide deck on your laptop and there's not enough screen room for your browser. In these cases, it helps to have a Chatter client app Installed.

Chatter Desktop is a Chatter client app that integrates your computer with Chatter. Chatter Desktop makes collaboration easier than ever. Want alerts when people you're following post something new? Just install Chatter Desktop and watch it display pop-up notifications for each update. Need to share a file with your coworkers? Just drag it to the Chatter Desktop interface.

To install Chatter Desktop:

1. At the top of any Salesforce page, click the down arrow next to your name. From the menu under your name, select **My Settings** or **Setup**—whichever one appears.

2. From the left panel, select one of the following:

   - If you clicked **My Settings**, select **My Settings** > **Desktop Add-Ons** > **Chatter Desktop**.
   - If you clicked **Setup**, select **Desktop Integration** > **Chatter Desktop**.

Starting a Group or Two

Now that you've enabled Chatter, encourage people to collaborate by creating public and private focus groups around common interests. For example, you can create groups for the sales, marketing, product development teams, and so on.

Groups are a great way for users to share information and files and ask questions. Instead of sending out a mass email, group members can post questions on the group's page; when a question is answered, it's answered for all group members. Groups give instant access to subject matter experts.

Try It Out: Create a Group

Chatter is all about sharing information and collaboration. Now that you've turned on feeds, one of the best ways to get people to collaborate is to create groups around common interests. Let's create a private collaboration group for the recruiters so they can collaborate on recruiting efforts and share information within the group in a secure way.

1. In Chatter, click **Groups** > **New Group**.

2. Use a descriptive name for your group—for example "Recruiting Team". You also have the option of adding a short description of the group.

3. Select **Private** if you want to create a group for just the recruiters. If you don't make the group private, any Chatter user in your organization can join. Similarly, because customers are users from outside your company, you probably don't want to allow them to join this particular group. If it makes sense to allow customers at a later point, you can always do so by changing the group's settings.

4. Click **Save**.

Creating a Private Collaboration Group

Group Edit
New Group

Help for this Page

Save   Cancel

Basic Information

| = Required Information

Group Name | Recruiting Team

Owner   Owner

Description   This is a private group for recruiters.

Group Access

○ **Public**   Everyone can see updates and join.

◉ **Private**   Only members can see updates. Membership requires approval.

☐ **Allow Customers**   You can invite customers to this group. ⓘ

Save   Cancel

You've created the group. Now you can simply add or invite members—in this case, recruiters—and maybe upload a snazzy picture for the group.

Introducing Notifications

For users who are frequently away from their desks, knowing when something in Salesforce needs their attention is incredibly important. If they use Salesforce1 on their mobile device, users can get notifications when certain events happen, such as when they receive approval requests or when someone mentions them in Chatter.

Three types of notifications can appear to Salesforce1 users.

• *In-app notifications* keep users aware of relevant activity while they're using Salesforce1. By tapping ☐, a user can view the 20 most recent notifications received within the last 90 days.

• *Push notifications* are alerts that appear on a mobile device when a user has installed the Salesforce1 downloadable app but isn't using it. These alerts can consist of text, icons, and sounds, depending on the device type. If an administrator enables push notifications for your organization, users can choose individually whether to receive push notifications on their devices.

• *Actionable notifications* are push notifications that include action buttons, so users can act directly from the notification without needing to open the Salesforce1 downloadable app. Depending on the type of device and how push notifications are configured, actionable notifications can even appear on the lock screen.

Try It Out: Enable Notifications

Let's make sure notifications are enabled, so we can trust that users will know when someone comments on one of their posts or mentions them somewhere in Salesforce.

1. From Setup, enter `Salesforce1 Notifications` in the `Quick Find` box, then select **Salesforce1 Notifications**

2. Select the notifications that you want your Salesforce1 users to receive.

3. Select actionable notifications so your Salesforce1 users can respond directly from certain types of push notifications without opening Salesforce1.

4. Click **Save**.

Look At What We've Done

As we did when we tested user access in Securing and Sharing Data on page 145, we'll have to log in as multiple users to test notifications.

First, let's create some Chatter activity.

1. If you aren't already, log in to Salesforce as Ben Stuart.

2. Open Mario Ruiz's profile. You can do this by entering his name in the global search box and clicking the recent record that appears below the box.

3. In the text box, enter `Can you share the candidates and applications for the SW Engineer position with me and @Melissa Lee? Thanks!`, and click **Share**.

4. Log in as Melissa Lee, and comment on that post: `Thanks in advance, @Mario Ruiz!`.

Now let's verify that our user received the right notifications in Salesforce1.

1. Log in to Salesforce1 as Mario Ruiz. Tap ⬚, and verify that you have two new in-app notifications: one from when Ben posted to your profile, and one from when Melissa mentioned you.

Notifications for Mario Ruiz

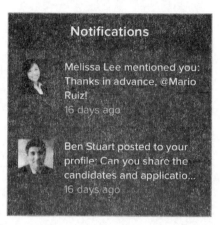

2. Log in to Salesforce1 as Ben Stuart. Verify that you have one new in-app notification from when Melissa commented on your post.

Introducing Actions

Now that we've turned on Chatter, we've seen what it can do for users who are communicating with each other directly. There's one more feature that takes advantage of Chatter to save your users time in their day-to-day tasks: *quick actions*, also known as simply *actions*. Create actions and add them to the Chatter publisher on the home page, on the Chatter tab, in Chatter groups, and on record detail pages. In Salesforce Classic, actions appear in the Chatter publisher. In Lightning Experience, actions appear in different areas of the user interface, depending on the action's type. In Salesforce1, actions appear in the action bar, its associated action menu, and as list-item actions.

Actions make it easier for your users to work directly from wherever they are in the app.

Example: For example, Megan Smith no longer has to go to the navigation menu, open the Contacts item, click New, and specify which account her new contact should be associated with. With actions, she can create a new contact for that account by simply clicking—or tapping—the associated action in either the Chatter publisher in the full site or in the action bar in Salesforce1. Actions do the work for her.

In the Chatter publisher, we already have a handful of *default actions*.

- Standard Chatter actions are included when Chatter is enabled.

- *Create actions* are actions that let users create records—like New Contact, New Opportunity, and New Lead. They respect your validation rules and field requiredness, and you can choose which fields display for each action.

- *Log a call actions* let users record the details of phone calls or other customer interactions. These call logs are saved as completed tasks.
- *Question actions* enable users to ask and search for questions about the records that they're working with.
- *Update actions* let users make changes to a record through its detail page

Most of these out-of-the-box actions aren't very helpful for users of our recruiting app, but we can easily customize this feature. In this section, we'll be personalizing the actions that appear for our users throughout the full site and Salesforce1.

With the platform, we can declaratively create three types of actions.

- Create actions
- Log a call actions
- Update actions

We can't create standard actions, but we can control whether they show up or not, as well as what order they show up in. For create and log a call actions, we can create either global or object-specific actions. For update actions, we can only create object-specific actions.

Try It Out: Create a Global Action

Global actions let users do tasks such as creating records or recording call details directly from the publisher on the Home tab, the Chatter tab, the action bar on the Salesforce1 feed, and Chatter groups. You can also add global create actions to record detail pages. Global create actions don't automatically establish a relationship between the record that's created and any other record. For example, if Ben Stuart uses a global create action on an account to create a contact, the action doesn't automatically associate the new contact with the account. However, object-specific actions do. We'll get to those later.

Let's create a global action.

1. From Setup, enter `Actions` in the `Quick Find` box, then select **Global Actions**.
2. Click **New Action**.
3. For `Action Type`, leave Create a Record selected.
4. For `Target Object`, select Position.
5. For `Record Type`, select Standard Position. We'll create an action for IT positions after we finish this action.
6. Leave `Label` blank for now.
7. For `Standard Label Type`, select New "Record Type". Notice that `Label` no longer appears. By selecting a value other than --None--, we're telling Salesforce to automate the label

of this action. The standard label type we selected uses the record type we selected to form the label: New Standard Position.

8. For Name, enter *New_Standard_Position*.

9. Enter a description.

10. Click **Save**.

Now let's configure the fields that will appear when a user selects this action.

Introducing Action Layouts

Just like we can customize object record pages with page layouts, we can customize actions using *action layouts*. Using the action layout editor, we can select the fields that will show up when a user clicks on an action.

The upper part of the editor contains a palette, and below the palette is the action layout. The palette contains fields from the action's target object that you can add to the action layout, except for the following unsupported field types:

- Record type fields
- Read-only field types such as roll-up summary, formula, and auto-number fields
- Read-only system fields such as `Created By` or `Last Modified By`

Inactive Fields

Fields that are already on the action layout still appear on the palette but are inactive. When you select an inactive field on the palette, Salesforce highlights the field on the action layout.

Field Type Conversion

If you convert a field's type from one that is supported for actions to a type that isn't supported, Salesforce removes the field from the action layout. If you convert the field back to a supported type without changing the action layout, Salesforce automatically adds the field back to the layout. If you edit the layout and then convert the field back to a supported type, add the field back to the layout manually.

Layouts Used for Log a Call Actions

A Log a Call action takes the active task page layout except under the following conditions:

- Suppose that your organization has a custom Log a Call action for an object. The custom action takes the custom action layout defined for it.
- Now suppose that your organization has a custom Log a Call global action. That action takes the custom layout defined for it, unless you also have a custom Log a Call action for an object. (A custom action on an object overrides a custom global action.)

To display the simpler New Task form to Salesforce1 users, enable the form in Activity Settings and ensure that the layout used includes a subject field.

Layout Auditing

Salesforce tracks action layout customization in the setup audit trail history.

Rich text area fields are supported only when you add them to one-column layouts, or as fields that span both columns in two-column layouts. If you add a rich text area field to only one column in a two-column layout, it appears as a plain text area, because there's not enough space to display the full rich text editor.

Try It Out: Customize an Action Layout

We want to minimize the number of fields on the action layout, so that users can focus on the most important information. For optimal usability, eight fields is a good limit. Adding more than 20 fields can severely impact user efficiency. We'll set predefined field values for `Status`, `Open Date`, and `Hire By`, so we won't add those fields to the layout.

1. Drag the following fields into the first column of the action layout.

   - `Type`
   - `Min Pay`
   - `Functional Area`

2. Drag the following fields into the second column.

   - `Hiring Manager`
   - `Location`
   - `Max Pay`
   - `Job Level`

Layout for New Standard Position Action

Position Title ☆ Sample Position Title	**Hiring Manager** Sample User
Type Sample Type	**Location** Sample Location
Min Pay $123.45	**Max Pay** $123.45
Functional Area ⇨ Sample Functional Area	**Job Level** ⇨ Sample Job Level

3. Click **Save**.

Try It Out: Add Predefined Field Values

A few fields still need to be filled out: `Status`, `Open Date`, and `Hire By`. These fields represent important details, but we don't need our users to fill them out every time they use the action. We know that every new position record should have a `Status` of New Position, an `Open Date` of the current date, and a `Hire By` of 90 days after the Open Date. Let's take care of those with predefined field values now from the detail page for the New Standard Position global action.

1. In the Predefined Field Values related list, click **New**.

2. For the `Field Name` drop-down list, select `Status`.

3. For the specific value, select New Position.

4. Click **Save**.

Setting the Predefined Value for a New Position's Status

Field Information	
Target Object	Position
Field Name	Status
Field Type	Picklist
Specify New Field Value	
A specific value	New Position

Now every position created using this global action will automatically have a `Status` of New Position. Users who are creating a position by using the action don't have to worry about selecting that field. They can focus on the variable information. Use the same steps to create predefined field values for `Open Date` and `Hire By` using this table.

Table 39: Additional Predefined Field Values

Field Name	New Field Value
Open Date	TODAY()
Hire By	TODAY() + 90

That's it! Now let's create a few more global actions. We currently have one for creating new standard positions, but what about IT positions? And our recruiters would also appreciate being able to easily create new candidate and job application records. Let's get busy!

Try It Out: Create More Global Actions

We'll start with a global action to create new IT positions. Repeat all the steps you completed to create the New Standard Position global action, but set the record type to IT Position. When that's done, use the following table to create the other two global actions.

Global Action	Action Information	Action Layout
New Candidate	• `Action Type:` Create a Record • `Target Object:` Candidate • `Standard Label Type:` New "Record" • `Name:` *New_Candidate*	Column 1: • First Name • Email • Education Column 2: • Last Name • Years of Experience • City
New Application	• `Action Type:` Create a Record • `Target Object:` Job Application • `Label:` New Application • `Standard Label Type:` --None--	• Candidate • Position • Cover Letter

Our New Candidate action doesn't need any predefined field values, since we can't predict the values of any of the fields. The New Application action, however, does. We know that every job application created from the publisher should be marked as new. So now create a predefined field value for New Application, automatically setting the `Status` field to New.

Introducing Global Publisher Layouts

Global publisher layouts determine which actions appear in the publisher in various pages throughout Salesforce, including the Home tab, Chatter tab, and Chatter group detail pages in the full site, as well as the action bar and action menu in Salesforce1. Global publisher layouts can include only global actions.

Note: Chatter groups without customers display the global publisher layout by default, unless you override it with a customized group publisher layout. In Chatter groups that allow customers, the publisher displays standard actions only, such as Post, File, Link, and Poll.

Now that we've created all the global actions needed for our recruiters, let's add them to a global publisher layout.

Try It Out: Customize a Global Publisher Layout

Before we begin, let's make sure we can add our actions to a global publisher layout. From Setup, enter "Chatter Settings" in the `Quick Find` box, then select **Chatter Settings** and select `Enable Actions in the Publisher`.

Now let's get to that layout.

1. From Setup, enter `Publisher Layouts` in the `Quick Find` box, then select **Publisher Layouts**.

Like page layouts and compact layouts, each global publisher layout can be assigned to a user profile. Because our recruiters have different needs from the rest of the company, let's create a custom layout with actions tailored to their typical tasks. We'll assign that layout to the Recruiter profile so that our standard employees, who don't often need to do things like creating candidates or job applications, aren't bogged down by irrelevant actions.

2. Click **New**.

3. Select Global Layout as the `Existing Publisher Layout` to clone.

4. For `Publisher Layout Name`, enter `Recruiter Layout`.

5. Click **Save**.

Let's get rid of the actions that aren't relevant to recruiters.

1. Drag **New Contact**, **Log a Call**, **New Opportunity**, **New Case**, and **New Lead** back to the palette.

2. Click the **Quick Actions** category in the palette.

3. Drag **New IT Position**, **New Standard Position**, **New Application**, and **New Candidate** into the Quick Actions in the Salesforce Classic Publisher section of the layout so that they appear after **Poll**.

   Actions in this section appear in the Chatter publisher in the full Salesforce site. But we also need to make sure that our recruiters have access to them in Salesforce1.

4. Click **Quick Save**.

5. In the Salesforce1 and Lightning Experience Actions section, click **override the predefined actions**.

6. Using actions from the Salesforce1 & Lightning Actions category of the palette, make the Salesforce1 and Lightning Experience Actions section match the Quick Actions in the Salesforce Classic Publisher section.

7. Click **Save**.

Now that we have a working publisher layout for recruiters, let's make sure they can see it by assigning the new layout to the Recruiter profile.

1. Click **Publisher Layout Assignment**.

2. Click **Edit Assignment**, and change the publisher layout for the Recruiter profile to Recruiter Layout.

3. Click **Save**.

Look At What We've Done

Before we move on to create the other type of action—object-specific—let's make sure our global actions are working as expected.

To test our changes, log in to Salesforce as Mario Ruiz, and verify that Mario can create an IT position, a standard position, a candidate, and a job application from the Chatter publisher. Check it out in Salesforce1 as well.

1. Log in to Salesforce as our recruiter, Mario Ruiz.

2. In the publisher on the Home tab, click **More**. The bottom four options should be New IT Position, New Standard Position, New Application, and New Candidate.

3. Click **New IT Position**. The fields that appear should match what we configured in the action layout.

Fields for a New IT Position in the Chatter Publisher

4. Fill in the fields, and click **Create**.

   As soon as we click **Create**, a feed Item is created.

Feed Item for New QE Engineer II Position

5. Click the position name for the new IT position.

6. Verify that our predefined field values have values assigned to them: `Status` should be New Position, `Open Date` should be today, and `Hire By` should be 90 days from today.

7. Return to the Home tab, and repeat these verification steps for the New Standard Position, New Application, and New Candidate actions.

Introducing Object-Specific Actions

But wait! That's not all. We can also create *object-specific actions*.

Like global actions, object-specific actions let users create records or log details about calls or other interactions. The key difference is that you can only add these actions to record detail pages, since they are automatically associated with a specific object.

When a user creates a record by using an object-specific create action, a feed item for that record appears:

- In the feed for the record on which the new record was created
- As the first entry in the feed for the new record
- In the Chatter feed of the user who created the record
- In the user profile feed for the user who created the record
- In the Chatter feed of any users who follow the record on which the record was created
- In the Chatter feed of any users who, through custom triggers or auto-follow rules for new records, automatically follow the new record

Try It Out: Create an Object-Specific Action

Object-specific actions will be very useful for our recruiters. If we add an action to the position record to create a new job application, users won't have to specify the position that new application is associated with. The platform will just know to associate it with the position record. Let's get to it! More efficiency is just around the corner.

1. From Setup, enter *Objects* in the Quick Find box, then select **Objects**, and then click **Position**.

2. In the Buttons, Links, and Actions related list, click **New Action**.

This should look familiar. The fields we need to fill out to create an object-specific action are almost identical to the ones we filled out for a global action. There's just one new field: Object Name. Because we are creating a new action on the Position object, the platform knows that the Object Name should be Position. This means that this action can only be added to page layouts for the Position object. Now let's fill in the rest of the fields.

3. For Action Type, select Create a Record.

4. For Target Object, select Job Application.

5. For Label, enter *New Application*.

6. Leave Standard Label Type set to its default value.

7. Click **Save**.

As soon as we save, we see the action layout editor for our new action. There are only a few fields on the Job Application object, so it should be easy to determine which fields we want to add to the layout. Since any job applications created using this action will be automatically related to the position the user has open, we don't need to add the Position field to the layout. Owner will be automatically assigned to the user who creates the record. As for Status, we can trust that any job applications created should be New by default, so we can take care of that field with a predefined field value.

> 📝 Note: You might get a message, warning you that there are required fields missing from the layout. In this case, that required field is `Position`, but don't worry! The platform will automatically associate the job application with the position we create it on, since this action will only be accessed from a position record.

That leaves only two fields, so add Candidate and Cover Letter to the layout, and save the layout.

Now let's assign a predefined field value to `Status` before we forget.

8. From Setup, enter `Objects` in the `Quick Find` box, then select **Objects**, and select **Position**.

9. In the Buttons, Links, and Actions related list, click **New Application**.

10. In the Predefined Field Values related list, click **New**.

11. For `Field Name`, select Status.

12. For the specific value, select New.

13. Click **Save**.

Try It Out: Create More Object-Specific Actions

Now that we've had some practice creating object-specific actions, let's add a few more.

Object	Action Information	Action Layout
Position	• `Action Type:` Create a Record • `Target Object:` Job Posting • `Label:` New Posting • `Standard Label Type:` --None--	• Employment Website
Candidate	• `Action Type:` Create a Record • `Target Object:` Job Application • `Label:` New Application • `Standard Label Type:` --None--	• Position • Cover Letter

Object	Action Information	Action Layout
Employment Website	• `Action Type:` Create a Record • `Target Object:` Job Posting • `Label:` New Posting • `Standard Label Type:` --None--	• Position
Job Application	• `Action Type:` Create a Record • `Target Object:` Review • `Standard Label Type:` New "Record" • `Name:` New_Review	• Rating • Assessment

Just one of these actions needs a predefined value, so let's take care of that now.

1. From Setup, enter `Objects` in the `Quick Find` box, then select **Objects**, and then click **Candidate**.

2. In the Buttons, Links, and Actions related list, click **New Application**.

3. Create a predefined field value that automatically sets `Status` to New.

Try It Out: Assign Object-Specific Quick Actions to Page Layouts

Unlike global quick actions, object-specific quick actions don't have a new type of layout. However, every page layout has a special place for them. The actions sections of the page layout editor look and act similar to the editor for global publisher layouts. All we have to do is drag actions from the palette and drop them into the right spot.

1. From Setup, enter `Objects` in the `Quick Find` box, then select **Objects**, and then click **Position**.

2. In the Page Layouts related list, click **Edit** next to IT Position Layout.

Notice that the Quick Actions in the Salesforce Classic Publisher section is empty. This page layout is using the global publisher layout assigned to each user's profile. Because we created object-specific actions, we can't add them to the global publisher layout. That's okay! To have our new actions appear on position records, we just need to override the global publisher layout.

3. In the Quick Actions in the Salesforce Classic Publisher section, click **override the global publisher layout**.

When we override the global publisher layout, the platform automatically provides some actions, such as standard Chatter actions like Post and File.

4. In the palette, click **Quick Actions**.

5. Drag Mobile Smart Actions back to the palette.

   Mobile smart actions are a set of pre-configured actions, just like default actions. However, they are only available in Salesforce1. Mobile smart actions appear as a single action element in the page layout editor. However, they appear in the action bar and action menu in Salesforce1 as distinct create actions. These distinct actions allow users to create records directly from the action bar.

   For custom objects like ours, these actions are New Task, New Contact, Log a Call, New Group, New Opportunity, New Case, and New Lead. We can't change which actions are included as part of a mobile smart actions bundle, so we're going to remove it and manually add actions that are relevant to this object. For more information, see "Mobile Smart Actions" in the Salesforce Help.

6. Drag actions from the palette to the Quick Actions in the Salesforce Classic Publisher section so that they're in this order.

   - New Application
   - New Candidate
   - New Posting
   - Post
   - New Task
   - New Note
   - File
   - Link

   Note: We have some duplicates, because we created a New Application global action and a New Application object-specific action. The Force.com platform helps us out with this—using the hover text over the actions. One of the actions is called New_Application, and the other is Position__c.New_Application. Our object-specific action is the second.

229

The name indicates that it's directly associated with the position object using the Position__c prefix. That means that this action can be added only to a position page layout.

Customizing the Actions Available on a Standard Position Record

Actions in this section appear in the Chatter publisher in the full Salesforce site. But we also need to make sure that our recruiters have access to these actions in Salesforce1.

7. Click **Quick Save**.

8. In the Salesforce1 and Lightning Experience Actions section, click **override the predefined actions**.

9. Using actions from the Salesforce1 & Lightning Actions category, make the Salesforce1 and Lightning Experience Actions section match the Quick Actions in the Salesforce Classic Publisher section.

10. Click **Save**.

11. Click **IT Position Layout** at the top of the palette, and select **Position Layout**.

12. Customize both action sections for the Position Layout so that they match the IT Position Layout.

Now let's add our object-specific actions for candidates, employment websites, and job applications to those page layouts. Go to each page layout, and add the actions to both action sections in the order indicated in this table.

Table 40: Summary of Quick Actions in Page Layouts

Object	Page Layout	Quick Actions
Candidate	Candidate Layout	• New Application
		• New Task
		• New Note
		• Post
		• File
		• Link

Object	Page Layout	Quick Actions
Employment Website	Employment Website Layout	• New Posting • New Task • New Note • Post • File • Link
Job Application	Job Application Layout	• New Review • New Task • New Note • Post • File • Link

Look At What We've Done

Now that we've created all of our object-specific actions and assigned them to the associated page layouts, let's make sure they're working in the Salesforce1 mobile app.

1. Launch Salesforce1, and log in as Mario Ruiz.

2. Open a position record by tapping **Positions** in the navigation menu and tapping one of your recent positions.

3. Tap the **New Application** action in the action bar.

4. Select a candidate, enter text for the cover letter, and then tap **Submit**.

We didn't have to specify that the new job application should be related to the position we have open, but the application appears in the position's Job Applications related list anyway. This is the power of object-specific actions.

A Position's Related Job Applications

5. From the position's related information page, tap **Job Applications** to see the items in that related list.

6. Tap the related item associated with our new job application to open that record.

7. Verify that the predefined field value we set is working as designed: `Status` should be set to New, even though we didn't manually select that when we created the record.

Now let's verify the other object-specific actions. From the action bar or action menu, make sure that:

- From a position record, we can create a new candidate.

- From a position record, we can create a new job posting. The posting is automatically associated with the position.

- From a candidate record, we can create a new job application. The application is automatically associated with the candidate, and its status is New.

- From an employment website record, we can create a new job posting. The posting is automatically associated with the employment website.

- From a job application record, we can create a new review. The review is automatically associated with the job application.

Summing Up

We've added Chatter and actions to our Recruiting app, but we've barely scratched the surface. With Chatter, you give your users the power to stay on top of everything that's happening in your company, and you enable them to easily collaborate and share information. With actions, you let your users more easily create and relate records. And because it's part of the Force.com platform, you can incorporate real-time feed updates, user profiles, groups, and more into all of your custom applications.

If you dig a little further, you can learn how to programatically add posts and comments, add feeds to custom pages, and even expose actions for integration with external systems.

These advanced subjects are beyond the scope of this book, but you can find out more by completing the Chatter Basics Trailhead module at https://trailhead.salesforce.com/en/module/chatter.

CHAPTER 9 Automating Business Processes

Robust application? Check. Secure data access? Check. Fast, fun, and collaborative? Check! Our hiring team at Universal Containers has never been more productive. The last chapter demonstrated how easy it is to collaborate in real time with Chatter. Now it's time to find ways to make our app more powerful.

Up to this point, we've created little more than a glorified database—it holds the information we need and lets us search for records based on various criteria, but it doesn't help our recruiters and hiring managers do their jobs more effectively. There's no automation that lets a recruiter know when the status of a candidate has changed or when a new position has been entered into the system. Chatter will let them know about the records they're following, but we want to build automation into our app to keep the processes moving forward.

Once again, the Force.com platform helps us out with more built-in functionality. In this case, the tools that we'll use to solve our process automation problem are called Process Builder and *approval processes*. We'll take a look at the various ways that we can use the Process Builder first, and then we'll tackle an approval process at the end of the chapter.

235

Introducing Process Builder

The Process Builder is a tool that lets you automate business processes using a convenient graphical representation of your process as you build it. Automated processes in the Process Builder consist of:

- Criteria that determine when to execute action groups and
- Immediate and scheduled actions to execute when those criteria are met.

Any change that causes a record to match the criteria automatically triggers the action group.

👁 **Example:** Say Ben Stuart, a software development manager, wants to extend an offer to Ethan Tran, a bright young candidate who's interested in the Software Engineer position. At Universal Containers, it's a recruiter's job to extend offers, but in this case, Mario Ruiz, the recruiter responsible for the Software Engineer position, doesn't know whether or not Ben has made a decision unless Ben emails or calls him directly.

Instead of relying on Ben to remember to tell Mario, let's automate it! We can set up a simple process that automatically assigns a task to the recruiter when a manager decides to extend an offer or reject a job application.

Automatically Assigning a Task to a Recruiter Using Workflow

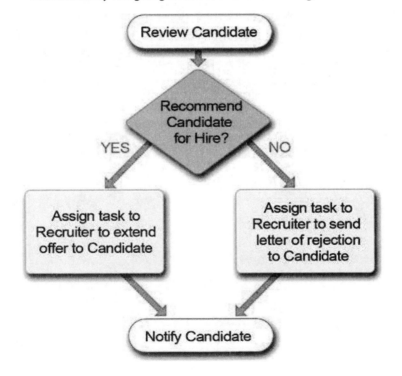

Pretty powerful, isn't it? In general, if we can come up with a condition that specifies when a particular event should happen, we can make it happen automatically with the Process Builder. Processes are one of the secret ingredients that will transform our Recruiting app from a glorified database into a fully functional tool that everyone finds useful.

Now that we've got a general idea of what processes are all about, let's take a closer look at what it takes to create a process.

Process Builder: A Closer Look

When you create a process in the Process Builder, you start by choosing an object, for example, a Position. Then you tell the Process Builder what to evaluate when someone creates or changes a Position record. For example, your process can check whether a Position has a status of **Open – Approved**. When it does, your process executes an action, like sending a company-wide email so everyone knows that a new position has opened in the company. You can define multiple criteria nodes in a single process and associate groups of actions with each criteria node.

The object you choose as the basis of your process influences the fields that are available for setting the criteria. For example, if we create a process for a Job Application object, we can set the criteria based on the values of fields like `Job Application Number` and `Status`. We can also set the criteria based on standard fields, such as `Record Owner` or `Created Date`, as well as fields based on the currently active user when the criteria is evaluated, such as their `Role` or `Time Zone`.

With the Process Builder, you can execute a wide range of actions, including:

* Create a record
* Update any related record
* Use a quick action to create a record, update a record, or log a call
* Launch a flow—flows are another automation tool ideal for complex branching logic
* Send an email
* Post to Chatter
* Submit for Approval

With the Process Builder, you can even schedule actions to trigger at specified times. If you need your process to do more than what those actions allow, you can even call Apex from a process. We won't be getting into Apex here, but just know that it's a very powerful and flexible way to add functionality to your process.

We'll look at all the ways that we can set criteria and define actions a little later. For now, just understand that the platform makes it very easy to create detailed processes that target specific situations.

Automating Our Recruiting App

Now that we've oriented ourselves to the different components involved with processes, see how we can use a process in our recruiting app.

We've already talked about one instance where an automated process gives us a big advantage: automatically assigning a task to a recruiter when the status of a job application changes to Rejected or Extend an Offer. This is a great start, but what else can we do?

If we look back at our last chapter on security and sharing, recall that we wanted to grant both recruiters and hiring managers permission to create new positions, but that ultimately we always wanted a recruiter to own those records because filling them is the recruiter's responsibility. We hinted in the security and sharing chapter that we could accomplish this with the Process Builder, and indeed we can! We simply need to use an **Update Records** action to change the record owner of a position record to a recruiter if it was originally created by a hiring manager. To prevent a single recruiter from getting overloaded with all these additional positions, we can also use another platform feature, *queues*, to divvy up the orphaned position records fairly. We'll place the record in a queue of other position records without owners, and then let individual recruiters claim the positions they want.

Let's also think about how position availability is advertised throughout Universal Containers. Like many organizations, Universal Containers prefers to fill positions with employee referrals, but employees often aren't aware of which positions are currently open. We can use an **Email Alerts** action to automatically send an email to every employee whenever a new position opens up. This way employees learn about positions as they become available and can immediately think of friends and family members who might be interested.

Sound good? While there are many more ways to use Process Builder to build a killer on-demand Recruiting app in the cloud, let's stick with these three for now since they'll give us a good example of the main types of actions that are available. To summarize what we'll be building:

1. A task that assigns a task to a recruiter when the status of a job application changes to Rejected or Extend an Offer

2. A field update that reassigns ownership of a position that's created by a hiring manager to a queue of position records without owners, so that individual recruiters can claim ownership of the positions they want

3. An alert that sends an email to every employee when a new position is created

Now let's get started!

Creating a Process That Assigns Tasks

As we create our process, we'll first want to define criteria that checks whether the `Status` field of a job application record is set to `Rejected`. Then we'll create an associated action that assigns a "Send Rejection Letter" task to the relevant recruiter. We'll then define a second criteria node that checks whether the job application `Status` field is set to "Extend and Offer." The associated action for this criteria node creates an "Extend Offer" task assigned to the relevant recruiter.

Try It Out: Create a Process and Define "Send Rejection Letter" Criteria

Let's start by creating our process and configuring what triggers the process to execute actions.

1. From Setup, enter *Process Builder* in the `Quick Find` box, then select **Process Builder**.

2. Click **New**.

3. Name the process `Recruiter Tasks`.

4. Press *TAB* to autofill the API name and then click **Save**.

Now that we've named our process, first we select the object that will be associated with our process. As we talked about earlier, every process must be associated with a single object. Because we need to trigger this process when the `Status` field of a job application record is set to `Rejected`, we'll choose the Job Application object.

5. Click **Add Object** and choose **Job Application** for the Object type. You can type in the Object field to filter the list of objects. For example, type *Job* to see objects that start with job.

6. Let's choose to start the process **when a record is created or edited** to ensure that the process evaluates our criteria any time the record changes. We'll make an additional selection when we define our criteria that also makes sure that if our criteria is already true, the process won't execute actions again if some unrelated change is made to the Job Application object. We'll explain that option when we get there.

7. Click **Save**.

Now it's time to define our criteria. Criteria are just a set of conditions that must be true before our process executes any actions.

8. Click **Add Criteria**.

9. Enter *Send Rejection Letter* for the criteria name.

10. For the criteria for executing actions, leave the selection as *Conditions are met*.

11. In the `Set Conditions` area, click in the `Field` area to select a field on the Job Application object.

12. Select **Status** and then click **Choose**.

13. Leave the operator and type as **Equals** and **Picklist**.

14. For the value, select **Rejected**.

    Now let's make sure that our process doesn't execute unwanted actions if an unrelated change is made to the record. For example, let's say a user changes the status field on a job application record. The process evaluates it and creates a `Send Rejection Letter` action for the recruiter. Good. That's what we want our process to do. Now let's say a user subsequently changes the Cover Letter field on the job application record. Because the record changed, the process evaluates it again and because the status field is still set to **Rejected**, it creates yet another `Send Rejection Letter` task for the recruiter. That's not good.

    There's an easy way to avoid this. The process can also check whether the record already met criteria before the last change was made to the record. If the criteria was already met the last time the record was saved, the process doesn't execute actions. By selecting this option, the process only executes actions if the record changes from not meeting our specific criteria to meeting criteria.

15. Click **Advanced** at the bottom of the side panel, and select **Yes** where you're asked `Do you want to execute the actions only when specified changes are made to the record?`. It's that easy!

240

Define Criteria for this Action Group

Criteria Name *

```
Send Rejection Letter
```

Criteria for Executing Actions *
- ○ Conditions are met
- ○ Formula evaluates to true
- ○ No criteria—just execute the actions!

Set Conditions

	Field *	Operator *	Type *	Value *	
1	[Job_Application... 🔍	Equals ▾	Picklist ▾	Rejected ▾	✕

➕ Add Row

Conditions *
- ○ All of the conditions are met (AND)
- ○ Any of the conditions are met (OR)
- ○ Customize the logic

▼ Advanced

Do you want to execute the actions only when specified changes are made to the record?

☑ Yes

16. Click **Save**.

At this point, we've just defined our "Send Rejection Letter" criteria. Now let's define the action that should execute when those criteria are true.

Try It Out: Add a "Send Rejection Letter" Action to Your Process

To create a task and assign it to the owner of the Job Application record, you'll add a **Create a Record** action to your process. When you add actions to a process, you have the option of creating immediate actions (**1**), which execute when the process is triggered, or you can schedule an action (**2**) to happen some time before or after an event, for example, one day before the created date, or three days after the last modified date.

Immediate and Scheduled Actions

For now, we just need to define a single action that executes as soon as our criteria are met.

1. Click **Add Action** in the Immediate Actions area (**1**).

2. Select **Create a Record**.

3. Enter `Rejection Letter Task` for the action name.

4. Select **Task** for the record type. Remember, you can type to filter this list.

   Notice that when you select the Task record type, some fields automatically display with empty values. These are required fields for a Task record. You can also add values for other Task fields that aren't required.

5. For the Priority field, set the value to **High**.

6. For the Status field, set the value to **Not Started**.

7. For the Assigned To ID field, click in the Type area and select **Reference** and then click in the Value area to choose a field to reference.

Reference a Field

8. Select **Owner ID** and then click **Choose**.

9. Let's also add a subject to our task.

    a. Click **Add Row**.

    b. Select **Subject** for the field.

    c. Leave the Type as **String** and enter `Send Rejection Letter` for the value.

10. Almost done. Let's add a due date for our task.

    a. Click **Add Row**.

    b. Select **Due Date Only** for the field.

    c. Select **Formula** for the type.

    d. Enter `[Job_Application__c].CreatedDate + 1` and click **Use this Formula**.

11. Click **Save**.

    Nice work! You've just created a process that checks whether a Job Application is rejected and, if true, creates a task for the owner to send a rejection letter. We could activate this process now, but let's add another criteria node and action so recruiters know to extend an offer when the Job Application status is set to Extend an Offer.

The remaining criteria and actions are similar to what we just did, so we'll pick up the pace for the rest of them, focusing just on the fields and options that are unique to each.

Try It Out: Create the "Extend an Offer" Criteria and Action

To wrap up our first process, we need to add another criteria node and action to our process for when the status of a job application is set to `Extend an Offer`. This is almost identical to the "Send Rejection Letter" criteria and action, so we'll just list the values that you'll need in the following two tables.

Tip: Keep in mind that a process evaluates criteria in the order represented on the canvas. Our process will first check whether the job application status field is set to Rejected. If that's true, the process executes our defined action. If not, the process evaluates the next criteria, in this case whether the status is set to Extend an Offer.

Table 41: Values for Creating the "Extend an Offer" Criteria

Field	Value
Criteria Name	Extend an Offer
Criteria for Executing Actions	Conditions are met
Set Conditions	Job Application: Status equals Extend an Offer
Conditions	All of the conditions are met (AND)
Advanced Option	Yes, execute actions only when specified changes are made to the record

Table 42: Values for Creating the "Extend an Offer" Immediate Action

Field	Type	Value
Action Type	default	Create a Record
Action Name	default	Extend an Offer Task
Record Type	default	Task
Priority	Picklist	High
Status	Picklist	Not Started
Assigned To ID	Reference	Job Application > Owner ID
Subject	String	Extend an Offer
Due Date Only	Formula	NOW() + 1

All done! Make sure the "Recruiting Tasks" process is activated, and let's go try it out. Just click **Activate** (**1**).

Look at What We've Done

Let's test our new "Send Rejection Letter" process and see what happens:

1. Click the Job Applications tab, and select a job application record.

2. Click **Edit**, and change `Status` to `Rejected`.

3. Click **Save**.

The Send Rejection Letter task automatically appears in the Open Activities related list on the Job Application detail page, as shown in the following image.

Open Activities Related List on Job Application Detail Page

Pretty neat, don't you think? Suddenly, our Recruiting app has become a lot more interactive and powerful!

Creating a Process That Updates Field Values

For our next use case, we want to create a process that ensures the owner of a new position record is always a recruiter. To do this, we're going to define a process that reassigns ownership of a position that's created by a hiring manager to a *queue* of position records without owners. When a position record is in that queue, individual recruiters can claim ownership of the positions they want. But before we jump ahead of ourselves, let's stop a moment. Just what, exactly, is a queue?

Introducing Queues

Much like a collection of items in a lost and found drawer, a queue is a collection of records that don't have an owner. Users who have access to the queue can examine every record that's in it and claim ownership of the ones they want.

Queues are traditionally used in sales and support organizations to distribute new leads and support cases to the employees who have the most availability. Because the platform natively supports queues for Leads, Cases, and any custom object, we can create a queue for the Recruiting app's Position object.

Try It Out: Create a Queue for Positions

We need to know the types of records that can be placed in the queue (in our case, Positions), and the users who are allowed to pull records out of it (in our case, Recruiters). Once we know those two things, defining the queue itself is just a matter of a few simple clicks:

1. From Setup, enter `Queues` in the `Quick Find` box, then select **Queues**.
2. Click **New**.
3. For `Label`, enter `Unclaimed Positions Queue`.
4. In the `Queue Email` text box, enter an email address for an individual or a distribution list, such as `recruiters@universalcontainers.com`.

   When you click in the `Queue Email` text box, the `Queue Name` text box is automatically populated.
5. Select `Send Email to Members`.

Notice here that if `recruiters@universalcontainers.com` was a real email distribution list that went to all recruiters, we wouldn't need to select `Send Email to Members`. We do it here only because `recruiters@universalcontainers.com` is a fake email address and can't be used for testing later.

You have two options for notifying queue members when new records are added to the queue depending on whether or not `Send Email to Members` is selected..

Send Email to Members not selected

- If you don't specify a queue email, individual queue members are always notified, regardless of the `Send Email to Members` checkbox.
- If you specify a queue email address, only that address is notified.

Send Email to Members selected

- If you don't specify a queue email, individual queue members are always notified, regardless of the `Send Email to Members` checkbox.
- If you specify a queue email address, that address *and* individual queue members are notified.

  Note that if an individual queue member also receives email sent to the specified queue email address, they'll receive duplicate notifications.

6. In the Supported Objects section, move Position into the Selected Objects list.

Defining a Queue

New Queue

Queue Edit   Save   Cancel

Queue Name and Email Address | = Required Information

Enter the name of the queue and the email address to use when sending notifications (for example, when a case has been put in the queue). The email address can be for an individual or a distribution list. When an object is assigned to a queue, only the queue members will be notified.

Queue Name: Unclaimed Positions Qu

Queue Email: recruiters@universalcor

Send Email to Members: ☑

If a queue email is not specified, individual queue members are always notified, regardless of the checkbox.

Supported Objects

Select the objects you want to assign to this queue. Individual records for those objects can then be owned by this queue.

Available Objects:
Candidate
Case
Employment Website
Job Appplication
Lead

Selected Objects:
Position

Add ▶   ◀ Remove

Queue Members

To add members to this queue, select a type of member, then choose the group, role, or user from the "Available Members" and move them to the "Selected Members." If the sharing model for all objects in the Queue is Public Read/Write/Transfer, you do not need to assign users to the queue, as all users already have access to the records for those objects.

Search: Roles and Subordinates ▾ for: ____ Find

Available Members:
Role and Subordinates: CEO
Role and Subordinates: Channel Sales Team
Role and Subordinates: Customer Support, International
Role and Subordinates: Customer Support, North America
Role and Subordinates: Dir Product Management
Role and Subordinates: Director QA
Role and Subordinates: Director, Channel Sales
Role and Subordinates: Director, Direct Sales
Role and Subordinates: Eastern Sales Team
Role and Subordinates: Installation & Repair Services
Role and Subordinates: Marketing Team
Role and Subordinates: Recruiter
Role and Subordinates: SVP, Human Resources
Role and Subordinates: SVP, Sales & Marketing

Add ▶   ◀ Remove

Selected Members:
Role and Subordinates: Recruiting Manager

Save   Cancel

As you can see, a single queue can handle multiple objects—the platform allows you to do this so that you don't have to define multiple queues for the same group of users.

7. In the Queue Members section, select `Roles, Internal and Portal and Subordinates` from the Search drop-down list.

8. Move `Role and Subordinates: Recruiting Manager` to the Selected Members list.

9. Click **Save**.

Perfect! We've just defined a new queue that can act as a temporary owner for all of the position records that are created by hiring managers. Whenever a position is placed in the queue, all recruiters are notified, and the appropriate person can claim ownership. All we need to do now is create the process that places those position records into the queue.

Try It Out: Create a Process That Updates Fields

Now that we've got our queue ready to go, we can get started creating our process.

1. Return to the Process Builder and create a new process.

2. Enter `Assign Position to Recruiter` for the process name. Press `Tab` to automatically enter the API name.

3. For the process description, enter `Reassign position records to a recruiter if they were created by another type of employee` and then save.

4. Click **Add Object**.

5. Select **Position** for the object type.

    While we know that recruiters should almost always own position records, we don't want to impede the organization if there's a special case in which a non-recruiter should own the record instead. Let's choose to evaluate this rule only when a record is created so that if an exception needs to be made, the process won't supersede any changes that were made by a recruiter.

6. In the **Start the process** section, select **only when a record is created**.

7. Save your changes.

    Finally, we need to make sure that this process executes our specified action whenever a position record is created by someone who isn't a recruiter or a recruiting manager. Let's define this criteria in our process.

8. Click **Add Criteria**.

9. Enter `Reassign Position to Queue` for the criteria name.

10. Leave the **Conditions are met** selected.

Now let's define our criteria conditions. We'll base our criteria on the role of the user that creates the position record. Whenever the role isn't a recruiter or recruiting manager, the process executes actions.

11. In the Set Conditions area:

    a. In the Field column select `Position > Created By ID > Role ID > Name`.

    b. Set the Operator column to `Does not equal`.

c. In the Type column, select `String`.

d. In the Value column enter `Recruiter`.

e. Click `Add Row`.

f. In the Field column select `Position > Created By ID > Role ID > Name`.

g. Set the Operator column to `Does not equal`.

h. In the Type column, select `String`.

i. In the Value column enter `Recruiting Manager`.

11. Click **Save**.

Nice work! Now our process checks whether a Position is created by someone who isn't a recruiter or recruiting manager.

Now let's create an Update Records action so our process changes the owner field on a Position record to the Unclaimed Positions Queue. Before we set up our action, let's first find the ID value for the Unclaimed Positions Queue so we can reference it in our Update Records action.

1. From Setup, enter `Queues` in the `Quick Find` box, then select **Queues**.

2. Click the **Unclaimed Positions Queue** in the `Queue Name` column.

3. In the address bar of your browser, copy the 15-digit ID number at the end of the page address, for example, `00GD0000001FMfB`. This is the ID for the queue.

Great. Now that we have the ID value for our queue, let's create the action in the Process Builder.

4. If you don't already have it open, return to the Process Builder and reopen your Assign Position to Recruiter process.

5. In the `IMMEDIATE ACTIONS` area on the canvas, click **Add Action**.

6. Select **Update Records**.

7. For `Action Name`, enter `Reassign Position to Queue`.

8. Click in the `Record Type` field.

9. Click **Select the Position__C record that started your process**, and then click **Choose**.

10. In the `Criteria for Updating Records` section, leave the **No criteria** option selected.

11. In the `Set new field values for the records you updated` section, select **Owner ID** for the field value.

12. For Type, leave **ID** selected.

13. For Value, paste the ID value copied from your browser. Remember, this is the queue's ID.

14. Click **Save**.

Nicely done! Before we leave this process behind, though, let's give it a second action—one that ensures that no positions will languish in the queue without being claimed by a recruiter. This time, we'll schedule the action so it executes at a later time.

Introducing Scheduled Actions

As we mentioned earlier, scheduled actions are actions that occur before or after a certain amount of time has elapsed (for example, seven days before the value of the `Hire By` field, or three days after the record was last modified).

For example, the goal of reassigning position records to the Unclaimed Positions queue is to have the appropriate recruiter take ownership. However, what if a position is placed in the queue and no recruiter claims it? Rather than leaving the position to languish unclaimed in the queue, we can define a scheduled action that alerts the recruiting manager if no recruiter claims a position record within a certain number of days. We'll also choose some advanced options to ensure that the manager is alerted only when necessary.

Neat, huh? Let's see how easy it is to schedule an action.

Try It Out: Create the "Notify Recruiting Manager" Scheduled Action

Before we create our scheduled action, let's go copy the ID value of the Recruiting Manager role so that we can assign the task to that role in our process.

1. From Setup, enter `Roles` in the `Quick Find` box, then select **Roles**.

2. Expand the `CEO` role and the `VP Human Resources` role so you can see the `Recruiting Manager` role in the role hierarchy. Click the `Recruiting Manager` role.

3. In the address bar of your browser, copy the 15-digit ID number at the end of the page address, for example, `00ED0000000xEVv`. This is the ID for the recruiting manager. We'll paste this ID value when we assign our task.

Now let's return to the Process Builder and open the Assign Position to Recruiter process.

Before we create an action that assigns a task, we must first specify a schedule. The schedule determines when the time-dependent actions should fire.

1. Click **Set Schedule**.

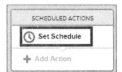

In this case, we want our recruiting manager to be notified three days after a position has been assigned to the Unclaimed Positions queue.

2. Use the text box and drop-down lists to specify *3 Days After Last Modified Date*.

3. Click **Save**.

Scheduling An Action

Set Time for Actions to Execute	❓

| ⦿ | 3 | Days ▾ | After ▾ | [Position__c].LastModifiedDate ▾ |
| ◯ | | Days ▾ | from now. | |

Our schedule is now shown on the scheduled actions node on the canvas. The **Add Action** button is now active, and we can define our action as usual.

Table 43: Values for Creating the "Assign Position to Recruiter" Scheduled Action

Field	Type	Value
Action Type	default	Create a Record
Action Name	default	Assign Unclaimed Position Record to Recruiter
Record Type	default	Task
Priority	Picklist	High
Status	Picklist	Not Started
Assigned To ID	ID	Paste the Recruiting Manager role value you just copied into the Value column.
Subject	String	Unclaimed Position
Due Date Only	Formula	[Position__c].CreatedDate + 4

Great! Now let's activate the process by clicking **Activate** (**1**).

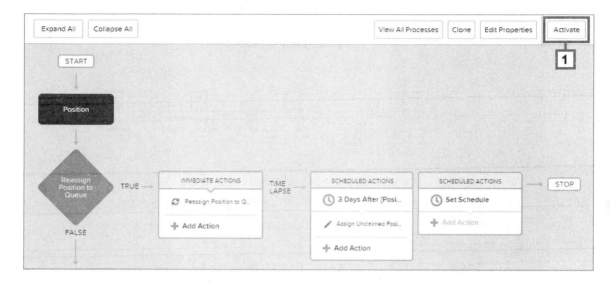

Look At What We've Done

Great! We've now got a process that moves position records created by non-recruiters to a queue of unclaimed positions, and if not claimed by a recruiter in three days, assigns a task to the recruiting manager.

To try it out, simply make sure that you're logged in as a hiring manager (such as Ben Stuart) and create a new position. As soon as you return to the detail page for the position, you'll see that the Unclaimed Positions Queue has automatically been assigned as the record owner, and that any user assigned to the Recruiter or Recruiting Manager role will have received an email notification.

To actually view the contents of the queue, click the Positions tab, and choose `Unclaimed Positions Queue` from the View drop-down list. Any recruiter or recruiting manager can click the **Accept** button on this page and take ownership of the new position.

Although our Assign Unclaimed Position Record to Recruiter task won't be activated for another three days, we can see that it's currently scheduled to fire by looking at the *Pending Scheduled Actions*, which lists all of the actions that are scheduled for the future.

To view it:

1. From Setup, enter `Flows` in the `Quick Find` box, then select **Flows**.

2. Scroll down to the Paused and Waiting Interviews list.

3. Click **Create New View** to specify which fields to display for scheduled actions in the Paused and Waiting Interviews list. We recommend displaying the following fields.

Pending Scheduled Actions

- Flow Name **(1)** corresponds to the process's `Process Name`.
- Paused Date **(2)** is the time at which the schedule started for the action group.
- Current Element **(3)** identifies the group of scheduled actions that Salesforce is waiting to execute.
- Type **(4)** indicates the type of a paused or waiting interview. Processes that are waiting to execute scheduled actions are of type Workflow.

Current Element displays `myWait_myRule_N`, where `N` is the number of the associated criteria and action group. For example, if Current Element displays `myWait_myRule_2`, Salesforce is waiting to execute the group of scheduled actions that are associated with the second criteria in the process.

As soon as a recruiter takes ownership of the new position record, this task is deleted from the workflow queue. Pretty slick, isn't it?

Now let's create another process that sends an email alert.

Adding an Action That Sends Email Alerts

For our final process, let's create an email alert and have the process reference that email alert to send a notification whenever a new position is created. We want all the employees at Universal Containers to know when there are new positions available so they have the best opportunity to bring in referrals.

For this action, there's a step that we'll need to handle first: we need to design a template for what the email alert should look like.

Introducing Email Templates

Just as the platform includes built-in tools for setting security permissions, tracking events and tasks, and building business logic with automated processes, it also provides a built-in tool for writing emails to users and contacts in your organization. *Email templates* allow you to create form emails that communicate a standard message, such as a welcome letter to new employees or an acknowledgement that a customer service request has been received.

To personalize the content of an email template, we can use *merge fields* to incorporate values from records that are stored in the system. For example, if we wanted to address an email recipient by their first name, we could write an email template.

```
Dear {!Contact.FirstName},

...
```

In this example, `{!Contact.FirstName}` is a merge field that brings in the first name of the contact to whom the email is addressed, so an email to John Smiley would read:

```
Dear John,

...
```

For our email alert, we can build an email template to notify users of new positions that have been added to the system. We can use merge fields to include information from the position record, such as its title and the required skills. Let's go do that now, and then we can add the email alert action to our process.

Try It Out: Build an Email Template

To build a new email template, we have to go to the Setup area.

1. From Setup, enter *Email Templates* in the `Quick Find` box, then select **Email Templates**.

Here you should see a list of all the email templates that have already been defined for your organization, including several sample templates from Salesforce.

2. Click **New Template**.

   We can choose to create a text, HTML, or custom email template. HTML and custom email templates are the same except that HTML templates allow you to specify a letterhead to give your email the same look and feel as other emails from the same source.

   To keep things simple, we'll stick with a plain-text email for now.

3. Select `Text`, and click **Next**.

255

Defining an Email Template

Edit Text Email Template   Help for this Page

Recruiting App: New Position Alert

Use merge fields to personalize your email content. You can add substitute text to any merge field. Substitute text displays only if the merge record does not contain data for that field. Enter substitute text after a comma in the merge field, for example, {!Contact.FirstName,Sir or Madam}. When you save the template, the merge field will appear in the email body of the template with the following syntax: {!NullValue(Contact.FirstName,"Sir or Madam")}. Click on the link below to see a sample email template.

View Sample Template

> Use this area to copy the codes for the merge fields.

Note that the Description field is for internal use only. It will be listed as the title of any email activities you log when sending mass email.

Available Merge Fields

Select Field Type	Select Field	Copy Merge Field Value
Position Fields	Position Title	{!Position__c.Name}

Copy and paste the merge field value into your template below.

Email Template Edit   Save   Save & New   Cancel

Email Template Information | = Required Information

Folder	Unfiled Public Email Templates
Available For Use	☑
Email Template Name	Recruiting App: New Po
Template Unique Name	Recruiting_App_New_P ⓘ
Encoding	General US & Western Europe (ISO-8859-1, ISO-LATIN-1)
Description	Send update email to all Universal Containers employees.
Subject	New Position Alert: {!Position__c.Name}
Email Body	{!Position__c.Responsibilities__c} Skills Required {!Position__c.Skills_required__c} Educational Requirements {!Position__c.Educational_Requirements__c} If you know of anyone great who might be able to fill this role, please contact the hiring manager, {!Position__c.Hiring_Manager__c}

> Paste your merge field codes into the Subject and Email Body areas of your email template.

Save   Save & New   Cancel

The New Template page lets us define the email template itself. The area near the top is where we'll generate the merge field codes for the fields in the email template below it, so let's skip past it for now and start with the Folder drop-down list.

4. In the Folder drop-down list, choose `Unfiled Public Email Templates`.

The Unfiled Public Email Templates folder is a standard, public folder available in every organization. By keeping the email template in a public folder, it'll be available to other users who have permission to view and edit email templates.

5. Select `Available For Use`.

This option will make our email template available when we create our email alert action.

6. For `Email Template Name`, enter *Recruiting App: New Position Alert.*

> Tip: To help keep your email templates organized, it's a good idea to preface any template name with the name of the app that uses it. Or, even better, you can create a public email template folder with the name of the app, such as Recruiting App Templates, and file all the relevant email templates in it.

7. For `Encoding`, accept the default of General US & Western Europe (ISO-8859-1, ISO-Latin-1).

8. For `Description`, enter *Send update email to all Universal Containers employees.*

Now we get to the heart of our email template—the email's subject and body text.

9. For `Subject`, enter *New Open Position Alert:*.

We want to put the title of the new position in the subject of our email, so we'll need to use our first merge field here, just after the colon in our subject. To get the proper code, we'll have to go back to the merge field area near the top of the page.

10. In the Select Field Type drop-down list, choose *Position Fields.*

Although there are many objects to choose from in the Select Field Type drop-down list, because we're creating an email template for a workflow rule, we're limited to the fields for the object that will be associated with that workflow—in our case, Position. That's because the workflow rule that uses this email template won't know about any records other than the position record that triggered the workflow rule. If we put in fields from another object, they'd be left blank in our email.

Now let's grab the field we want.

11. In the Select Field drop-down list, choose *Position Title.*

In the `Copy Merge Field Value` text box, a merge field code appears for Position Title. We can copy and paste it to the end of our subject line so the subject now looks like: `New Open Position Alert: {!Position__c.Name}`. When an email is generated from this template, `{!Position__c.Name}` will be replaced with the relevant position title.

Easy, right? Now let's finish the remainder of our email.

12. In the email body, enter the following text.

```
There's a new position open at Universal Containers!

Title: {!Position__c.Name}
Functional Area: {!Position__c.Functional_Area__c}
```

```
Location: {!Position__c.Location__c}

Job Description
{!Position__c.Job_Description__c}

Responsibilities
{!Position__c.Responsibilities__c}

Skills Required
{!Position__c.Skills_Required__c}

Educational Requirements
{!Position__c.Educational_Requirements__c}

If you know of anyone great who might be able to fill this role,
 please contact the hiring manager,
{!Position__c.Hiring_Manager__c}.

Thanks!
```

13. Click **Save**.

That's it for our email template. Now that it's done, we just need to create the email alert that uses our new email template.

1. From Setup, enter *Email Alerts* in the *Quick Find* box, then select **Email Alerts**.

2. Click **New Email Alert**.

3. For *Description*, enter *Email New Position Alert*. Press TAB to automatically fill in the unique name.

4. For *Object*, select **Position**. This associates the email alert with the position object.

5. Next to the *Email Template* field, click the lookup icon (🔍), and select **Recruiting App: New Position Alert**.

6. In the Recipient Type Search field, choose *Role and Subordinates*.

7. In the Available Recipients list, select *Role and Subordinates: CEO* and click **Add**.

8. Skip the remaining fields and click **Save**.

   Nice job! Now we're ready to create a new process with an email alert action.

Try It Out: Create a Process that Sends an Email

Now that we've built our email template and email alert, we're ready to create a process with an `Email Alerts` action. We could add the email alerts action to the existing process we've already created, but we need the process to send the email alert whenever a position is open and approved. Therefore, in our new process we want to evaluate a position record any time it's created or edited instead of only when the record is created. That way, any subsequent changes to the record, like changing the status to approved, trigger the process. We'll create our new process using the same basic steps we've been using. Let's get started.

1. Go to the Process Builder and create a new process.

2. Enter `New Position Notification` for the process name. Press `TAB` to automatically enter the API name.

3. For the process description, enter `Notifies all employees that a new position is available` and then save the process.

4. Use the Position object to start your process and start the process **when a record is created or edited**.

   Let's define our criteria so that it sends an email alert whenever a position record is open and approved.

   Table 44: Values for Creating the "New Position Notification" Criteria

Field	Value
Criteria Name	Check for Open and Approved Status
Criteria for Executing Actions	Conditions are met
Set Conditions	Position: Status equals Open - Approved
Conditions	All of the conditions are met (AND)
Advanced Option	Yes, execute actions only when specified changes are made to the record

   Now we can add our `Email Alerts` action.

5. In the IMMEDIATE ACTIONS area, click **Add Action**.

6. Select **Email Alerts**.

7. For `Action Name`, enter `Email New Position Alert`.

259

8. For `Email Alert`, enter *Email New Position Alert* and select the `Email New Postion Alert`.

9. Click **Save**.

And that's all there is to it! To test out this process, all you need to do is activate it and then create a new position record with a status of Open - Approved. Within a few seconds, all users within your organization will receive an email letting them know that a position has just been created. Go ahead—try it!

Introducing Approvals

Now that we've automated parts of our business using processes, let's take a look at another business logic tool that the platform provides: *approval processes.*

Approval processes let you specify a sequence of steps that are required to approve a record. Each step allows one or more designated approvers to accept or reject a record. The steps can apply to all records for the object associated with the process, or just to records that meet certain requirements. Like processes you create in Process Builder, approval processes also let you specify actions—like sending an email alert, updating a field value, or assigning a task—that should occur whenever a record is approved, rejected, first submitted for approval, or recalled.

Approval Processes Consist of Steps and Actions

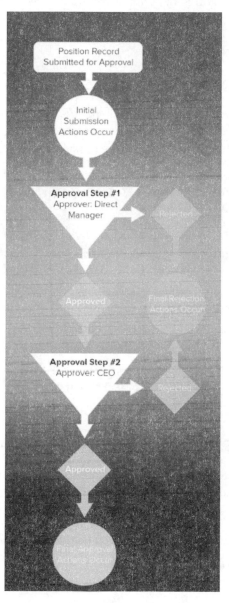

Your org has a three-tier process for approving expenses. This approval process automatically assigns each request to right person in your org, based on the amount requested.

For our recruiting app, we're going to define a similar approval process to submit new positions for approval. We want to make sure that a manager approves any position that his or her employee creates, and that any position with a minimum salary of more than $150,000 is approved by the CEO. Let's get started.

Planning for Approval Processes

In most cases you'll find that you have to do a little advance planning before implementing an approval process on your own. The checklist available from "Set Up an Approval Process" in the Salesforce Help outlines the things that you should think about and the components you should build before diving in.

For this approval process, the only preliminary step we need to do is define an email template that can be used to notify the designated approver that he or she has a pending approval request.

Beyond the Basics

If Chatter is enabled for your organization, your users can receive approval requests as posts in their Chatter feed. You can also customize the way approval requests appear in the feed by creating post templates and associating them with your approval processes. For more information about how this works, see "Where Do Approval Request Posts Appear?" in the Salesforce Help.

Since we turned on notifications for Salesforce1, your users can receive in-app and push notifications when someone submits a record for approval. Individual users can opt in or out of approval request notifications in both email and Salesforce1 via the `Receive Approval Request Emails` user field. For more information, see "Approval User Preferences" in the Salesforce Help.

Try It Out: Create an Email Template for Approvals

Since we've already talked about email templates in Introducing Email Templates on page 255, we'll simply include the values that we want to use for the template in the following table. You can build it from Setup by entering `Email Templates` in the `Quick Find` box and then selecting **Email Templates**.

Table 45: The "Recruiting App: New Position Requires Approval" Email Template

Parameter	Value
Template Type	Text
Available For Use	Selected
Email Template Name	*Recruiting App: New Position Requires Approval*
Encoding	General US & Western Europe (ISO-8859-1, ISO-LATIN-1)

Parameter	Value
Description	*Send notification email to designated approver when new position record requires approval.*
Subject	*New Position Requires Approval*
Email Body	*A new position record has been submitted for your approval. Please visit the link below and either approve or reject it.* *{!Position__c.Link}* *Thanks!*

Try It Out: Create an Approval Process

Now that we've finished our preparation, we're ready to define the approval process itself. The approval process definition acts as a framework for the approval steps and actions that we'll define later.

1. From Setup, enter `Approval Processes` in the `Quick Find` box, then select **Approval Processes**.

2. From the Manage Approval Processes For drop-down list, choose `Position`.

There are two different wizards that we can use to create a new approval process: a Jump Start Wizard and the Standard Setup Wizard. The Jump Start Wizard sets several default values for us and only requires input for the most crucial fields: the approval assignment email template, filter criteria to enter the approval process, and the designated approvers. The Standard Setup Wizard, on the other hand, allows us to configure every possible option for our approval process. We'll stick with the latter for now so we can take a look at all of the options that are available.

3. From the **Create New Approval Process** drop-down button, choose **Use Standard Setup Wizard**.

4. In the `Process Name` field, enter `Approve New Position`.

5. In the `Description` field, enter `Ensure that a manager approves any position that his or her employee creates, and that any position with a minimum salary of more than $150,000 is approved by the CEO.`

6. Click **Next**.

After entering the name and description, our next step is to specify the conditions that determine which positions need approval. As with processes, we can do this by either defining a set of criteria or creating a formula. Let's define the criteria so that all positions created by a user other than the CEO must be approved by at least a direct manager.

7. In the first row of filter criteria, select `Current User: Role not equal to CEO`.

8. Click **Next**.

9. From the `Next Automated Approver Determined By` drop-down list, select `Manager`.

The `Manager` field is a standard field on the User object that designates the user's manager. The field establishes a hierarchical relationship between users, which prevents you from selecting a user that directly or indirectly reports to his or herself. This manager will be the designated approver for the first step of our approval process.

Alternatively, you could have selected the `Create New Hierarchical Relationship Field` option in the drop-down list to define a new custom *hierarchical relationship* lookup field on the fly. The hierarchical relationship field type is specifically designed for the User object, and mimics the behavior of the standard `Manager` field by associating one user with another without indirectly associating that user to him or herself. For this approval process, though, the standard `Manager` field is perfect, so let's move on.

Specifying the Approver Field

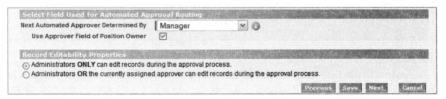

10. Select the `Use Approver Field of Position Owner` checkbox.

The `Use Approver Field of Position Owner` checkbox becomes editable when you select Manager in the `Next Automated Approver Determined By` drop-down list. When you select this checkbox, the approval request is routed to the user specified in the `Manager` field on the record owner's user record. If you don't select this checkbox, the approval request is routed to the manager of the user submitting the record. In our case, we want to obtain approval from the position owner's manager, so select this checkbox.

11. In the Record Editability Properties area, choose `Administrators ONLY can edit records during the approval process`.

Record editability allows you to specify whether a record that's been submitted for approval can be edited by the approver before being approved. Since we don't want managers to change the positions that a hiring manager or recruiter creates without alerting the owner, we'll only let administrators perform edits while a record is in our approval process.

12. Click **Next**.

13. In the `Approval Assignment Email Template` lookup field, select **Recruiting App: New Position Requires Approval**.

14. Click **Next**.

Our next step in defining the approval process is specifying which fields should be displayed on the Approval page layout, which the approver sees when he or she approves or rejects a record. Each approval process has its own page layout, and, unlike other page layouts, the Approval page layout can only be configured from within its approval process.

15. Move the following fields from Available Fields to Selected Fields.

- Position Title
- Owner
- Hiring Manager
- Type
- Location
- Hire By
- Job Description
- Min Pay
- Max Pay

Defining the Record Approval Page Layout

On this page we can also specify whether approval history information should be displayed on the Approval page layout. This information shows whether this record was submitted for approval in the past, who the designated approvers were, and whether it was approved or rejected.

16. Select `Display approval history information in addition to the fields selected above`.

Finally, before leaving this page, we can specify security settings to determine whether approvers can access an external version of the approval page from any browser, including those on mobile devices, without logging in to Salesforce. Unless it's a mandatory requirement for your approvers, it's better not to choose this option because you won't be able to add approval steps that let users manually select the next approver. We'll leave the default choice selected for now.

17. Click **Next**.

The last page of the New Approval Process wizard allows us to choose who should be allowed to submit position records for approval. Again, we'll just leave the default Position Owner selected, because there's no reason for another user to have this power.

The last two options on this page allow us to place the Approval History related list on all Position page layouts and give users the ability to recall pending approval requests after they've submitted them. The Approval History related list is the same history related list that we included on the Approval page layout, so we'll also include it on the Position detail page. From this related list users can also click the **Recall Approval Request** button to withdraw their pending approval requests. If we didn't enable this last option, only administrators would have access to the **Recall Approval Request** button.

18. Select `Add Approval History Related List to All Position Page Layouts`.

19. Select `Allow submitters to recall approval requests`.

20. Click **Save**.

Phew! We've finished defining the framework for our approval process, but we won't be able to activate it until we've given it some steps and some actions to fire when records are actually approved or rejected. Let's move on to those now.

21. Select `Yes, I'd like to create an approval step now`.

22. Click **Go!**

Try It Out: Create Approval Steps

As we said earlier, every approval process consists of a set of steps that are required to approve a record, and each step allows one or more designated approvers to accept or reject the submitted record. In other words, every round of "signatures" that you need to get a record approved must have a corresponding step in the approval process. An approval step consists of:

- One or more designated approvers
- Optional filter criteria, so that only records that meet certain conditions will require approval at that step
- Optional step approval actions that execute regardless of the outcome of the whole approval process
- Optional step rejection actions that execute regardless of the outcome of the whole approval process
- Optional step recall actions that execute if the record is recalled

For our New Position approval process, we'll need to define two steps—one that requires approval from the record submitter's manager for all new position records, and one that requires additional approval from the CEO for position records with minimum salaries in excess of $150,000. Let's define the first step for all new position records now.

Because we selected `Yes, I'd like to create an approval step` now at the end of the Standard Approval Process wizard in the last section, we're already at the beginning of the New Approval Step wizard. If we weren't, we could return to the same wizard with the following steps:

1. From Setup, enter `Approval Processes` in the `Quick Find` box, then select **Approval Processes**.

2. In the Inactive Approval Processes related list, click **Approve New Position**.

3. In the Approval Steps related list, click **New Approval Step**.

In this first step, we want the approval request to go to the Position owner's manager:

4. In the `Name` field, enter `Manager Approval`.

5. In the `Description` field, enter `Every new position record must be approved by the Position owner's manager`.

6. In the `Step Number` field, enter `1`.

The `Step Number` field specifies the order in which multiple steps should be processed. By assigning this as Step 1, it will be the first to execute when the approval process is triggered.

7. Click **Next**.

The Specify Step Criteria area allows us to define the criteria or create a formula that filters the records that require approval during this step. Because we've already filtered out position records that are owned by the CEO from the whole approval process, this step does not need any additional filtering.

8. Click **Next**.

Finally, we have to select the assigned approver for this step, and specify whether his or her delegate is allowed to approve the request as well. Because this is the Manager Approval step, it clearly makes sense to accept the default option of `Automatically assign using the custom field selected earlier. (Manager)`. However, because position records aren't particularly sensitive, it's okay for managers to assign delegated approvers. So managers who go on vacation, or who receive large quantities of approval requests, can share their work with another employee.

9. Select `The approver's delegate may also approve this request`.

10. Click **Save**.

Having completed our first approval step, we're faced with another choice: to create optional approval or rejection actions for this step, or to return to the approval process detail page. While we ultimately need to specify *final* approval and rejection actions that occur when the approval process ends one way or the other, there's nothing in particular that needs to happen after this first step that we can't specify elsewhere. Let's return to the detail page for our approval process and define our second approval step for positions with minimum salaries of more than $150,000.

11. Select `No, I'll do this later. Take me to the approval process detail page to review what I've just created.`

12. Click **Go!**.

13. In the Approval Steps related list, click **New Approval Step**.

Once again we're back in the New Approval Step wizard, but this time it includes a summary of the previous step that we created. This helps us to remember where we are in our approval process.

Defining a Second Approval Step

14. In the `Name` field, enter `CEO Approval`.

15. In the `Description` field, enter `Every new position record with a minimum salary over $150,000 must be approved by the CEO.`

16. In the `Step Number` field, enter `2`.

17. Click **Next**.

For this approval step, we only want to send positions with a minimum salary over $150,000 to the CEO. Additionally, we want to exclude any records that the CEO has already approved (for example, because one of the CEO's direct reports created the record).

18. Select the `Enter this step if the following` radio button, then choose `criteria are met` from the drop-down list.

19. In the first row of filters, enter `Position: Min Pay greater or equal 150000`.

 Tip: As a shortcut, you can specify 150,000 as 150k.

20. In the second row of filters, enter `Current User: Manager not equal to Cynthia Capobianco` (the acting CEO in Universal Containers Role Hierarchy on page 179).

21. Click **Next**.

Finally, we need to select the approver (the CEO), and specify what should happen if he or she rejects this request.

22. Select the `Automatically assign to approver(s)` radio button.

23. In the drop-down list below the radio button, select `User`, click the lookup icon (🔍), and choose the name of the CEO in your organization (Cynthia Capobianco).

We're keeping this approval process fairly simple, but if we wanted to, we could use the **Add Row** and **Remove Row** links to send the approval request to multiple approvers in this step. We could also select `Related Users` in the first drop-down list in the row to add an approver who is listed in fields on the submitted record. For example, since this is an approval process for Position records, we could add the position's hiring manager to the list of approvers.

24. Below the **Add Row** and **Remove Row** links, select `Approve or reject based on the FIRST response`.

If this step was requesting approval from multiple users, the radio buttons below the **Add Row** and **Remove Row** links would determine whether the approval request needed unanimous approval, or if the record would be approved or rejected based on the first user to respond to the request.

25. Select `The approver's delegate may also approve this request`.

The next section allows us to specify what to do with the record if it's rejected at this step. Because the position record is locked from editing during the approval process, it makes the most sense to perform the final rejection.

26. Select `Perform all rejection actions for this step AND all final rejection actions. (Final Rejection)`.

27. Click **Save**.

Once again, we're faced with a choice to define approval or rejection actions for this particular step. Let's circumvent those, and return to the approval process detail page to define our initial submission, final approval, and final rejection actions for the whole process.

28. Select `No, I'll do this later. Take me to the approval process detail page to review what I've just created.`

29. Click **Go!**

Try It Out: Create Approval Actions

Now that we've finished defining our approval process steps, we're nearly done. All that remains is to specify the *approval actions* that should occur whenever a record is initially submitted, or when it's finally approved or rejected.

Just like the actions in a process, approval actions allow you to create and assign tasks, update fields, and send email updates. They can be associated with the approval process as a whole or with individual approval steps.

271

The Approval Process Detail Page

Approval Processes
Position: Approve New Position
« Back to Approval Process List

Process Definition Detail   Edit ▾   Clone   Deactivate   View Diagram

Process Name	Approve New Position	**Active**	✓
Unique Name	Approve_New_Position	**Next Automated Approver Determined By**	Manager of Record Owner
Description	Ensure that a manager approves any position that his or her employee creates, and that any position with a minimum salary of more that $150,000 is approved by the CEO.		
Entry Criteria	Current User: Role NOT EQUAL TO CEO		
Record Editability	Administrator ONLY	**Allow Submitters to Recall Approval Requests**	✓
Approval Assignment Email Template	Recruiting App: New Position Requires Approval		
Initial Submitt...			
Create...		Modified By	Jane Smith, 8/19/2010 2:36 PM

> Approval actions can also be associated with individual approval steps.

Initial Submission Actions ⓘ   Add Existing   Add New ▾

Action	Type	Description
	Record Lock	Lock the record from being edited
Edit | Remove	Field Update	Set Status to Pending Approval

Approval Steps ⓘ

Action	Step Number	Name	Description	Criteria	Assigned Approver	Reject Behavior
Show Actions | Edit	1	Manager Approval	Every new position record must be approved by the Positions owner's manager.			Final Rejection
Show Actions | Edit	2	CEO Approval	Every new position record with a minimum salary over $150,000 must be approved by the CEO.	(Current User: Manager NOT EQUAL TO Jane Smith)		Final Rejection

> You can define approval actions that occur when a record is initially submitted, finally approved, or finally rejected.

Final Approval Actions ⓘ   Add Existing   Add New ▾

Action	Type	Description
Edit	Record Lock	Lock the record from being edited
Edit | Remove	Field Update	Set Status to Open Approval

Final Rejection Actions ⓘ   Add Existing   Add New ▾

Action	Type	Description
Edit	Record Lock	Unlock the record for editing
Edit | Remove	Field Update	Set Close Date to Today
Edit | Remove	Field Update	Set Status to Closed - Not Approved

Recall Actions ⓘ   Add Existing   Add New ▾

Action	Type	Description
	Record Lock	Unlock the record for editing

Because defining an approval action is similar to the way we created actions in our processes, we'll quickly step through updating the `Status` field to Pending Approval when a position is initially submitted and then leave our other approval actions as exercises.

1. If you're not on the approval process detail page already, from Setup, enter `Approval Processes` in the `Quick Find` box, then select **Approval Processes**, and then click **Approve New Position**.

2. In the Initial Submission Actions related list, click **Add New**, and select **Field Update**.

3. In the `Name` field, enter `Set Status to Pending Approval`.

4. In the `Description` field, enter `While a position is in an approval process, its status should be set to Pending Approval`.

5. In the `Field to Update` drop-down list, select Status.

6. In the Picklist Options area, select `A specific value` and choose Pending Approval from the list.

7. Click **Save**.

Now, to finish up the rest of the approval process, define the remaining approval actions on your own according to the values in the following table.

Table 46: Additional Approval Actions

Category	Type	Values
Final Approval Actions	Field Update	Name: Set Status to Open Approved
		Field to Update: Status
		A specific value: Open - Approved
Final Rejection Actions	Field Update	Name: Set Status to Closed - Not Approved
		Field to Update: Status
		A specific value: Closed - Not Approved
Final Rejection Actions	Field Update	Name: Set Close Date to Today
		Field to Update: Close Date
		Use a formula to set the new value: `TODAY()`

Try It Out: Activate Our Approval Process

We're all done with defining our Approve New Position approval process, but in order to test it one final step remains: we've got to activate it. Before we do so, however, be careful! Once an approval process has been activated, its approval steps can no longer be edited, even if you deactivate it. The only way to make changes is to clone the existing approval process and make edits in the cloned one.

Once you're ready to test the approval process:

1. From Setup, enter `Approval Processes` in the `Quick Find` box, then select **Approval Processes** to return to the approval process list page.

2. Click **Activate** next to the Approve New Position approval process.

The Approve New Position approval process automatically moves to the Active list, and a new field is displayed: `Process Order`. This field is important if we're trying to use more than one approval process at a time because it tells us the order in which each approval process will be evaluated.

Look At What We've Done

As we've seen, approval processes are inherently complex and take a bit of work to set up. You have to walk through multiple screens and set several parameters, making it difficult to visualize and understand the approval process holistically.

Fortunately, the Force.com platform has a Process Visualizer that renders each approval process as a flowchart. The flowchart contains all of the critical details for each approval process, including the steps necessary for a record to be approved, the designated approvers for each step, the criteria used to trigger the approval process, and the actions that take place when a record is approved, rejected, recalled, or first submitted for approval.

To access the Process Visualizer, click the **View Diagram** button at the top of any approval process detail page.

The Process Visualizer

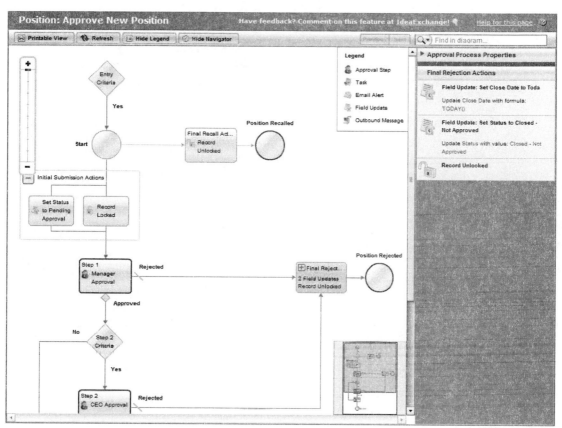

Now let's test our approval process:

1. From Setup, enter `Users` in the `Quick Find` box, then select **Users** and edit the user record for your Recruiting Manager to fill in the `Manager` field so the approval chain is properly set up. Set Phil Katz's manager to Amy Lojack (the Product Manager).

2. Log in to your app as Phil Katz, and create a new position.

Notice that after clicking **Save**, the detail page displays a **Submit for Approval** button in the new Approval History related list.

The Submit for Approval Button

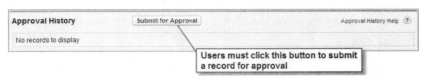

3. Click **Submit for Approval** and then click **OK**.

Clicking the **Submit for Approval** button causes several things to happen. First, the record is locked from editing, as shown by the lock icon at the top of the page. Additionally, two new entries appear in the Approval History related list showing who submitted the record and the current approval assignment. Finally, the manager of the position owner receives an email reporting that there's a new position to approve.

A Submitted Position Record

Position
Test Position
« Back to List: Users

Customize Page | Edit Layout | Printable View | Help for this Page

Job Applications [0] | Open Activities [0] | Activity History [0] | Notes & Attachments [0] | Employment Websites [0] | Approval History [2]

Position Detail   🔒 Unlock Record | Edit | Delete | Clone

Position Title	Test Position	Owner	George Abitbol [Change]
Status	Pending Approval	Location	San Francisco, CA
Type	Part Time	Open Date	6/4/2010
Functional Area	Human Resources	Hire By	9/2/2010
Job Level	HR-200		
Travel Required	☐		

This icon shows that users cannot edit the record.

| Created By | George Abitbol, 6/4/2010 4:11 PM | Last Modified By | George Abitbol, 6/4/2010 4:12 PM |
| Hiring Manager | | | |

▼ **Compensation**

| Min Pay | $151,000.00 | Max Pay | $160,000.00 |

▼ **Description**

Job Description
Responsibilities
Skills Required
Educational Requirements

▼ **Required Languages**

| Java | ☐ | C# | ☐ |
| JavaScript | ☐ | Apex | ☐ |

🔒 Unlock Record | Edit | Delete | Clone

Job Applications   New Job Application   Job Applications Help (?)
No records to display

Open Activities   New Task | New Event   Open Activities Help (?)
No records to display

Activity History   Log A Call | Mail Merge | Send An Email   Activity History Help (?)
No records to display

Notes & Attachments   New Note | Attach File   ...s Help (?)
No records to display

Two new entries appear in the Approval History related list

Employment Websites   New Job Posting   Employment Websites Help (?)
No records to display

Approval History   Recall Approval Request   Approval History Help (?)

Action	Date	Status	Assigned To	Actual Approver	Comments	Overall Status
Step: Manager Approval (Pending for first approval)						⏱ Pending
Reassign	Approve / Reject	6/4/2010 4:12 PM	Pending	Cynthia Capoblanca	Cynthia Capoblanca		
Approval Request Submitted						
	6/4/2010 4:12 PM	Submitted	George Abitbol	George Abitbol		

When the manager next logs in and visits the record, an **Approve/Reject** button is visible on the Approval History related list. She can click this button to see the approval request and approve or reject the record, with comments.

4. Log in as Amy Lojack, the direct manager who is responsible for approving the request.

5. Click **Approve/Reject** in the Approval History related list on the record, enter any optional comments, and then click **Approve**.

💡 Tip: To make accepting and rejecting approval requests more convenient, consider adding the Items to Approve related list to the default Home tab layout.

1. From Setup, enter `Home Page Layouts` in the `Quick Find` box, then select **Home Page Layouts**.

2. Click **Edit** next to the Dashboard Home Page Default or DE Default.

3. Select `Items to Approve` and click **Next**.

4. Arrange the `Items to Approve` component on the page layout by moving it up and down the Wide (Right) Column list as desired.

5. Click **Save**.

The Approval Request Page

If the approver accepts the record, it progresses to the next step of the approval process (if its `Min Pay` field is greater than $150,000 and the CEO still hasn't approved it), or else the position's `Status` field is set to Open - Approved. The record details remain locked to protect them from being changed, but recruiters can still associate the position with job applications, tasks, or other activities. If the record is rejected, its status is set to Closed - Not Approved, the `Close Date` field is set to today's date, and the record is unlocked in case it just needs a simple edit before it reenters the approval process. With just a few minutes of work, we've built an effective business process that will make all of Universal Containers' users more effective.

Summing Up

Check out our Recruiting app now! By leveraging the platform's built-in process automation and approval process tools, we've transformed our app from a glorified database into a fully functional application that provides real value to its users.

Next we'll tackle something that provides real value to our executive users: reports and dashboards that give our users a complete analytical picture of how the recruiting program at Universal Containers is going.

CHAPTER 10 Analyzing Data with Reports and Dashboards

We've come a long way with our Recruiting app—not only do we have custom objects to store our data, we also defined security and sharing rules to protect that data, while making it easier for the hiring team to collaborate. And we added automation by implementing several business processes with workflow and approvals. We've built a functional application in the cloud, and we haven't even written a single line of code!

Now it's time to turn our attention to the needs of the Universal Containers managers and executive staff. Because they need to keep track of many different aspects of the business, we need a way to give them a bird's-eye view of the company's recruiting activity without forcing them to delve into piles and piles of data. To do this, we'll create a set of custom reports for our Recruiting app and then build a dashboard that allows users to view summaries of key Recruiting app statistics every time they log in.

Introducing Reports

We can help users monitor and analyze the data that's being generated in their organization by building *reports*. Reports are summaries of the data that's stored in an app. They consist primarily of a table of data, but can also include data filters, groupings, and a customized graph.

While a comprehensive set of reports is included with every organization to provide information about standard objects, such as contacts and accounts, we can also build custom reports that highlight interesting metrics about the data stored in our custom objects.

For example, an executive at Universal Containers might have the following questions about recruiting.

- On average, how many days does it take for each recruiter to fill a position?
- Which functional areas have the most open positions?
- Which positions have been open for more than 90 days?
- Which positions are getting the most candidates?
- Which employees conduct the most interviews?
- What does the job application pipeline look like for each open position?
- Who have we hired in the last 90 days?

We can answer all of these questions and more by creating custom reports in the Reports tab of the app. Although this tab isn't visible by default in our Recruiting app, any user can click the arrow tab on the right side of the tab bar to display all available tabs, and then navigate to the reports area by clicking **Reports**.

A Sample Report

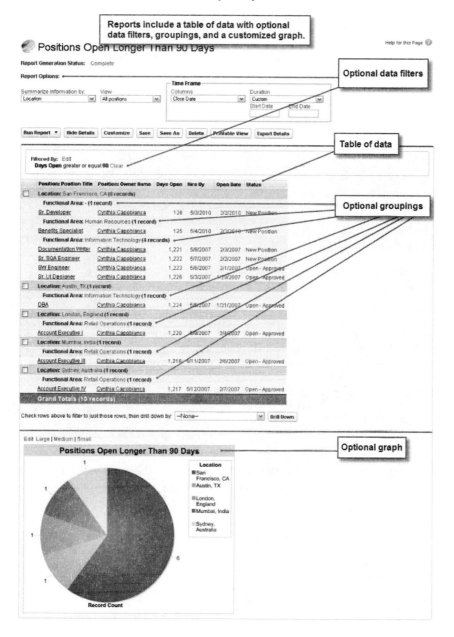

Reports include a table of data with optional data filters, groupings, and a customized graph.

Positions Open Longer Than 90 Days

Optional data filters

Table of data

Optional groupings

Optional graph

Report Formats

The platform supports four different report formats, each with varying degrees of functionality and complexity.

- *Tabular reports* are the simplest and fastest way to look at your data. Similar to a spreadsheet, they consist simply of an ordered set of fields in columns, with each matching record listed in a row. While easy to set up, they can't be used to create groups of data or graphs. Consequently, they're best used just for tasks like generating a mailing list.

    Tip: Use tabular reports when you want a simple list or a list of items with a grand total.

- *Summary reports* are similar to tabular reports, but also allow users to group rows of data, view subtotals, and create charts. For example, in the sample Employee Interviewer reports that appear in the following screenshot, the summary report groups the rows of reviews by the possible values of the `Owner Name` field, allowing us to see at a glance subtotals of how many times the two interviewers have talked to candidates and entered reviews for them.

   While a little more time-consuming to set up, summary reports give us many more options for manipulating and organizing the data, and, unlike tabular reports, they can be used in dashboards. Summary reports are the workhorses of reporting—you'll find that most of your reports tend to be of this format.

    Tip: Use summary reports when you want subtotals based on the value of a particular field or when you want to create a hierarchically grouped report, such as sales organized by year and then by quarter.

- *Matrix reports* allow you to group records both by row and by column. For example, in the following sample Employee Interviewer reports, the matrix report groups the review rows by the possible values of the `Owner Name` field, and also breaks out the possible values of the `Position` field into columns. Consequently, the report gives us summarized information such as the number of times an interviewer has interviewed candidates and entered reviews for a particular position. These reports are the most time-consuming to set up, but they also provide the most detailed view of our data. Like summary reports, matrix reports can have graphs and be used in dashboards.

    Tip: Use matrix reports when you want to see data by two different dimensions that aren't related, such as date and product.

- *Joined reports* let you create different views of data from multiple report types. In a joined report, data is organized in blocks. Each block acts like a "sub-report," with its own fields, columns, sorting, and filtering. You can add a chart to a joined report. For example, in the following sample, the joined report pulls data from two report types related to the Positions object. Together, the report shows applications received from job ads posted for each position.

Tip: Use joined reports to group and show data from multiple report types in different views.

Tabular, Summary, Matrix, and Joined Reports Offer Different Options for Viewing Data

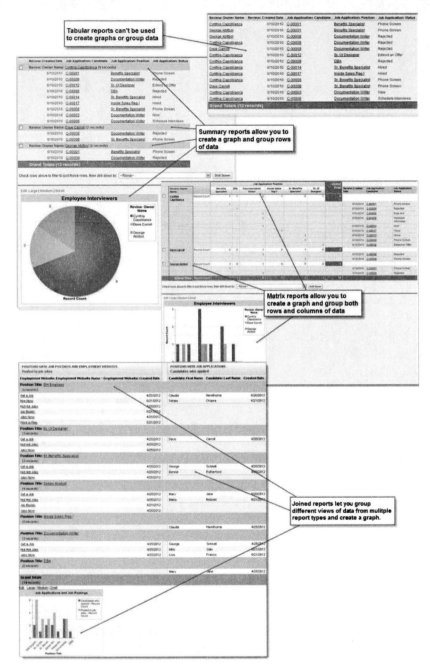

Tabular reports can't be used to create graphs or group data

Summary reports allow you to create a graph and group rows of data

Matrix reports allow you to create a graph and group both rows and columns of data

Joined reports let you group different views of data from mulitple report types and create a graph.

Setting Up the Recruiting App for Reports

Before we get started building reports, we first need to take care of a couple tasks that will make our reports easy to find in the Recruiting app. We need to add the Reports tab to the default tab display along with our Positions, Candidates, and Job Applications tabs. We'll also need to create a folder for storing all the reports that we create. While both of these tasks are purely optional, they'll go a long way towards improving the experience of our Recruiting app users.

Try It Out: Add the Reports Tab

First we'll start by adding the Reports tab to the set of default tabs that are displayed for every Recruiting app user. To do so, we need to revisit the Recruiting app that we created way back in Building a Simple App on page 31.

1. From Setup, enter `Apps` in the `Quick Find` box, then select **Apps**.
2. Click **Edit** next to the Recruiting app.
3. In the Choose the Tabs section, add Reports to the Selected Tabs list.
4. Optionally, select `Overwrite users' personal custom app customizations`.

   If you choose this option, the Reports tab is automatically added to the tab bar by default for all users. If you've already deployed your app and you'd rather not overwrite existing users' changes, leave this option unchecked. Users can manually add the Reports tab to their personal tab bar by clicking the **+** tab.

5. Click **Save**.

Perfect! Now let's visit the Reports tab to perform our next task: creating a folder for Recruiting reports.

Try It Out: Create a Recruiting Reports Folder

On the Reports tab, you see recently viewed reports and dashboards organized in report or dashboard folders. You can quickly browse the Folders pane or search what you're looking for. To see all items, or only reports for example, you can filter the list view. Every organization, by default, has standard folders, some that contain report templates.

Unfiled Public Reports is a standard folder all users can access. As an administrator, you can store reports in that folder to share with everyone in your organization. You can make any other folder public, by sharing it with all users. Personal folders (also standard folders) such as Personal Custom Reports and Personal Dashboards are an exception. They contain reports or dashboards private to each user and can't be accessed by others.

The Reports Tab and Folders

To let users access your reports, make the folder that stores the reports accessible to them. Let's create a folder to organize reports that your users can find easily.

1. In the Reports tab, click ![icon] next to the Folders pane and choose **New Report Folder**.

2. In the `Report Folder Label` field, enter `Recruiting Reports`. `Folder Unique Name` autopopulates with `Recruiting_Reports`. Leave this default value.

3. Click **Save**.

4. Next to the Recruiting Reports folder, click ![icon] and select **Share**.

> 📝 Note: If you don't see the Share option, you just need to turn on folder sharing. From Setup, enter `Folder Sharing` in the `Quick Find` box, then select **Folder Sharing**, and make sure `Enable access levels for sharing report and dashboard folders` is selected.

You can share all of the contents of a report folder by selecting one of the options at the top of the dialog: Users, Roles, Roles and Subordinates, or Public Groups. We want everyone at Universal Containers to be able to see, but not change, the reports in this folder.

5. Click **Roles and Subordinates**.

6. Next to CEO, click **Share**.

7. Make sure that the level selected in the Access column is **Viewer**. This allows all users in your company to view this folder and the reports in it, but allows only administrators to modify the reports inside the folder or add new reports to it.

8. Click **Done** to save our settings, and then click **Close**.

Great—we're now ready to create our first report.

Creating a Summary Report

To get started, we'll create a summary report that answers the question, "Which functional areas have the most new or open positions and in what region?" This report will include the title, hiring manager, location, and status of each position, as well as a pie chart that presents the data visually. As we do this, we'll skip over some of the more complicated reporting options so we can quickly create a report that fits our requirements. Our second example will then define a more complex matrix report that shows off some of the more advanced reporting features.

Because this report is going to use so many different reporting features, we'll break down the procedure into three parts:

1. Creating a summary report

2. Adding columns and filters

3. Adding a chart

Try It Out: Create a Summary Report

To create our summary report, we'll start by opening the report builder, a powerful visual editor for reports.

1. On the Reports tab, click **New Report**.

The first step in creating a report is choosing the right report type. A *report type* defines the set of records and fields available to a report based on the relationships between a primary object and its related objects. Reports display only records that meet the criteria defined in the report type. Your administrators may have set up custom report types for you, or you can select from the available standard report types.

To help with navigation in this screen, all objects and relationships are grouped in categories like Accounts & Contacts or Customer Support Reports. The custom objects and relationships that we built for our Recruiting app can be found in Other Reports.

 Note: The Other Reports category contains all reports based on custom objects. If you've built a custom object that's related to a standard object, such as Account or Contact, you'll also be able to report on your custom object in the standard object's category.

2. From the Create New Report page, double click on the Other Reports category.

The Other Reports Category in the Create New Report Page

Objects that have a many-to-one relationship with another object, like Job Applications and Positions, can either be selected on their own or in the context of their relationship with the other object. For example, if we select Job Applications with Position, our report will count job application records, but can filter, group, or display fields from the related position records as well. This will come in handy a little later when we build reports that count job application records. But because we need to count position records in our report and positions aren't on the many side of a relationship, we'll stick with a standalone positions report for now.

3. Select Positions.

4. Click **Create**.

Custom Report in Report Builder

Now that we've chosen the report type, we can customize the report. Note that we can't go back and change the report type. To do that, you have to start with a whole new report. The report builder's Preview pane displays a limited set of data; we can also run the report at any time to see if we have the results we're looking for. For example, let's see what a baseline positions report looks like without any customizations.

5. Click **Run Report**.

A Positions Report with No Customizations

> 📝 Note: The Show drop-down list defaults to My Positions. If you are logged in as a user who does not own any positions, select All Positions before you click **Run Report**. The report will then display all the positions to which you have access.

As you can see, without specifying any details, we already have a list of position records with a Grand Total at the bottom. This is the equivalent of what we might see if we were creating a tabular report without additional columns. Now let's take this basic report to the next level.

   6. Click **Customize** to return to the report builder.

When creating a new report, we first need to choose the format of the report that we want to create. The default is tabular. Because we want to group rows of open positions by functional area, we'll create a summary report.

   7. Click **Tabular Format** and select **Summary** to change the format.

Now we want to group our rows of data by the `Functional Area` field.

   8. Find `Functional Area` in the Fields pane and drag it to the grouping drop zone in the Preview pane. When you have lots of fields, using Quick Find is usually fastest.

Adding a Grouping for a Report

Say we want to see positions also grouped by region. While the Location field gives us city and state, we want to group data geographically by regions, like USA, UK, and Asia Pacific. By categorizing the location field into buckets, we get a field that can be used for the grouping.

9. Drag `Location` from the Field pane into the preview after Position Name.

10. Click ⌄ on Location, and select **Bucket this Field**.

11. Type `Region` in the `Bucket Field Name`.

12. Click **New Bucket**, type `USA`, and press Enter.

13. Select:

- `San Francisco, CA`
- `Austin, TX`
- `Boulder, CO`
- `New York, NY`

14. Click **Move To**, and from its drop-down select **USA**.

15. Click **New Bucket**, type UK, and press Enter.

16. Move `London, England` into the UK category.

17. Move the remaining items into an Asia Pacific bucket.

18. Click **OK**.

Creating a Bucket Field

When done, locations are categorized regionally, and you have a bucket field called Region, which appears in the Field pane. However, we don't need to do anything, because the Platform has automatically added it to the left of Position Name.

Bucket Fields in the Report Preview

We're closer now! Our report still only lists position names, but now they're grouped by functional areas and by region. Also, each grouping has a record count subtotal in parentheses. These counts will be the basis of the pie chart that we'll add later.

Try It Out: Add Columns and Filters

Now, lets select and order the fields shown, and set the filters that restrict the set of records included in the report.

In addition to `Position Title` and `Location`, we also want to display the `Hiring Manager` and `Status` fields for each record. To select multiple fields or columns, press CTRL (Windows) or Command (Mac).

1. In report builder, drag the following fields into the preview.

   - `Hiring Manager`
   - `Status`

   You can also double-click fields to add them to the end of the report.

2. Reorder columns by dragging them. When you're done, the order should be:
   - Position Title
   - Location
   - Hiring Manager

- Status

Adding a Column Using Drag-and-Drop

We're even closer to our goal. However, the `Status` field shows us that the report includes some position records that have already been filled. Since we only want to view the new and open ones, we need to set some filters. Filters define the set of records to be included in the report; for example, you can include only records created this month or only records that belong to a certain user. With standard filters, you can quickly filter by record owner or date field. With field filters, you can filter on any field in the report. Because we want to view open positions across the entire organization and not just positions that we own (by default, all custom reports include "My" records only), we need to set two filters.

3. In the Show drop-down, select `All Positions`.

4. Click **Add** > **Field Filter**.

5. Define a filter for `Status equals New Position, Pending Approval, Open - Approved`.

6. Click **OK**.

💡 Tip: Notice that whenever you choose a checkbox field or a picklist field, like `Status`, in your filter, a lookup icon (🔍) shows up next to the filter row. Click the icon to view valid values for that field and quickly insert the ones by which you want to filter.

Using this filter of `Status equals New Position, Pending Approval, Open - Approved` means that our report will include only those position records with one of these three statuses. Note that the comma between the three `Status` values is treated as an OR function, so this one filter is the same as using these three filters.

- Status equals New Position, OR
- Status equals Pending Approval, OR
- Status equals Open - Approved

▪▪ Beyond the Basics

Did you know you can filter on a bucket field?

Say you want to view data for non-UK regions. You can add a filter for the bucket field, `Region` that you created to group data in the last exercise. You can filter bucket fields like any other field in the report. You would set the filter in this example as: *Region does not contain UK*.

As you add more filters, by default, they're applied cumulatively on the report using the AND function. That means, only data that meets all the filter conditions is displayed. But you can control how filters behave by using **Filter Logic** from the Add drop-down.

Try It Out: Add a Pie Chart

The final step is to display a chart with the report. In our case, we want a pie chart.

1. Click `Add Chart` and choose the pie chart type.

The chart builder automatically knows that we want the values to be the record count, and the wedges to be the different functional areas. That's because chart values correlate to a report's summary fields, and pie chart wedges correlate to a report's groupings. Since we have a second grouping by `Region`, we can choose a different field to display in the wedges. But we'll keep the default selections.

Now let's finish up our chart and generate our final report.

2. Click **OK**.

Summary Report Showing Open Positions by Region and Functional Area

When the report is run, you have several options for viewing data.

- Group, summarize data by a different field. For example instead of `Functional Area`, you can summarize by `Hiring Manager`.
- Export data into an Excel spreadsheet or CSV (comma separated values) format.
- Clear any filters applied.
- Refine results with standard filters such as date or range.

Because our report meets all of our criteria, let's save it to the Recruiting Reports folder.

3. Near the top of the report, click **Save**.

4. In the `Report Name` field, enter *Open Positions by Functional Area and Region*.

5. In the `Report Description` field, enter *Which functional areas have the most new or open positions by region?*

6. In the `Report Unique Name` field, enter *Open_Positions_by_Functional_Area* if that's not already the value.

7. From the `Report Folder` drop-down list, select Recruiting Reports.

8. Click **Save**.

Now if we view the Recruiting Reports folder, we can see our new summary report. Next, we'll make a matrix report that takes advantage of some of the more advanced reporting features.

Creating a Matrix Report

For our next report, we'll answer the question, "On average, how many days does it take each recruiter to fill a position with or without required travel?" This report will use a matrix format to highlight the difference that mandatory travel makes in how long it takes for positions to be filled. Looking at data only for this year and the last, the report will include:

- Record counts for each position a recruiter owns
- A custom summary formula for the percentage of a recruiter's positions that require travel
- A time-based filter that restricts the data only to positions that were created this year or last
- A color-coded field summary for the average number of days positions remain open:
  - Averages of less than 30 days are color-coded green
  - Averages of between 30 and 60 days are color-coded yellow
  - Averages of more than 60 days are color-coded red

Because this report is going to use so many different reporting features, we'll break down the procedure into four parts:

1. Creating a matrix report
2. Adding custom summary fields
3. Adding columns and filters
4. Adding a chart and conditional highlighting

Try It Out: Create a Matrix Report

To create the matrix report, we'll use the report builder again, this time highlighting steps that are different from how we defined the summary report.

1. In the Reports tab, click **New Report**.

Once again, we'll be creating a report that counts position records.

2. From the list, click the "+" to expand Other Reports.
3. Select Positions, and click **Create**.

Because we want to directly compare individual recruiter performance for positions that do and do not require travel, we'll use a matrix report. That way we can group the rows of positions by recruiter, and columns of positions by whether or not they require travel.

4. From the Format drop-down, select `Matrix`.

Specifying Groupings in a Matrix Report

Now let's group by both rows and columns. Notice the two sets of drop zones for matrix reports.

5. From the Fields pane, drag `Position: Owner Name` to the row grouping drop zone.

6. Now, drag `Travel Required` to the column grouping drop zone.

Our report now breaks out the possible values for the `Travel Required` field in the columns dimension. Recruiters are also broken out in the row dimension, but because all custom reports query just the report creator's data by default (that is, "My" records only), only one recruiter is listed in the report so far. Let's keep going.

Try It Out: Add Summary Fields

In the next step, we want to specify which numerical or checkbox field values to include in our report, and how each of them should be summarized in subtotals and grand totals. Though record count is always summarized as a sum total, we can summarize other numerical and checkbox fields in different ways.

For example, it doesn't make sense to sum the values of the `Days Open` column—the resulting total wouldn't provide much value. However, if we calculate the average for `Days Open`, we'd know roughly how long positions stay open.

For our report, we need to include three different types of summaries: record count, average days open, and a formula that calculates the percentage of records requiring travel. While the first two are standard summary fields, the third will require a visit to the Custom Summary Formula editor. Let's start with the first two. By default, the report already adds `Record Count`, so let's add the average for the number of days a position stays open.

1. Find the `Days Open` field and drop it into the matrix.

2. In the Summarize dialog, select `Average`.

Now, let's create that formula to calculate the percentage of records requiring travel.

3. Double-click **Add Formula**. You'll see the Custom Summary Formula editor.

The Custom Summary Formula Builder

The formula editor lets us define a new formula based on the summarizable fields in the report. In our case, we want to include a summary that shows the percentage of position records that require travel in any given segment. To make this calculation we need to divide the sum of records that require travel by the sum of all records:

4. In the `Column Name` field, enter *Travel Required Percentage*.

5. In the `Description` field, enter *The percentage of total position records that require travel.*

6. In the `Format` drop-down list, choose *Percent.*

7. In the `Decimal Places` drop-down list, choose *0.*

8. For `Where will this formula be displayed?`, choose *At all summary levels.*

Now, let's write our formula. Similar to other formula editors in the platform, this provides tools to make make it easier.

9. In the Formula section, click **Summary Fields** and select `Travel Required`, then select Sum.

The formula editor displays the following API representation of those values:

```
Position__c.Travel_Required__c:SUM
```

10. Click the **Operators** drop-down and select **Divide**.

11. Click **Summary Field** and select `Record Count`.

The final formula looks like this:

```
Position__c.Travel_Required__c:SUM / RowCount
```

We can quickly verify that the formula is correct by checking its syntax before saving.

12. Click **Check Syntax**.

13. Click **OK**.

Try It Out: Add Columns and Filters

In the next steps, we'll select report columns, then define our filters. Because we're already familiar with adding columns, let's zip through that step first.

 Note: Before you can add fields to a matrix report, make sure Details is selected under the **Show** drop-down list. If details aren't shown, you can only add summary fields.

1. Add the following report columns by double-clicking them.

   * `Functional Area`

   * `Status`

   `Position: Position Title`, `Days Open` and `Travel Required` should already be part of your report.

For our report, we want to define three filters: one to include all positions, one to include only those positions created in the last year, and one to include those with a `Status` of Open - Approved or Closed - Filled.

2. In the Show drop-down list, choose `All Positions`.

3. In the Date Field filter select `Position: Created Date`.

Notice that all other date fields defined on the Position object are also available in the Date Field filter, including `Close Date`, `Hire By`, and `Open Date`.

4. For **Range**, choose `Current and Previous CY` (meaning this and last calendar year). The start and end dates are populated automatically.

Now let's add a field filter based on the status.

5. Click **Add**.

6. Create this filter.

   `Status equals Open - Approved, Closed - Filled`

7. Click **OK**.

Filtering the Matrix Report

⠿ **Beyond the Basics**

Cross filters let you filter on a report's child objects using a straightforward WITH or WITHOUT condition. For example, you only want to see data for positions that have job applications. You can add a **Cross Filter** from the Add drop-down on the Fields pane like this: `Positions with Job Applications`. You can sub-filter the `Job Applications` object to refine results further.

Adding a Cross Filter

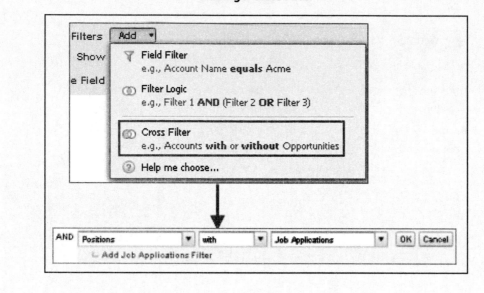

Try It Out: Add a Chart and Conditional Highlighting

We're almost done. Now, in addition to creating a horizontal bar chart that shows the average number of days open, recruiters, and whether the position requires travel, we also want to conditionally highlight data to help us quickly analyze which recruiters are performing well and which need to work on filling their positions faster.

1. Click **Add Chart**.

2. Select the Vertical Bar Chart type.

3. In the `Y-Axis` drop-down list, choose `Average Days Open`.

4. In the `X-Axis` drop-down list, choose `Position: Owner Name`.

5. In the `Group-By` drop-down list, choose `Travel Required` and keep the side-by-side grouping format.

6. Leave the `Plot additional values` checkbox empty.

A *combination chart* plots multiple sets of data on a single chart. Each set of data is based on a different field, so values are easy to compare. You can also combine certain chart types to present data in different ways in a single chart. The report we're building doesn't need a combination chart, but they are useful when comparing data, charting trends, and so forth.

7. Click the Formatting tab.

8. In the `Chart Title` field, enter *Avg Days to Hire With and Without Travel.*

9. Click **OK**.

All three of our summary fields are available to highlight, but we just want to emphasize one: `Average Days Open`. That's because we want to highlight which recruiters are closing positions in less than 30 days, less than 60 days, or more than 60 days.

10. Click the **Show** drop-down list and select **Conditional Highlighting**.

Adding Conditional Highlighting to Show Changes in Data

11. In the first row, set `Select Field` to `Average Days Open`.

12. In the first color picker, select a shade of green. This is the low color.

13. In the first text field, enter *30*. This is the low breakpoint.

14. In the second text field, enter *60*. This is the high breakpoint.

15. In the third color picker, select a shade of red. This is the high color.

16. Click **OK**.

17. Click **Run Report**.

Viewing the Results of the Matrix Report

Our report shows at a glance how well our recruiters fill positions and how long, on average, positions stay open. Conditional highlighting shows which positions are taking longer to fill—generally those requiring travel. Let's quickly save this report before moving on.

18. Click **Customize** to return to the report builder.

19. Near the top of the report, click **Save**.

20. In the `Report Name` field, enter `Avg Days to Hire With and Without Travel`.

The `Report Unique Name` field is automatically populated.

21. In the `Report Description` field, enter `On average, how many days does it take each recruiter to fill a position with or without required travel?`

22. From the `Report Folder` drop-down list, select `Recruiting Reports`.

23. Click **Save**.

24. Click **Close**, and then click **Save & Close** to return to the Reports tab.

💡 **[other]:** Did you know you can add charts to more than just reports and dashboards? You can give users valuable information directly on the pages they visit often. To do that, just embed report charts in detail pages for standard or custom objects. When users see charts on pages, they can make decisions based on data they see in the context of the page without going elsewhere to look for it.

For more information about embedding charts into page layouts, see "Add a Report Chart to a Page Layout" in the Salesforce Help.

As we've seen, custom reports can provide a lot of interesting data, giving insight into the challenges that an organization faces. However, unless a user visits these reports often, much of their benefit remains untapped. How can we give users a way of keeping tabs on the information in reports without wasting their time? The answer, as we'll see next, lies with dashboards.

Introducing Dashboards

A *dashboard* shows data from source reports as visual components, which can be charts, gauges, tables, metrics, or Visualforce pages. The components provide a snapshot of key metrics and performance indicators for your organization. Each dashboard can have up to 20 components. Users can view any dashboard available in a public folder in their organization, such as Company Dashboards, and can select a favorite, whose first three components display on the Home tab.

To put it mildly, users *love* the summarized views they get with dashboards, and no good Force.com app is complete without at least one.

A Sample Recruiting Dashboard

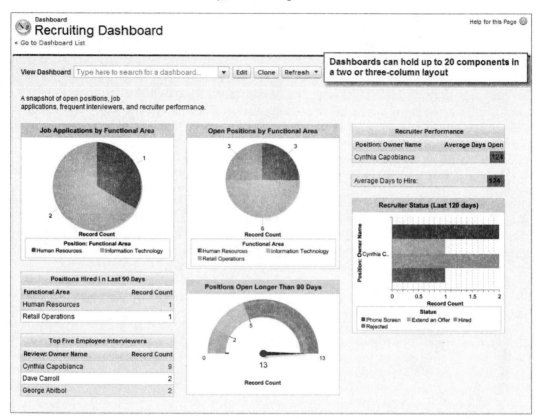

Try It Out: Create Additional Reports

We'll be creating a small-scale recruiting dashboard in this chapter, but before we do, let's use our new report-building skills to create a few more reports. Because we're already familiar with how report builder works, we'll just outline the specifics of a few reports in the following table—you can either create them on your own, or just familiarize yourself with the options.

💡 **Tip:** Want to click along with our dashboard instructions but don't want to spend your time creating all these new reports? Just create the Positions Open Longer Than 90 Days report in the first row. However, if you're interested in recreating the sample dashboard displayed here, you'll need to create the other four as well.

Table 47: Additional Recruiting Report Specifications

Report Name	Question	Report Type	Options
Positions Open Longer Than 90 Days	*Which positions have been open for more than 90 days?*	Positions	Format: Summary Report
			Summarize information by: Location and then by Functional Area
			Columns: Position: Position Title, Position: Owner Name, Status, Open Date, Hire By, Days Open
			Filters: All Positions; Days Open greater or equal 90
			Chart Type: Pie
			Chart Wedges: Functional Area
			Chart Title: Positions Open Longer Than 90 Days
Job Applications by Functional Area	*Which positions are getting the most candidates?*	Job Applications with Position	Format: Summary Report
			Summarize information by: Position: Functional Area and then by Position: Position Title
			Columns: Job Application Name, Job Application Status
			Filters: All job applications; Position: Status equals Open - Approved
			Chart Type: Vertical Column
			X-Axis: Position: Functional Area
			Chart Title: Job Applications by Functional Area
Employee Interviewers	*Which employees conduct the most interviews?*	Job Applications with Reviews	Format: Summary Report
			Summarize information by: Review: Created By
			Columns: Job Application: Job Application Number, Job Application:

Report Name	Question	Report Type	Options
			Position, Job Application: Status, Review: Created Date
			Filters: All job applications
			Chart Type: Pie
			Chart Title: Employee Interviewers
Recruiter Status	*What does the job application pipeline look like for each recruiter and open position?*	Job Applications with Position	Format: Matrix Report
			Subtotal Rows by: Position: Owner Name and then by Position: Position Title
			Subtotal Columns by: Job Application Status
			Columns: Job Application: Job Application Number
			Filters: All job applications; Job Application: Last Modified Date Last 120 Days; Position: Status equals Open - Approved, Closed - Filled
Positions Hired in Last 90 Days	*Who have we hired in the last 90 days?*	Positions	Format: Summary Report
			Summarize information by: Functional Area
			Columns: Position: Position Title, Position: Owner Name, Hiring Manager, Job Level, Location, Close Date
			Filters: All positions; Close Date Last 90 Days; Status equals Closed - Filled

Try It Out: Create a Dashboard

Now that we've got a set of reports to reference, we're ready to create a small Recruiting dashboard. To do so, we'll be working in the Reports tab.

First we need to create a folder to hold our dashboards. We'll use the same steps that we used to create a folder to hold our reports.

1. In the Reports tab, click ⬛▾ next to the Folders pane and choose **New Dashboard Folder**.

2. In `Dashboard Folder Label`, enter `Recruiting Dashboards`. The `Folder Unique Name` field automatically populates with `Recruiting_Dashboards`.

3. Click **Save**.

4. Next to the Recruiting Dashboards folder, click ▾ and select **Share**.

5. At the top of the dialog, click **Roles and Subordinates**.

6. Next to CEO, click **Share**.

7. Make sure the level selected in the Access column is **Viewer**. This allows all users in your company to view this folder and the reports in it, but allows only administrators to modify the reports inside the folder or add new reports to it.

8. Click **Done** to save our settings, and then click **Close**.

Now we'll create a dashboard.

1. On the Reports & Dashboards page, click **New Dashboard**.

The Dashboard Edit Page

Once we specify the dashboard properties, we can add components.

2. Click **Dashboard Properties**.

3. In the `Title` field, enter `Recruiting Dashboard`.

4. The `Dashboard Unique Name` field autopopulates with Recruiting_Dashboard.

5. Select the Recruiting Dashboards folder to save it in.

6. Click **OK**.

7. For the dashboard description—the editable field near the top of the page—enter `A snapshot of open positions, job applications, frequent interviewers, and recruiter performance.`

Each dashboard has a running user, whose security settings determine which data to display in a dashboard. All users with access to the folder see the same data, regardless of their own personal security settings.

The running user's security settings only apply to the dashboard view. Once a user drills down into a source report or detail page off the dashboard, the user will view the data based on his or her normal security settings.

For example, suppose a system administrator with the "Modify All Data" permission is the running user for our recruiting dashboard. In this case, every recruiting-related record is counted in all of the report totals on our dashboard, including users who'd normally be restricted from viewing certain records (like those assigned to the Standard Employee profile). Although those users would be able to see the summary data for all records in the dashboard, if they navigated to the source reports, they'd see just the records they have access to.

When you're designing a dashboard, keep the dashboard's audience in mind. Ask whether any of the information is sensitive and how much you want them to see. If you do give a user access to dashboards that include more data than he or she normally has permission to view, be sure to communicate that they might see different values when they click through the dashboard to view the associated reports. And if you need to restrict a dashboard from certain users, just save it to a restricted-access folder.

Beyond the Basics

Did you know you can set up a *dynamic dashboard* that shows users data according to their own security settings?

Say you want to show the same set of dashboard components to different sets of users, each with a different level of visibility. You'd potentially have to set up dozens of dashboards with the right running user for each, and store them in separate folders. With dynamic dashboards, administrators can accomplish the same thing without having to create and maintain all those extra dashboards and folders. A single dynamic dashboard can display a standard set of metrics across all levels of your organization.

To find out more, see "Provide Individualized Views of a Dashboard" in the Salesforce Help.

For our recruiting dashboard, the data that we'll be showing in the dashboard isn't particularly sensitive. Consequently, we'll choose a system administrator as the running user, and save the dashboard to a public folder.

8. In the `View dashboard as` field in the upper right of the screen, enter the name of your user, since you have system administrator privileges. This sets the running user for the dashboard.

We now have an empty dashboard that's ready to be filled with components.

Adding Dashboard Components

We haven't yet defined any components, but it's easy to add and reorder them in dashboard builder.

Components come in five varieties.

Icon	Type	Description
	Charts	Displays a bar, column, line, pie, donut, or funnel chart—or any chart contained in a report.
	Tables	Displays a table that contains values and totals from columns in the report.
	Metrics	Displays the grand total from a report, along with a label that you enter.
	Gauges	Shows the grand total of a report as a point on a "fuel-tank" type of scale.
	Visualforce Pages	Displays any Visualforce dashboard component in your organization.

Try It Out: Add a Chart Component

Let's start by adding a chart that shows the number of open positions by functional area:

1. Drag a pie chart component onto the left column of your dashboard.
2. Click **Edit Title**, and enter `Open Positions by Functional Area`.

3. Click the Data Sources tab and find and select the Open Positions by Functional Area report.

4. Drag the report and drop it onto the pie chart component.

> **Tip:** Click ✎ on the pie to open the component editor. On the Component Data tab, notice that `Values` and `Wedges` for the pie are autofilled. This is because record count and the `Functional Area` field are used in the source report chart. On the other hand, if the source report didn't have a chart, Values and Wedges would automatically pick up record count and the first grouping in the report.

The Dashboard Component Edit Page

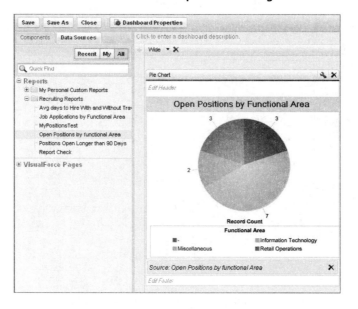

Ta-da! We now have a pie chart in our dashboard! If a user clicks on the chart, they're taken to the report from which the chart was generated.

Try It Out: Add a Gauge Component

Now let's create a gauge component that shows us how we're doing with positions that have been open for longer than 90 days.

1. Click the Components tab.

2. Drag a gauge component onto the middle column of your dashboard.

3. Click **Edit Title**, and enter `Positions Open Longer Than 90 Days`.

4. Click the Data Sources tab and find and select the Positions Open Longer Than 90 Days report.

5. Drag the report and drop it onto the gauge component.

Now, let's change how our gauge looks. Just like the conditional highlighting in our matrix report, this gauge can display different colors depending on the total count of positions that have been open too long. We want a green color if there are fewer than two positions, yellow if there are between two and five, and red if the value is over five.

6. Click ✎ on the gauge to open the component editor.

7. Click the Formatting tab and set the following fields.

Formatting the Gauge Component

- For `Minimum`, enter `0`.
- For `Low Range Color`, pick a shade of green.
- For `Breakpoint 1`, enter `2`.
- For `Middle Range Color`, leave the shade of yellow selected.
- For `Breakpoint 2`, enter `5`.
- For `High Range Color`, pick a shade of red.
- For `Maximum`, enter `10`.

8. Click **OK**.

Perfect! Our recruiting dashboard now contains two components.

Try It Out: Add a Table Component

Now let's create a table component that shows us the average number of days it takes a recruiter to fill a position with or without travel.

1. Click the Components tab.

2. Drag a table component onto the right column of your dashboard.

3. Click **Edit Title**, and enter `Recruiter Performance`.

4. Click the Data Sources tab, and find and select the Avg Days to Hire With and Without Travel report.

313

5. Drag the report and drop it onto the table component.

6. Click 🔧 on the table to open the component editor.

7. Click the Formatting tab.

Make sure **Show Chatter Photos** is selected. This displays each recruiter's Chatter profile picture in the table.

Just like its underlying source report, we can add conditional highlighting to our table component to highlight recruiter performance levels. We want a green color if the recruiter needs fewer than 45 days, yellow if he or she needs between 45 and 75 days, and red if the value is over 75.

8. Set the following fields for conditional highlighting.

- For `Low Range Color`, pick a shade of green.

- For `Breakpoint 1`, enter *45*.

- For `Middle Range Color`, leave the shade of yellow selected.

- For `Breakpoint 2`, enter *75*.

- For `High Range Color`, pick a shade of red.

9. Click **OK**.

Table Component

Try It Out: Add a Metric Component

Finally, let's create a metric component that shows us the average number of days it takes all recruiters to fill a position.

1. Click the Components tab.

2. Drag a metric component onto the right column of your dashboard and drop it below the table we just created.

3. Click the Data Sources tab and find and select the Avg Days to Hire With and Without Travel report.

4. Drag the report and drop it onto the metric.

Because metric components consist of a single value, they don't need a title. Instead, we give them a label much like any other field that you see in the platform.

5. In the label field, enter *Average Days to Hire*.

> 📝 Note: Did you notice that we're using the same report that we used for our table? This metric is just another visualization of the data in that report.

6. Click ⚒ on the metric to open the component editor.

7. Click the Component Data tab. Notice that the metric value is autopopulated with the column summary total used in the chart of the source matrix report.

Finally, let's add more conditional highlighting to showcase values.

8. Click the Formatting tab and set the following fields.

- For *Low Range Color*, pick a shade of green.
- For *Breakpoint 1*, enter *45*.
- For *Middle Range Color*, leave the shade of yellow selected.
- For *Breakpoint 2*, enter *75*.
- For *High Range Color*, pick a shade of red.

9. Click **OK**.

▪▪ **Beyond the Basics**

Did you know you can filter components across the dashboard for multiple views of data?

Dashboard filters give you the flexibility of directly manipulating dashboard information on the fly instead of filtering each underlying report. Click **Add Filter** in the dashboard builder to create a dashboard filter and its values. A dashboard can have up to three filters. In this dashboard, for example, you can create a filter called *Function* on the Functional Area field. When viewing the dashboard, users can pick different filter values like Finance or Human Resources to see data for each job function across the dashboard. To learn more, search "Add a Dashboard Filter" in the Salesforce Help.

Adding a Dashboard Filter

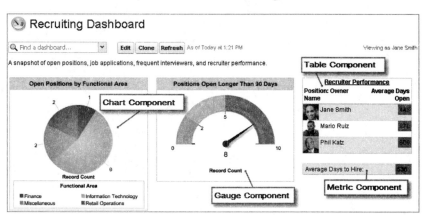

We've now got a simple, four-component dashboard for our Recruiting app! (Your dashboard might look slightly different.) Let's save our dashboard.

10. Click **Close**, then click **Save & Close**. You can also click **Save** if you want to update the title or description, or change the folder.

Four Components on the Recruiting Dashboard

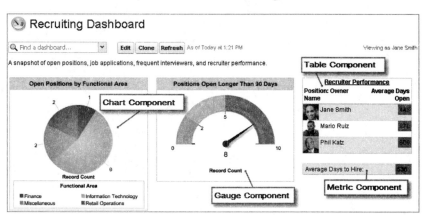

If you click the Home tab, you can add the dashboard's first row to your home page. Be sure to add the dashboard section to your Home tab layout and then select the dashboard you want to appear in that section: the Recruiting Dashboard you just created.

1. From Setup, enter `Home Page Layouts` in the `Quick Find` box, then select **Home Page Layouts**.

2. Select `Dashboard Snapshot`, and click **Next**.

3. Leave the component in their default order, and click **Save**.

4. On the Home tab, click **Customize Page** in the upper right corner of the Dashboard component.

5. Select `Recruiting Dashboard` from the Dashboard Snapshot drop-down list.

6. Click **Save**.

And because we saved the dashboard in a public folder, any user can add it to his or her Home tab, too.

As you can see, once we created the reports for our Recruiting app, adding them to a dashboard was a piece of cake. It's so easy, that we'll leave the remainder of the components as an exercise for you to try on your own—see how close you can come to recreating A Sample Recruiting Dashboard on page 306.

Refreshing Dashboards

Dashboards reflect a snapshot of your data at a specific time. On the Home tab, that time is indicated in the upper left corner on the Dashboard component; on the Reports tab, it's indicated in the upper right corner. You can refresh your dashboards on either tab by clicking **Refresh**.

If you are using Enterprise, Unlimited, or Performance Edition, you can schedule dashboards to refresh automatically at specific times, and upon completion, receive an email notification that includes the refreshed dashboard.

Scheduling a dashboard refresh is easy. On the Reports tab, simply click the down arrow on the **Refresh** button and select **Schedule Refresh...**, then, indicate who should receive the notification email and the time you want the refresh to occur.

Introducing Mobile Dashboards

The information we've packed into our Recruiting Dashboard can be useful to a lot of people—even recruiters away from their desks. Before we get into Salesforce1 again, we need to make sure dashboards are enabled for mobile. If Dashboards aren't in the navigation menu, users won't see them at all. Let's take a quick look at the configuration for our mobile navigation.

1. From Setup, enter `Navigation` in the `Quick Find` box, then select **Salesforce1 Navigation**.

This is the page that dictates what the navigation menu in Salesforce1 looks like. The first item in the list becomes our users' landing page in Salesforce1, and since this configuration is the same for all of our users, we want the first item to be something useful for everyone. The usefulness principle extends throughout the configuration: we want to put the items that users want most at the top.

The *Today* element corresponds to an app that helps users plan for and manage their day by integrating calendar events from their mobile device with their Salesforce tasks, contacts, and accounts. Available in the Salesforce1 downloadable apps only.

The *Smart Search Items* element, which becomes a dynamic list of recently used objects, can expand into a set of eight or more menu items in the mobile experience, and it might end up pushing other elements below the scroll point if you put it near the top of the menu. Anything you put above the Smart Search Items element appears in the unlabeled first section of the navigation menu. Anything you put below the Smart Search Items element appears in the Apps section of the navigation menu.

2. Arrange the items in the Selected area using the **Up** or **Down** arrows like so:

- Today
- Tasks
- Chatter
- Smart Search Items
- Dashboards

Now that we're sure dashboards appear in Salesforce1 for our organization, let's see how dashboards work on a mobile device.

1. Launch Salesforce1.

2. From the navigation menu, tap **Dashboards**.

3. From the list of recent dashboards, tap **Recruiting Dashboard**.

The Recruiting Dashboard in Salesforce1

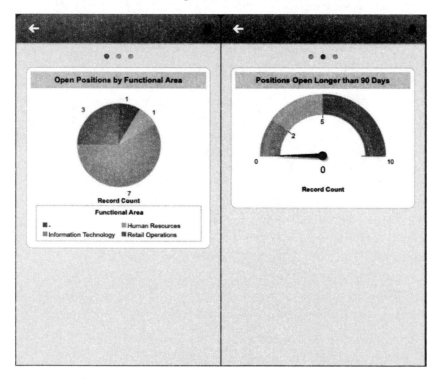

Our dashboard looks a little different in a mobile context. Instead of seeing all three columns in one view, we see all of each column in a single view. To see other columns, we can swipe left or right. To see the details for a component, we can tap on one. In this component view, we can tap on data points to see their values highlighted.

Introducing Custom Report Types

While dashboards are an excellent way of rendering data, many users will need information that's more granular and unique to their job function, so they'll need to create their own reports. You'll want to control which data they can access for their reports, and make it easy for them to create reports that are useful. You can do both of these by creating custom report types.

Custom report types define the criteria from which your users can run and create reports. When you create a report type, you specify the objects, relationships, and fields that users can select for their reports.

How are custom report types useful in our Recruiting app? Well, our recruiters will appreciate it if we give them an easy way to scan for positions to which candidates have applied. In addition, the recruiters will probably want to see which of those job applications have reviews. That way, they'll know if any positions are on the verge of closing.

Try It Out: Create a Report Type

We've spent most of this chapter on the Reports tabs. Now it's time to return to the Setup menu.

1. From Setup, enter `Report Types` in the `Quick Find` box, then select **Report Types**.

2. If you see an introductory splash page, just click **Continue**.

3. Click **New Custom Report Type**.

The custom report type that we're creating will include data from three different objects: Position, Job Application, and Review. Positions will be the focus of the recruiters, though, so let's make Position the primary object in this report type.

4. In the `Primary Object` drop-down list, select `Positions`.

Next, we'll give this report type an intuitive name and categorize it so it's easy for users to find it. We'll also enter a description so users who select the report type will know its function.

5. In the **Report Type Label** field, enter `Positions with Reviewed Job Applications`.

6. In the **Report Type Name** field, enter `Positions_with_Reviewed_Job Applications` if it is not there already.

7. In the **Description** field, enter `Which positions have job applications that have been reviewed?`

8. In the **Store in Category** drop-down list, select `Other Reports`.

When creating a report type, set its status to `In Development` if you want to test it before making it available to all your users; however, the report type we're creating does not require much testing, so let's deploy it.

9. Select `Deployed`.

10. Click **Next**.

The platform uses a graphical hierarchy and set diagrams (also called Venn diagrams) to let us easily specify which related records from other objects we want to include in the report results.

11. Click the white box under box A (Positions). Box B appears.

12. On box B, select Job Applications from the drop-down list, and leave `Each "A" record must have at least one related "B" record` selected.

Report Type Hierarchy and Set Diagram for Positions and Job Applications

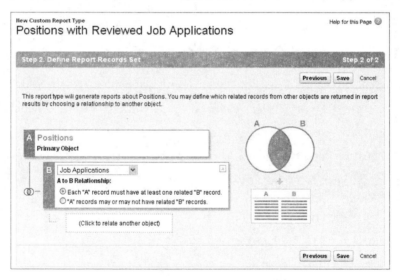

By leaving this option selected, we've indicated that we want this report type to only include position records for which there are job applications. Notice how the set diagrams on the right change to reflect our selection.

13. Click the white box under box B (Job Applications). Box C appears.

14. On box C, select Reviews from the drop-down list, and leave `Each "B" record must have at least one related "C" record` selected.

Report Type Hierarchy and Set Diagram for Positions, Job Applications, and Reviews

We've further narrowed the scope of our report to only include job applications that have reviews.

15. Click **Save**.

Our custom report type is nearly finished. In fact, we could technically say it's done now, but there's something we can do to make it even more convenient for our users: we can reorganize how the fields display in the Fields pane of the report builder.

This report type incorporates three objects (Position, Job Application, and Review), each containing many fields. A user creating a report using this custom report type will likely be overwhelmed by all of those fields, so let's remove the ones they won't need, and move the important ones to the top. We can also specify which ones are selected by default.

16. On the Custom Report Type detail page, scroll down to the Fields Available for Reports related list and click **Edit Layout**.

The page that appears is similar to the page layout editor we used in Enhancing the Simple App with Advanced Fields, Data Validation, and Page Layouts on page 57. You can reorder fields by dragging them, create and delete sections, and so forth. You can also double-click the fields to change their label and specify whether they should be checked by default.

(!) Important: If a field isn't in a section, it won't be available to users when they generate reports from this report type.

Let's reorganize the page.

17. Create a new section called *Position, Job Application, and Review Fields*.

18. In the Positions section, change the label of the following fields by double-clicking the field name and editing it in the dialog that opens.

- `Created By` to `Position Created By`
- `Created Date` to `Position Created Date`
- `Status` to `Position Status`

19. In the Job Applications section, change the label of the following fields by double-clicking the field name and editing it in the dialog that opens.

- `Created By` to `Job Application Created By`
- `Created Date` to `Job Application Created Date`
- `Status` to `Job Application Status`

20. In the Reviews section, change the label of the following fields by double-clicking the field name and editing it in the dialog that opens.

- `Created By` to `Review Created By`
- `Created Date` to `Review Created Date`

21. Move the following fields from the Positions section into the Position, Job Application, and Review Fields section.

- `Position Name`
- `Created By`
- `Created Date`
- `Days Open`
- `Functional Area`
- `Hire By`
- `Hiring Manager`
- `Open Date`
- `Status`
- `Travel Required`

22. Move the following fields from the Job Applications section into the Position, Job Application, and Review Fields section.

- `Job Application Name`
- `Average Rating`

- Created By
- Created Date
- Number of Reviews
- Status

Notice that we didn't include the `Candidate` field. We left it out because this report type is available to all users, including hiring managers. As mentioned in the previous chapter, a hiring manager might try to poach candidates that apply for other jobs, so it's best not to reveal candidate names in reports.

23. Move the following fields from the Reviews section into the Position, Job Application, and Review Fields section.

- Review Name
- Created By
- Created Date
- Rating

24. Make the following fields checked by default.

- Days Open
- Hiring Manager
- Job Application Name
- Open Date
- Position Name
- Review Name

25. Delete the individual Positions, Job Applications, and Reviews sections.

26. Click **Save**.

Your custom report type is ready! To try it out, go to the Reports tab, click **New Report**, and select the Other Reports report type category. The Positions with Reviewed Job Applications report type is in the list below.

Look At What We've Done

Check out our Recruiting app now! We've met almost all of the requirements we talked about at the beginning of the book, but we're not there yet. In the next chapter, we're going to move beyond the platform's point-and-click tools, like security and workflow, and introduce Visualforce and the SOAP API. These features provide the key to incorporating functionality from all over the Web and will help us create a truly powerful application in the cloud. In fact, once you've mastered the tools available in the platform, these tools will be the way that you can let your creativity soar—the functionality of any app you build on the platform will be limited only by the Web itself!

CHAPTER 11 Moving Beyond Point-and-Click App Development

Up to this point, we've built a compelling app using various parts of the platform. We've created a data model to store our recruiting information, put workflow and approval logic in place to help manage the data, and built reports and a dashboard to help share the data. The fact that we were able to quickly put all of these pieces together without writing any code is a testament to the power of the Force.com platform.

A tremendous amount of research and thought has gone into the design of the platform. Salesforce has strived to anticipate the various business application needs of 21st century companies, and has addressed many of those needs with simple yet powerful declarative, point-and-click tools that nontechnical users can use to achieve unique business goals. However, it is impossible for one company to provide a single solution that's a perfect fit for everyone. That's why Salesforce has made it easy for developers to write code that builds upon the Force.com platform's point-and-click functionality. Once you learn how to program for the Force.com platform, you'll find that you can create apps for the Cloud that do just about anything you can dream up. The sky's the limit!

"Programming-phobia" is common for people without computer science backgrounds, and it's likely that many readers will want to put this book down as soon as they see the words "code" and "variable." Relax! When you read this chapter, you'll discover just how fun and easy programming for the Force.com platform can be. Also, bear in mind that the intent of this chapter isn't to make you a programmer (although it's a great place to start). Instead, this chapter will just give you a taste of what it's like to enhance your app with some very simple programming. If you don't feel like typing any code yourself, just copy and paste the code samples from the files included in the `RecruitingApp-9_0.zip` file, which you downloaded in Expanding the Simple App Using Relationships on page 97.

With the sample code and a few mouse clicks, we'll be able to swiftly enhance our app by adding:

- Candidate Map—An interactive map that shows the locations of the candidates that have applied for a particular position
- Mass Update Status—The ability to update the `Status` field on multiple job applications at the same time

Let's begin!

Introducing Mash-Ups and Web Services

If we revisit the requirements of our Recruiting app, we'll see that we still need to implement an interactive map that shows the locations of the candidates that have applied for a particular position. Clearly no such functionality is available by default in the platform, and we certainly don't have time to build our own mapping engine. Is this type of functionality even possible?

Of course it's possible! Because the Force.com platform runs on the Web, we can leverage the power of other websites to implement features that would never be available just through our platform alone. This means that with a little code, we can *mash up* our own recruiting data with an interactive map website, such as Google Maps, and place this functionality in our own app.

To implement a mash-up, we'll first need to understand a little about the technology that makes it possible: Web services. A *Web service* is the mechanism by which two applications that run on different platforms, that were written in different languages, and that are geographically remote from each other, can exchange data using the Internet. Web services makes data exchange between two such applications as straightforward as two processes exchanging data on a single computer.

The way that data is exchanged between two Web services is similar to the way data is exchanged between a Web browser like Microsoft Internet Explorer and a Web server. Just as a Web browser uses a common network protocol (HTTP over TCP/IP) to download HTML files hosted on a Web server, a Web service can also use this same network protocol to download data from another Web service. The key difference is the actual data that is sent and received—Web services use XML instead of HTML.

The online world has a vast array of Web services, many of which are free. For our Candidate Map feature, we'll utilize the Google Maps service, which let you easily embed interactive maps in your apps. If we can find a way to pass candidate addresses from our app to the Google Maps service, Google will take care of all the mapping functionality, saving us from worrying about how our app will render an interactive map. We'll just need to figure out how to pull that rendered map into our app.

> **Note:** The Force.com platform also has its own powerful Web services API, which includes the SOAP API. With the SOAP API, you can customize and integrate your Salesforce organization using the language and platform of your choice. The SOAP API defines a Web service that enables full, reliable access to all of the data in your organization, including the ability to read, create, update, and delete records.
>
> Because the SOAP API is only used behind the scenes for our Candidate Map feature, this book does not go into detail about it; however, you can learn about it in the *SOAP API Developer Guide*, at `www.salesforce.com/us/developer/docs/api/index.htm`.

Introducing Visualforce

So how do we pass our candidate's addresses to the Google Maps service? And after Google Maps service renders an interactive map that plots those addresses, how do we pull that map into our app?

These requirements may seem intimidating, but they're actually quite easy to meet, thanks to Visualforce. Visualforce is a powerful and flexible framework for customizing your app's user interface far beyond what's available using the platform's point-and-click tools. It's the most efficient way to combine data from multiple Force.com objects, blend data from Web services into your apps, or customize the logic that dictates the behavior of your app's user interface. When you use Visualforce, you'll see your productivity increase, and you'll find that you can create just about any type of browser-based user interface you can imagine.

The Visualforce framework consists of a tag-based markup language, similar to HTML. In the Visualforce markup language, each Visualforce tag corresponds to a user interface component. Need a related list? Simply add the `<apex:relatedList>` component tag. Want to display a record's details? Just use the `<apex:detail>` tag.

The following graphic shows a few of the most commonly used Visualforce tags and how they correspond to user interface components. Over 125 tags exist, ranging from large components, such as a detail section of a standard page, to small components, like a single field or link. You can learn about them all in the *Visualforce Developer's Guide*, at `developer.salesforce.com/docs/atlas.en-us.pages.meta/pages/`.

Sample Visualforce Components and Their Corresponding Tags

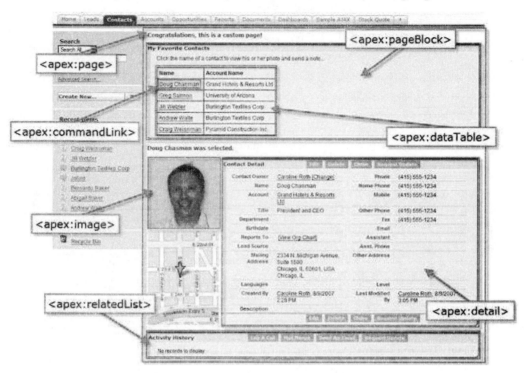

The behavior of Visualforce components can either be controlled by the same logic that is used in standard Salesforce pages, or you can associate your own logic written in Apex. Apex is Salesforce's programming language that runs in the cloud on Force.com servers.

Don't panic! You won't need to learn how to write Apex to create any of the features described in this book. Visualforce comes with a rich component library that allows you to quickly build pages without having to code a lot of functionality yourself. And because Visualforce markup is ultimately rendered into HTML, you can use Visualforce tags alongside standard HTML, JavaScript, Flash, AJAX, or any other code that executes within an HTML page. This means that we can create our Candidate Map by simply creating a Visualforce page that uses some basic Visualforce markup and JavaScript to pass our candidate addresses to the Google Maps service.

 Note: To learn more about Apex, see the *Force.com Apex Code Developer's Guide*, at
developer.salesforce.com/docs/atlas.en-us.apexcode.meta/apexcode/.

Introducing Visualforce Development Mode

Creating Visualforce pages is quick and easy, and there are two ways to do it: from Setup, enter `Visualforce Pages` in the `Quick Find` box, then select **Visualforce Pages**, or enable Visualforce development mode and navigate to a "blank" page.

In this book, we'll use Visualforce development mode to create and edit our Visualforce pages because it has several features that are quite handy. One of those is the special development footer on every Visualforce page. The footer lets you access a page markup editor that includes tools you can use to search for values, jump to a certain line in your code, and undo and redo changes. The page editor also offers highlighting and auto-suggest for component tags and attributes, and has a link to the component reference documentation, which includes descriptions and examples for every Visualforce component.

While you're in Visualforce development mode, you can create a new page just by entering a unique URL in your browser's address bar. And as you add code to your Visualforce page, you'll be able to save it and see your changes instantly rendered in your browser!

Visualforce Development Mode

Try It Out: Enabling Visualforce Development Mode

1. At the top of any Salesforce page, click the down arrow next to your name. From the menu under your name, select **My Settings** or **Setup**—whichever one appears.

2. From the left panel, select one of the following:

- If you clicked **My Settings**, select **Personal** > **Advanced User Details**.
- If you clicked **Setup**, select **My Personal Information** > **Personal Information**.

3. Click **Edit.**

4. Select the `Development Mode` checkbox.

5. Click **Save**.

Implementing the Candidate Map

Now that we've been introduced to Web services and Visualforce, we're ready to implement the mash-up piece for our Recruiting app: the Candidate Map. Our requirements state that we need to generate a map for all the candidates that have applied for a particular position so that we can better understand potential relocation costs associated with a new hire. Since Universal Containers has offices all over the country, this map will also help us assign candidates to an office if a particular position is open in more than one location.

Try It Out: Create a Visualforce Page

Now that we're in development mode, let's create a Visualforce page called CandidateMap by simply modifying the URL in our browser.

Salesforce URLs typically look something like this:
`https://`*`yourDomain`*`.my.salesforce.com/001/o`, where *`yourDomain`* is the name of your Salesforce custom domain. You can create a new Visualforce page by removing everything to the right of the `.my.salesforce.com/` part of the URL and replacing it with `apex/` followed by the name of the page you want to create.

1. In the address bar of your browser, replace everything to the right of `salesforce.com/` with `apex/CandidateMap.`

    > ⚠ Warning: Don't change anything to the left of `salesforce.com/`, as this information is specific to the instance of the Force.com platform that you're using, and changing it will prevent you from creating the Visualforce page.

The resulting URL should look something like this:
`https://`*`yourDomain`*`.my.salesforce.com/apex/CandidateMap.`

2. Press **Enter**.

The following Visualforce error page appears indicating that the page doesn't exist yet. Again, that's okay—this gives us a chance to exercise one of the other handy features of development mode, the *quick fix*. A quick fix is a way of creating something on the fly, right when we need it. In this case, even though

331

the CandidateMap page doesn't exist yet, development mode gives us a quick fix link to create it on the fly. Clicking the link is the equivalent of going to Setup, navigating to the Visualforce page section, clicking **New**, entering the name of the page, and clicking **Save**.

Visualforce Error Page

3. Click the **Create Page CandidateMap** link.

CandidateMap Visualforce Page

Congratulations! You've created your first Visualforce page! Now it's time to add some Visualforce markup so it displays our candidate map.

Try It Out: Write Visualforce Markup

In the footer at the bottom of your new Visualforce page, click **CandidateMap** to display the Visualforce development mode page editor. This editor displays all the markup for the page you're currently viewing—make sure to adjust the width of the bar so that you can see all the content.

Visualforce Development Mode

You'll notice that the page editor has default content.

```
<apex:page >
  <!-- Begin Default Content REMOVE THIS -->
  <h1>Congratulations</h1>
  This is your new Page: CandidateMap
  <!-- End Default Content REMOVE THIS -->
</apex:page>
```

The default content contains the Visualforce component tag `<apex:page>` on the first line and the closing tag, `</apex:page>`, on the last line. Just like elements in other markup languages, Visualforce component tags have a start tag, such as `<apex:page>`, and an end tag that is identical to the start tag except that it has a forward slash, such as `</apex:page>`.

The `<apex:page>` tag represents a single Visualforce page. All of the other content you want displayed on a page must be wrapped inside the start and end `<apex:page>` tags. As discussed earlier, content can be other Visualforce tags, plain text, merge fields, HTML, JavaScript, and so forth. For example, in the default content there are comments marked by the `<!--` and `-->` symbols, the HTML `<h1>` header tag, and plain text.

Let's change the look and feel of the page so it matches the style of the Position object, the object that's most closely tied to our candidate map. We can do this just by setting an attribute on the `<apex:page>`

tag. As with HTML tags, attributes on Visualforce tags configure the style or behavior of what the tag represents.

The attribute we need to set is `standardcontroller`. In Visualforce, controllers determine the style of the page, how the page acts when a user clicks a button, and the data that should be displayed in a page. Simply by setting the value of the `standardcontroller` attribute to the Position object, we're configuring our page to look and behave like the position pages, and display position data.

1. Place your cursor just inside the closing bracket of the `<apex:page>` tag, press the spacebar, and type `standardcontroller="Position__c"`. The result should look like:

    ```
    <apex:page standardcontroller="Position__c">
    ```

    > **Tip:** You can develop your own controllers, but the Force.com platform also includes a standard controller for every object, including custom objects that you create. It's another one of the benefits of Force.com!

Note that the format for setting an attribute is the name of the attribute followed by the equals sign (=), then the value of the attribute enclosed in quotes. Also, remember that the unique API names of custom objects have two underscores (__) and the letter c at the end.

Let's save our work so we can see our changes applied.

2. Click the save icon (💾) on the page editor, or press CTRL+S.

When you save your markup, the Force.com platform checks to make sure it's valid and lets you know if there are errors. If the markup is valid, the new version of your Visualforce page is saved and rendered in your browser.

Can you see how your page is different from before? Setting the `standardcontroller` attribute changed the look and feel of the default Visualforce page so that the Positions tab is selected.

Before and After Setting the `standardcontroller` Attribute

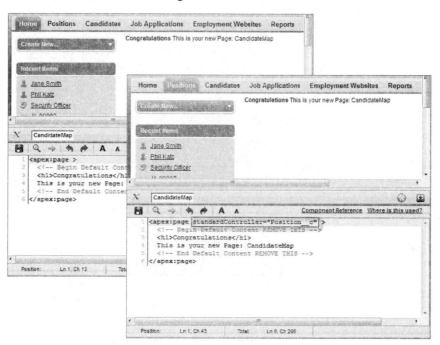

Next, let's remove the default HTML on our Visualforce page and replace it with something relevant to our Candidate Map, such as a brief description of the page just in case the purpose of the map isn't immediately obvious to users.

3. Delete the following markup:

```
<!-- Begin Default Content REMOVE THIS -->
<h1>Congratulations</h1>
This is your new Page: CandidateMap
<!-- End Default Content REMOVE THIS -->
```

4. Enter the following markup between the start and end `<apex:page>` tags.

```
This map shows the locations of candidates who have applied for
the <b>{!Position__c.Name}</b> position.
```

The result should look like:

```
<apex:page standardController="Position__c">
This map shows the locations of candidates who have applied for the
```

```
<b>{!Position__c.Name}</b> position.
</apex:page>
```

The description includes the `{!Position__c.Name}` merge field enclosed in the `<b>` HTML tag. We've used merge fields quite a bit while building our app. They were in our email template and some of our formulas. Now, we're using them once again, this time side by side with HTML and Visualforce component tags.

5. Click the save icon ( ) on the page editor.

Right now, our merge field isn't displaying because the Candidate Map is out of *context*, that is, there's no specific position record from which it can grab the data. Don't worry about that for now—we'll learn how to set context later. For now just trust that the `{!Position__c.Name}` merge field will render the position name, and the `<b>` HTML tag will make it bold.

Our Visualforce page is now ready for us to add our interactive map!

Try It Out: Add the Map to Our Visualforce Page

The interactive map functionality that is essential to our Candidate Map feature can be achieved with a blend of Visualforce markup and JavaScript that accesses the Google Maps service. As promised, you don't have to learn JavaScript to get the Candidate Map working. Instead, we'll use the sample code in the `RecruitingApp-9_0.zip` file you downloaded from Salesforce Developers in Expanding the Simple App Using Relationships on page 97.

1. In the `RecruitingApp-9_0.zip` file, locate the file `CandidateMapSample` and open it in your favorite text editor.

   ⓘ **Important:** Make sure that Word Wrap or any feature that might add line breaks to the code is turned off in your text editor. You must preserve the original line breaks in the code sample. New line breaks caused by word wrapping features in text editors can break the code and prevent the code sample from working correctly.

   Also, be aware that copying code from Adobe PDF files can also cause code to break, so avoid copying code from PDF versions of this book.

2. Select the entire content of the file, and copy and paste it into the page editor at the bottom of your CandidateMap Visualforce page. The `CandidateMapSample` file contains the Visualforce markup you added in the steps above, so just replace everything in the page editor with the entire sample in the file.

3. Click the save icon ( ) on the page editor.

The interactive map should appear on your CandidateMap Visualforce page, but with an error message and without plots. This is because the Candidate Map is still out of context and the page can't figure out which candidates to show. We can fix this by simply adding the CandidateMap Visualforce page to our position page layouts.

Try It Out: Add the Candidate Map to Position Page Layouts

Adding Visualforce pages to page layouts is as simple as adding fields or sections to page layouts. And once we add the CandidateMap Visualforce page to our position page layouts, the map will automatically plot the locations of the candidates who apply to each position. It'll work like magic!

We have two page layouts for the Position object and we'll want the map to appear on both. Let's start by adding the page to the original position page layout (Position Layout).

If you have any standard position records that use the Position Layout, navigate to one of those positions and click the **Edit Page Layout** link in the upper right corner of the record. If you don't have any standard position records:

1. From Setup, enter `Objects` in the `Quick Find` box, then select **Objects**.
2. Click **Position**.
3. In the Page Layouts related list, click **Edit** next to Position Layout.

The Position Layout is ready to edit. Let's create a section on the page layout for the CandidateMap Visualforce page.

4. In the palette, select the Fields category.
5. Drag the Section user interface element from the palette to just below the Description section on the page layout. The Layout Properties popup window appears.
6. In the `Section Name` text box, enter `Candidate Map`.
7. In the Display Section On Header area, select both the `Detail Page` and `Edit Page` checkboxes.
8. In the `Layout` drop-down list, choose `1-Column`.
9. Click **Ok**.

Now let's move the CandidateMap Visualforce page into our new section.

10. Select the Visualforce Pages category on the palette.

Notice that the palette lists our CandidateMap Visualforce page as a user interface element.

11. Drag the CandidateMap user interface element from the palette to the Candidate Map section on the page layout.

The Candidate Map JavaScript generates a map that is 400 pixels high and spans the width of the screen. This is just large enough to be useful without consuming too much room on the screen. The default properties of the Visualforce page user interface element need to be adjusted to accommodate the map. Otherwise, there might be odd spacing around the map and distracting scrollbars.

Let's fix the Visualforce page user interface element properties to accommodate the size of the generated map, as well as the text we added to the top of the CandidateMap Visualforce page. (In case you don't remember, the text is "This map shows the locations of candidates who have applied for the {!Position__c.Name} position.")

12. Double-click the CandidateMap element to access its properties.

13. Set the width to `100%`.

14. Set the height to `405`.

The height is always in pixels, while the width can be specified either in pixels or as a percentage. Setting the height to 405 pixels allows 400 pixels for the map and five more pixels for the text. Perfect!

15. Leave the `Show scrollbars` and `Show label` checkboxes deselected.

16. Click **OK** to exit the user element properties.

17. Click **Save** on the page layout.

Repeat all of the above steps for your other Position object page layout, the IT Position Layout.

Try It Out: Enable the Candidate Map for Mobile

One last thing before we test out the map. Let's make sure the map will show up for our users, whether they're accessing a position record from the full site or from a mobile device. On the detail page for each Visualforce page, there's a checkbox that enables it for Salesforce mobile apps.

1. From Setup, enter `Visualforce Pages` in the `Quick Find` box, then select **Visualforce Pages**.

2. Click **CandidateMap**. You can click the link under either the Label or Name columns. Both will go to the associated detail page.

3. Click **Edit**.

4. Select `Available for Salesforce mobile apps`, and click **Save**.

Once you finish, it's time to test the Candidate Map!

Try It Out: Test the Candidate Map

Navigate to any position record with one or more candidate applications. (If you haven't created any job applications in your app, now would be a good time.) After you bring up a position record, scroll down to see the Candidate Map in action!

Our Working Candidate Map

Responsibilities	Design, create, update, and deliver documentation for UCI's applications
Skills Required	* At least 5+ years writing technical documentation for a software development company * Exceptional technical writing and editing skills * Proven ability to write documentation for both non-technical business users and administrators * Ability to consistently meet deadlines and deliver high-quality materials * Proven track record of innovation for making online documentation more usable and useful for customers * Strong experience using XML tools to write single-source documentation for both online help and PDF distributio * Ability to learn quickly and adjust priorities in a dynamic environment with short release cycles * Demonstrated ability to adhere to existing styles and processes, and contribute towards improving them as necessary * Strong team player and able to work with documentation management to establish goals and priorities * Bachelor's degree
Educational Requirements	- Bachelor's Degree

▼ Candidate Map

This map shows the locations of candidates who have applied for the Documentation Writer position.

Launch Salesforce1 to see how the Candidate Map looks mobile. When you bring up a position record, swipe to the record detail view and scroll down to see the map. We can't interact with the map on the record details page. To do so, tap the map to open it in another page. Everything looks in order!

Notice how the Candidate Map Visualforce page is embedded within our Recruiting app just like the other functionality we built using the platform's declarative, point-and-click tools. Also notice that the map automatically displays only candidates who applied to this position.

With very little programming and a few clicks, we've mashed up the Google Maps service with Force.com and made the result look as if it were made expressly for our Recruiting app. Couple SOAP API with the thousands of Web services that are available on the Internet today, and the possibilities are limited only by our imaginations!

Implementing the Mass Update Status Button

The Candidate Map feature we just added is both useful and flashy. It'll help recruiters do their jobs more efficiently while adding an eye-catching graphic to an otherwise plain collection of data. The next feature we're going to implement is not as aesthetically appealing, but is much more useful and likely to save your users an incredible amount of time.

Picture yourself as a recruiter at Universal Containers. You're working on filling a highly-coveted position that's garnered hundreds of job applications and you've finally zeroed in on the three top candidates. However, before you can go further you need to reject the job applications submitted by all of the other candidates for the position—a task that could take hours if you have to open every one of those job application records and set the `Status` to rejected. What can you do?

Fortunately, creating tools that perform mass actions on data is yet another of the innumerable ways you can build upon the platform's functionality. With a few lines of Visualforce and the platform's point-and-click tools, we can enhance the Recruiting app in a way that will dramatically increase our users' productivity. When we're done, the daunting task of updating the `Status` field on multiple job applications will be reduced from hours of tedium to a few seconds of easy mouse clicking.

Planning the Mass Update Status Feature

The objective is simple: create a way to update the `Status` field on multiple job applications in a single operation. We just need to work out a few logistics to make sure the implementation goes smoothly. For example, where in our app will users go to access the Mass Update Status functionality? And how will they perform the actual update?

When designing a new feature, it's important to consider the context in which users will access it. Since the purpose of the Mass Update Status feature is to update the `Status` field on multiple job applications for a single position, it's most likely that users will want to perform this operation while viewing a position record. Therefore, it makes the most sense to provide access to the Mass Update Status feature from position records.

So where exactly on a position record should we provide access to the feature? Well, back in Expanding the Simple App Using Relationships on page 97, we added a Job Applications related list to our position records that made it easy for users to quickly identify all of the job applications submitted for a position. We could leverage that list by adding a checkbox next to each job application so that users can select the group of job applications they want to update. Then we could add an **Update Status** custom list button that lets users update the `Status` fields on all of the selected job applications in one fell swoop.

Once we're done, the feature will work something like this.

1. Open a position record and scroll down to the Job Applications related list.

2. In the Job Applications related list, select the checkboxes next to the job applications you want to update.

Job Applications Related List

	Action	Job Application Number	Candidate	Status	Created Date	Owner First Name	Owner Last Name
☐	Edit | Del JA-00002		C-00008	Rejected	2/4/2010	Cynthia	Capobianca
☐	Edit | Del JA-00008		C-00003	New	6/10/2010	Cynthia	Capobianca
☐	Edit | Del JA-00009		C-00008	Schedule Interviews	6/10/2010	Cynthia	Capobianca

Job Applications — New Job Application — Update Status — Job Applications Help (?)

3. Click the **Update Status** button.

The Mass Update Status page appears.

Mass Update Status Page

Mass Update the Status of Job Applications

Save   Cancel

Change

Status   --None--

Selected Applications

Job Application Number	Position Title	Candidate Name	Status
JA-00008	Documentation Writer	Chris McGuire	New
JA-00009	Documentation Writer	George Schnell	Schedule Interviews
JA-00002	Documentation Writer	George Schnell	Rejected

Save   Cancel

4. Choose a value for the Status field.

5. Click **Save**.

It may sound like this will take an astounding effort to implement, but it's really quite simple. All you need to do is create the Mass Update Status page with some basic Visualforce markup, and add a custom list button to the Job Applications related list on position records. You'll be done before you know it!

Try It Out: Create the Mass Update Status Page

We'll begin implementing the Mass Update Status feature by creating the Visualforce page that lets users choose the value with which the `Status` field is updated. To make this page even more usable, we'll include a table that shows the `Job Application Number`, `Position Title`, `Candidate Name`, and `Status` of each selected job application.

1. In the address bar of your browser, replace everything to the right of `salesforce.com/` with `apex/MassUpdateStatus`.

The resulting URL should look something like this:
`https://`*yourDomain*`.my.salesforce.com/apex/MassUpdateStatus`, where *yourDomain* is the name of your Salesforce custom domain. Remember to modify only the part of the URL after `.my.salesforce.com/`.

2. Press **Enter**.

3. Click the **Create Page MassUpdateStatus** link.

We now have a new Visualforce page called MassUpdateStatus. Next, we'll add the Visualforce markup that implements the Mass Update Status functionality.

To enter our markup, we'll use the Visualforce development mode page editor just as we did before. But this time around, we won't need any JavaScript; Visualforce will be able to do it all!

4. In the footer at the bottom of the MassUpdateStatus Visualforce page, click **MassUpdateStatus** to display the Visualforce development mode page editor. Adjust the width of the editor to display all of the content.

5. Delete all of the default markup in the Visualforce development mode page editor and replace it with the following markup. Remember that instead of typing, it's easiest to copy and paste the code from the `MassUpdateStatusSample` file located in the `RecruitingApp-9_0.zip` file you downloaded from `https://developer.salesforce.com/page/Force_Platform_Fundamentals`.

```
<apex:page standardController="Job_Application__c"
    recordSetVar="applications">
  <apex:sectionHeader title="Mass Update the Status
      of Job Applications"/>
  <apex:form>
    <apex:pageBlock>
      <apex:pageMessages />
      <apex:pageBlockButtons>
        <apex:commandButton value="Save"
            action="{!save}"/>
        <apex:commandButton value="Cancel"
```

```
          action="{!cancel}"/>
      </apex:pageBlockButtons>
      <apex:pageBlockSection title="Status Update"
          collapsible="false">
        <apex:inputField value=
            "{!Job_Application__c.Status__c}"/>
      </apex:pageBlockSection>
      <apex:pageBlockSection title="Selected Job
          Applications" columns="1">
        <apex:pageBlockTable value="{!selected}"
            var="application">
          <apex:column value="{!application.name}"/>
          <apex:column value=
              "{!application.position__r.name}"/>
          <apex:column headerValue="Candidate Name">
            <apex:outputText value=
                "{!application.candidate__r.
                First_Name__c & ' ' & application.
                candidate__r.Last_Name__c}"/>
          </apex:column>
          <apex:column value=
              "{!application.Status__c}"/>
        </apex:pageBlockTable>
      </apex:pageBlockSection>
    </apex:pageBlock>
  </apex:form>
</apex:page>
```

> **Tip:** In this sample code, notice that some components don't have close tags. If there are no other components nested within a component, you can "close" the tag by putting a forward slash at the end of the start tag, like: `<apex:sectionHeader/>`.

6. Click .

Understanding the MassUpdateStatus Visualforce Markup

Let's take a moment to discuss the main Visualforce tags we just added to our MassUpdateStatus page. Although we won't go into all of the use cases for each component or discuss every attribute in depth, you'll get a better understanding of how Visualforce works.

Tip: To see general descriptions and examples for all of the Visualforce components and their attributes, click the **Component Reference** link in the upper right corner of the Visualforce development mode page editor.

`<apex:page>`

As with all Visualforce pages, the MassUpdateStatus page must begin with an `<apex:page>` component. Notice the tag has the same `standardController` attribute used in our interactive Candidate Map feature, although this time it is set to the Job Application object (`Job_Application__c`). This makes sense because the Mass Update Status feature updates a field on job application records, not position records.

The component also has a `recordSetVar` attribute. We use this attribute to change the `standardcontroller` so that it accommodates a set of records rather than a single record.

`<apex:sectionHeader>`

The `<apex:sectionHeader>` component adds a header to the top of the page. The component's `title` attribute determines the text in the header.

`<apex:form>`

The `<apex:form>` component establishes a section on the page in which users can enter data and submit it by clicking a button or link. It's like an invisible container, similar to a `<form>` element in HTML.

`<apex:pageBlock>`

The `<apex:pageBlock>` component designates an outlined area on the page similar to the areas on detail pages that contain sections.

`<apex:pageMessages>`

The `<apex:pageMessages>` component allocates space for standard system messages (such as those that notify users when a file is being saved) and validation rule errors. These messages already exist in the Force.com platform, so you don't have to create them—you just have to use this component to make room for them in case the platform needs to display them.

`<apex:pageBlockButtons>`

The `<apex:pageBlockButtons>` component allocates space for a set of buttons on the page. Its subcomponents specify what the buttons do and how they are labeled.

`<apex:commandButton>`

Each `<apex:commandButton>` component creates an individual button inside the `<apex:pageBlockButtons>` component. The Mass Update Status page uses two `<apex:commandButton>` components: one to create a **Save** button and a second to create a **Cancel** button. The buttons are styled like standard Salesforce buttons.

The `value` attribute on the `<apex:commandButton>` component determines the words that appear on the button (such as "Save" or "Cancel"), while the `action` attribute determines the operation that occurs when the button is clicked. When setting the `action` attribute, you must use merge field syntax. For example, to configure the button to save the data entered on the page, set the `action` attribute to `{!save}`.

Each button appears twice on our MassUpdateStatus page—once at the top of the area allocated by the `<apex:pageBlock>` component and once at the bottom. This is a precautionary measure built into the `<apex:pageBlockButtons>` component to ensure that the button functionality is apparent to users, even if the page block is large.

`<apex:pageBlockSection>`

The `<apex:pageBlockSection>` component can be used within `<apex:pageBlock>` components to create a section on a page similar to the sections found on page layouts. On this page, the `<apex:pageBlockSection>` component is used twice.

The first instance of the `<apex:pageBlockSection>` component has a `title` attribute that's set to "Status Update." This text will appear at the top of the section. It also has a `collapsible` attribute that determines whether users can collapse and expand the section by clicking an arrow to the left of the title. We don't want users to accidentally collapse this page block section, so the attribute is set to "false."

The second `<apex:pageBlockSection>` component creates a section that has a table showing the job applications selected for updating. Its `title` attribute is set to "Selected Job Applications." Also, its `columns` attribute is set to "1."

 Tip: Unlike page layouts, a section on a Visualforce page can have more than two columns. However, the platform's stylesheets are optimized to accommodate one or two columns, so it's best not to exceed that limit.

`<apex:inputField>`

The `<apex:inputField>` component renders the `Status` field from the Job Application object on our page. Use `<apex:inputField>` components to create HTML input elements for any Salesforce field. All you need to do is set the component's `value` attribute to the API name of the Salesforce object and field.

`<apex:pageBlockTable>`

The `<apex:pageBlockTable>` component renders a table containing field values from multiple records of a specific object. For our feature, we need to set two of this component's attributes: `value` and `var`.

The `value` attribute tells the table which set of records contains the values to display. In this instance, we set the attribute to the expression `{!selected}` to enable the table to display values from the selected job applications.

The second attribute, `var`, creates a name that components within the table can use to reference individual records in the record set without actually referring to each record by name.

`<apex:column>`

The `<apex:column>` components inside the `<apex:pageBlockTable>` determine the columns of the table and the job application fields each column displays. For three of the four `<apex:column>` components, we just need to set the `value` attribute to an expression that references the field using the value of the `<apex:pageBlockTable>` component's `var` attribute followed by the API name of the field. For example, the following expression displays the values of the `Job Application Number` field:

```
{!application.name}
```

For the `Candidate Name` field, though, we need to do a bit more because the field is actually a combination of the `First Name` and `Last Name` fields from the Candidate object. To combine these fields, we use an `<apex:outputText>` component inside an `<apex:column>` component and set its `value` attribute to an expression that combines the `First Name` and `Last Name` fields from the Candidate object.

```
<apex:column headerValue="Candidate Name">
  <apex:outputText value="{!application.
      candidate__r.First_Name__c & ' ' &
      application.candidate__r.Last_Name__c}"/>
</apex:column>
```

When you generate column fields in this manner, the `value` attribute on the `<apex:column>` component is not set, so the table doesn't know what to use as the column header. Rectify this by setting the `headerValue` attribute on this `<apex:column>` component.

⁞⁞ Beyond the Basics

Did you know you can add a Chatter feed to a Visualforce page?

Say you want to add the Chatter feed for a position to its detail page. You can simply use the `<chatter:feed>` standard component:

```
<apex:page standardController="Position__c">
  <chatter:feed entityId="{$!Position__c.id}">
  <apex:detail />
</apex:page>
```

To find out more, see the Visualforce Developer's Guide.

Try It Out: Create a Custom List Button

Now that our Mass Update Status Visualforce page is complete, we're ready to create the button that users will click to access it.

The platform gives us the option of creating two types of buttons.

Detail Page Buttons
Buttons that appear on detail pages in the Button Section of the page layout.

List Buttons
Buttons that appear in list views, search result layouts, or related lists.

We need a button that users can click in the Job Applications related list on position records, so let's create a list button.

1. From Setup, enter *Objects* in the Quick Find box, then select **Objects**.

2. Click **Job Application**.

You might be wondering why we chose the **Job Application** object instead of the **Position** object, given that the button will appear on position records. The reason is that you create list buttons on the object that is being listed.

3. In the Buttons, Links, and Actions related list, click **New Button or Link**.

Custom Button Edit Page

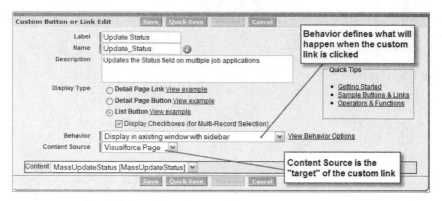

The custom button edit page should look familiar, since it closely resembles the formula editor that we saw previously.

4. In the `Label` text box, enter *Update Status*.

5. In the `Name` text box, accept the default value of *Update_Status*.

6. In the `Description` text box, enter *Updates the Status field on multiple job applications*.

We now have the option to specify whether we are creating a detail page link, detail page button, or list button. We've already decided to create a list button, but keep these other options in mind for future apps.

7. Select *List Button* as the `Display Type`.

When we selected the *List Button* option, did you notice the `Display Checkboxes (for Multi-Record Selection)` checkbox that appeared beneath it? By leaving this option selected, the platform knows to put checkboxes next to the records in the related list.

8. Leave the `Display Checkboxes (for Multi-Record Selection)` checkbox selected.

Next, the `Behavior` picklist lets you choose what happens when a user clicks the button. We know we want the button to open the Mass Update Status page, but we can specify whether the page opens in a new window or in the existing window, and whether or not it is has a sidebar and header. You can even configure the button to execute some JavaScript if necessary. For our app, it makes the most sense to configure the button to open the Mass Update Page in the existing window, and to leave the sidebar and header there as well.

9. In the `Behavior` picklist, select *Display in existing window with sidebar*.

Now we need to specify the content we want to display. To do this, we'll first need to indicate the type of content we want to display in the `Content Source` picklist.

10. In the `Content Source` picklist, select *Visualforce Page*.

When you select the *Visualforce Page* option, the bottom section of the custom list button edit page displays a `Content` picklist. The picklist contains the Visualforce pages in your organization that have a standard controller set to the object for which you are creating the button.

11. In the `Content` drop-down list, select *MassUpdateStatus[MassUpdateStatus]*.

12. Click **Save**.

13. Click **OK**.

After clicking **OK**, you are reminded that no users will be able to access the button until it is added to a page layout. This is because creating a custom button is similar to adding a custom field to an object—even if it's defined in the database, nobody will be able to see it until you explicitly add it to a page layout.

Try It Out: Add a Custom List Button to a Page Layout

Let's finish up our Mass Update Status feature by adding the Update Status list button to our Position page layouts.

1. From Setup, enter *Objects* in the `Quick Find` box, then select **Objects**.

2. Click **Position**.

3. In the Page Layouts related list, click **Edit** next to the page layout you want to edit first.

4. Click the wrench icon (🔧) in the Job Application related list to edit its properties.

5. In the Related List Properties window, click the **Buttons** bar at the bottom to expand the Buttons section.

Custom Button Edit Page

Here we can specify the standard and custom buttons that the related list displays. The Update Status button we just created should appear in the Available Buttons list.

6. Select the Update Status button and click **Add** to move it to the Selected Buttons list.

7. Click **OK** to exit the Related List properties window.

8. Click **Save**.

Repeat the above procedure for the other Position page layout.

> Note: We're not going to enable this Visualforce page for Salesforce mobile apps. Since Salesforce1's related lists don't display buttons, our users won't be able to access the Mass Update Status page from a mobile device.

Once that's done, the Mass Update Status feature is ready to test!

Try It Out: Test the Mass Update Status Feature

To test the Mass Update Status feature, navigate to a position record to which multiple candidates have applied, and scroll down to the Job Applications related list. Notice that the **Update Status** button is there, and checkboxes appear next to the job application numbers, just as we planned.

Now select a few job applications and click the **Update Status** button. Our Mass Update Status Visualforce page appears. Notice that the lower half of the page lists the job applications we selected on the previous page.

Mass Update Status Page Displaying Selected Applications

In the **Status** picklist, choose the new status for the selected records, and click **Save**. Salesforce updates all of the selected records with the new value.

The feature Is a success!

CHAPTER 12 Learning More

In this chapter ...

- Salesforce Developers
- Salesforce Trailhead
- Help and Training Options
- Multimedia
- AppExchange Partner Program
- What Do You Think?

This book has introduced some of the native technologies associated with the Force.com platform. We've created a fully functional Recruiting app, and we've introduced Visualforce and the SOAP API to show you how it can be used to build composite apps. But there's only so much we can cover in a single book—we skipped over many other powerful tools and options, and didn't talk about how you can share your own apps with others on the AppExchange. Indeed, we'd be surprised if you didn't have more questions about how you can take advantage of all that the platform has to offer!

Fortunately there are a number of ways you can learn more about the platform.

Salesforce Developers

Salesforce Developers is Salesforce's free developer program for the Force.com platform. The Salesforce Developers website at `developer.salesforce.com` is a developer community where you can learn, access key resources, and discuss a diverse set of topics related to Force.com, Database.com, Heroku, and other related Salesforce platforms with other developers in the community. Application development topics include Apex, Visualforce, integration APIs, database topics, packaging and distribution of your applications, and many more.

There are many ways to use and contribute to Salesforce Developers, including:

* Read and contribute technical articles that explain development topics.
* Download and contribute sample code.
* Read our blogs, subscribe to our RSS feeds, or become a blogger yourself.
* Read and contribute to the Salesforce Developers Discussion Boards.
* Read the monthly Force.com Developer News email newsletter.
* Register for an event in our event calendar or watch and listen to archived multimedia events.
* Participate in special programs such as developer previews to get a first hand look at what's coming.
* Watch technical webinars that help you get up to speed with new features.

Salesforce Trailhead

Trailhead is the easiest—and most fun—way to learn Salesforce. With more than 30 trails made up of more than 100 modules, Trailhead allows you to learn the Force.com platform and other aspects of Salesforce at your own pace. Trailhead uses interactive challenges that you complete in your own Developer Edition org to test your skills at the end of each unit. When you complete modules, you earn badges that you can display proudly on your Salesforce Developers profile.

To learn more about the Force.com platform, complete the Admin Beginner trail at https://trailhead.salesforce.com/trail/force_com_admin_beginner. Once you've mastered the Admin Beginner trail, try your hand at the Admin Intermediate and Admin Advanced trails at https://trailhead.salesforce.com/trail/force_com_admin_intermediate and https://trailhead.salesforce.com/trail/force_com_admin_advanced, respectively.

Help and Training Options

In addition to the Salesforce Developers website, the platform itself offers lots of help and training options:

- **Find answers to your questions.** Click **Help** at the top of any page in the application. Enter your keywords in the Search box and press Enter. The search returns online help topics, knowledge base solutions, and recommended training classes that match the keywords you entered.

- **Take online training.** Select the Training tab of the Help & Training window, choose your role and geographic location, and click **View Classes!** to find free online training classes. More than fifteen online training classes are available to you on-demand, 24/7!

- **Attend a class.** A number of examples in this book have been provided by Salesforce Training & Certification and are drawn from the expert-led training courses available around the world. Salesforce training courses provide an opportunity to get hands-on experience with the Force.com platform and Salesforce applications, and prepare you to become Salesforce Certified. To learn more or register for a class, visit `www.salesforce.com/training`.

- **Download tip sheets and best practice guides.** Select the Help tab of the Help & Training window and click **Tips** in the task bar to view and download tip sheets, implementation guides, and best practices for specific features.

Multimedia

Thanks to the hard work of our colleagues on the Salesforce.com Community and Force.com websites, we have an impressive number of podcasts and videos available. Our podcasts and videos keep the Force.com platform community connected by providing free access to a wide range of best practices, case studies, and product- and platform-focused digital audio content.

Find podcasts on our iTunes channel by searching for "salesforce" in the iTunes Music Store. To find our videos, go to the `https://developer.salesforce.com/content/type/Tech+Talk/` on the Salesforce Developers website.

Access to expert Force.com platform and CRM-related luminary interviews, thought-leadership presentations, roundtable discussions, and best practices are just a click away. Happy listening and watching!

AppExchange Partner Program

With the emergence of The Business Web™, companies can offer their services and applications to businesses over the Internet as easily as retailers and auctioneers can connect with online consumers. As AppExchange partners, more than 150 companies are already participating in this new chapter of computing by making their offerings available on The Business Web via the AppExchange. The AppExchange partner program makes it easy for both new and established businesses to join this growing community of cloud computing providers. Visit the Partner Program website at `www.salesforce.com/partners/` and join the Force.com AppExchange partner program today!

What Do You Think?

Well that about sums it up. Did you like what you've read? Has it inspired you to create your own on-demand apps and enter the world of cloud computing? We certainly hope so! We welcome any comments you might have—indeed, we count on your feedback and ideas. Go to the Salesforce Developers discussion boards at `community.salesforce.com/sforce?category.id=developers` or email us at `developerforce@salesforce.com` and let us know what you think!

GLOSSARY

A | B | C | D | E | F | G | H | I | J | K | L | M | N | P | O | Q | R | S | T | U | V | W | X | Y | Z

A

Activity

An event, a task, a call you've logged, or an email you've sent. You can relate an activity to other records, such as an account, a lead, an opportunity, or a case. In an org with Shared Activities enabled, you can relate an activity to multiple contacts. Tasks can also be generated by workflow rules and approval processes configured by a Salesforce admin.

Administrator (System Administrator)

One or more individuals in your organization who can configure and customize the application. Users assigned to the System Administrator profile have administrator privileges.

Advanced Function

A formula function designed for use in custom buttons, links, and s-controls. For example, the INCLUDE advanced function returns the content from an s-control snippet.

Reporting Snapshot

A reporting snapshot lets you report on historical data. Authorized users can save tabular or summary report results to fields on a custom object, then map those fields to corresponding fields on a target object. They can then schedule when to run the report to load the custom object's fields with the report's data.

Reporting Snapshot Running User

The user whose security settings determine the source report's level of access to data. This bypasses all security settings, giving all users who can view the results of the source report in the target object access to data they might not be able to see otherwise.

Reporting Snapshot Source Report

The custom report scheduled to run and load data as records into a custom object.

Reporting Snapshot Target Object

The custom object that receives the results of the source report as records.

Apex

Apex is a strongly typed, object-oriented programming language that allows developers to execute flow and transaction control statements on the Force.com platform server in conjunction with calls to the Force.com API. Using syntax that looks like Java and acts like database stored procedures, Apex enables developers to add business logic to most system events, including button clicks, related record updates, and Visualforce pages. Apex code can be initiated by Web service requests and from triggers on objects.

Apex Controller

See Controller, Visualforce.

Apex Page

See Visualforce Page.

App

Short for "application." A collection of components such as tabs, reports, dashboards, and Visualforce pages that address a specific business need. Salesforce provides standard apps such as Sales and Call Center. You can customize the standard apps to match the way you work. In addition, you can package an app and upload it to the AppExchange along with related components such as custom fields, custom tabs, and custom objects. Then, you can make the app available to other Salesforce users from the AppExchange.

App Menu

See Force.com App Menu.

AppExchange

The AppExchange is a sharing interface from Salesforce that allows you to browse and share apps and services for the Force.com platform.

Application Programming Interface (API)

The interface that a computer system, library, or application provides to allow other computer programs to request services from it and exchange data.

Approval Action

See Automated Actions.

Approval Process

An approval process automates how records are approved in Salesforce. An approval process specifies each step of approval, including who to request approval from and what to do at each point of the process.

Auto Number

A custom field type that automatically adds a unique sequential number to each record. These fields are read only.

B

Boolean Operators

You can use Boolean operators in report filters to specify the logical relationship between two values. For example, the AND operator between two values yields search results that include both values. Likewise, the OR operator between two values yields search results that include either value.

C

Class, Apex

A template or blueprint from which Apex objects are created. Classes consist of other classes, user-defined methods, variables, exception types, and static initialization code. In most cases, Apex classes are modeled on their counterparts in Java.

Clone

Clone is the name of a button or link that allows you to create a new item by copying the information from an existing item, for example, a contact or opportunity.

Cloud Computing

A model for software development and distribution based on the Internet. The technology infrastructure for a service, including data, is hosted on the Internet. This allows consumers to develop and use services with browsers or other thin clients instead of investing in hardware, software, or maintenance.

Combination Chart

A combination chart plots multiple sets of data on a single chart. Each set of data is based on a different field, so values are easy to compare. You can also combine certain chart types to present data in different ways on a single chart.

Component, Visualforce

Something that can be added to a Visualforce page with a set of tags, for example, `<apex:detail>`. Visualforce includes a number of standard components, or you can create your own custom components.

Component Reference, Visualforce

A description of the standard and custom Visualforce components that are available in your organization. You can access the component library from the development footer of any Visualforce page or the *Visualforce Developer's Guide*.

Controller, Visualforce

An Apex class that provides a Visualforce page with the data and business logic it needs to run. Visualforce pages can use the standard controllers that come by default with every standard or custom object, or they can use custom controllers.

Controller Extension

A controller extension is an Apex class that extends the functionality of a standard or custom controller.

Controlling Field

Any standard or custom picklist or checkbox field whose values control the available values in one or more corresponding dependent fields.

Custom App

See App.

Custom Controller

A custom controller is an Apex class that implements all of the logic for a page without leveraging a standard controller. Use custom controllers when you want your Visualforce page to run entirely in system mode, which does not enforce the permissions and field-level security of the current user.

Custom Field

A field that can be added in addition to the standard fields to customize Salesforce for your organization's needs.

Custom Help

Custom text administrators create to provide users with on-screen information specific to a standard field, custom field, or custom object.

Custom Links

Custom links are URLs defined by administrators to integrate your Salesforce data with external websites and back-office systems. Formerly known as Web links.

Custom Object

Custom records that allow you to store information unique to your organization.

Custom Report Type

See Report Type.

Custom Settings

Custom settings are similar to custom objects and enable application developers to create custom sets of data, as well as create and associate custom data for an organization, profile, or specific user. All custom settings data is exposed in the application cache, which enables efficient access without the cost of repeated queries to the database. This data can then be used by formula fields, validation rules, flows, Apex, and the SOAP API.

See also Hierarchy Custom Settings and List Custom Settings.

Custom View

A display feature that lets you see a specific set of records for a particular object.

D

Dashboard

A *dashboard* shows data from source reports as visual components, which can be charts, gauges, tables, metrics, or Visualforce pages. The components provide a snapshot of key metrics and performance indicators for your organization. Each dashboard can have up to 20 components.

Database

An organized collection of information. The underlying architecture of the Force.com platform includes a database where your data is stored.

Database Table

A list of information, presented with rows and columns, about the person, thing, or concept you want to track. See also Object.

Data Loader

A Force.com platform tool used to import and export data from your Salesforce organization.

Decimal Places

Parameter for number, currency, and percent custom fields that indicates the total number of digits you can enter to the right of a decimal point, for example, 4.98 for an entry of 2. Note that the system rounds the decimal numbers you enter, if necessary. For example, if you enter 4.986 in a field with `Decimal Places` of 2, the number rounds to 4.99. Salesforce uses the round half-up rounding algorithm. Half-way values are always rounded up. For example, 1.45 is rounded to 1.5. −1.45 is rounded to −1.5.

Delegated Administration

A security model in which a group of non-administrator users perform administrative tasks.

Delegated Authentication

A security process where an external authority is used to authenticate Force.com platform users.

Dependency

A relationship where one object's existence depends on that of another. There are a number of different kinds of dependencies including mandatory fields, dependent objects (parent-child), file inclusion (referenced images, for example), and ordering dependencies (when one object must be deployed before another object).

Dependent Field

Any custom picklist or multi-select picklist field that displays available values based on the value selected in its corresponding controlling field.

Detail

A page that displays information about a single object record. The detail page of a record allows you to view the information, whereas the edit page allows you to modify it.

A term used in reports to distinguish between summary information and inclusion of all column data for all information in a report. You can toggle the **Show Details/Hide Details** button to view and hide report detail information.

Developer Edition

A free, fully-functional Salesforce organization designed for developers to extend, integrate, and develop with the Force.com platform. Developer Edition accounts are available on developer.salesforce.com.

Development Environment

A Salesforce organization where you can make configuration changes that will not affect users on the production organization. There are two kinds of development environments, sandboxes and Developer Edition organizations.

Salesforce Developers

The Salesforce Developers website at developer.salesforce.com provides a full range of resources for platform developers, including sample code, toolkits, an online developer community, and the ability to obtain limited Force.com platform environments.

Document Library

A place to store documents without attaching them to accounts, contacts, opportunities, or other records.

E

Email Alert

Email alerts are actions that send emails, using a specified email template, to specified recipients.

Email Template

A form email that communicates a standard message, such as a welcome letter to new employees or an acknowledgement that a customer service request has been received. Email templates can be personalized with merge fields, and can be written in text, HTML, or custom format.

Enterprise Application

An application that is designed to support functionality for an organization as a whole, rather than solving a specific problem.

Enterprise Edition

A Salesforce edition designed for larger, more complex businesses.

Entity Relationship Diagram (ERD)

A data modeling tool that helps you organize your data into entities (or objects, as they are called in the Force.com platform) and define the relationships between them. ERD diagrams for key Salesforce objects are published in the *SOAP API Developer's Guide*.

Event

An event is an activity that has a scheduled time. For example, a meeting, or a scheduled phone call.

F

Field

A part of an object that holds a specific piece of information, such as a text or currency value.

Field-Level Security

Settings that determine whether fields are hidden, visible, read only, or editable for users. Available in Professional, Enterprise, Unlimited, Performance, and Developer Editions.

Field Dependency

A filter that allows you to change the contents of a picklist based on the value of another field.

Field Update

A field update is an action that automatically updates a field with a new value.

Filter Condition/Criteria

Condition on particular fields that qualifies items to be included in a list view or report, such as "State equals California."

Folder

A *folder* is a place where you can store reports, dashboards, documents, or email templates. Folders can be public, hidden, or shared, and can be set to read-only or read/write. You control who has access to its contents based on roles, permissions, public groups, and license types. You can make a folder available to your entire organization, or make it private so that only the owner has access.

Force.com

The Salesforce platform for building applications in the cloud. Force.com combines a powerful user interface, operating system, and database to allow you to customize and deploy applications in the cloud for your entire enterprise.

Force.com App Menu

A menu that enables users to switch between customizable applications (or "apps") with a single click. The Force.com app menu displays at the top of every page in the user interface.

Force.com IDE

An Eclipse plug-in that allows developers to manage, author, debug and deploy Force.com applications in the Eclipse development environment.

Web Services API

A Web services application programming interface that provides access to your Salesforce organization's information. See also SOAP API and Bulk API.

Foreign Key

A field whose value is the same as the primary key of another table. You can think of a foreign key as a copy of a primary key from another table. A relationship is made between two tables by matching the values of the foreign key in one table with the values of the primary key in another.

Formula Field

A type of custom field. Formula fields automatically calculate their values based on the values of merge fields, expressions, or other values.

Function

Built-in formulas that you can customize with input parameters. For example, the DATE function creates a date field type from a given year, month, and day.

G

Global Variable

A special merge field that you can use to reference data in your organization.

A method access modifier for any method that needs to be referenced outside of the application, either in the SOAP API or by other Apex code.

Group

A groups is a set of users. Groups can contain individual users, other groups, or the users in a role. Groups can be used to help define sharing access to data or to specify which data to synchronize in Salesforce for Outlook configurations or Lightning Sync configurations.

Users can define their own personal groups. Administrators can create public groups for use by everyone in the organization.

Group Edition

A product designed for small businesses and workgroups with a limited number of users.

H

Hierarchy Custom Settings

A type of custom setting that uses a built-in hierarchical logic that lets you "personalize" settings for specific profiles or users. The hierarchy logic checks the organization, profile, and user settings for the current user and returns the most specific, or "lowest," value. In the hierarchy, settings for an organization are overridden by profile settings, which, in turn, are overridden by user settings.

Home Tab

Starting page from which users can choose sidebar shortcuts and options, view current tasks and activities, or select another tab.

Hover Detail

Hover detail displays an interactive overlay containing record details. Details appear when users hover over a link to that record in the Recent Items list on the sidebar, or in a lookup field on a record detail page. Users can quickly view information about a record before clicking to view or edit the record. The record's mini page layout determines which fields are included in the hover details. Users can't customize which fields appear.

I

ID

See Salesforce Record ID.

Integrated Development Environment (IDE)

A software application that provides comprehensive facilities for software developers including a source code editor, testing and debugging tools, and integration with source code control systems.

Immediate Action

A workflow action that executes instantly when the conditions of a workflow rule are met.

Import Wizard

A tool for importing data into your Salesforce organization, accessible from Setup.

Instance

The cluster of software and hardware represented as a single logical server that hosts an organization's data and runs their applications. The Force.com platform runs on multiple instances, but data for any single organization is always stored on a single instance.

J

Junction Object

A custom object with two master-detail relationships. Using a custom junction object, you can model a "many-to-many" relationship between two objects. For example, you may have a custom object called "Bug" that relates to the standard case object such that a bug could be related to multiple cases and a case could also be related to multiple bugs.

K

No Glossary items for this entry.

L

Layout

See Page Layout.

Length

Parameter for custom text fields that specifies the maximum number of characters (up to 255) that a user can enter in the field.

Parameter for number, currency, and percent fields that specifies the number of digits you can enter to the left of the decimal point, for example, 123.98 for an entry of 3.

Letterhead

Determines the basic attributes of an HTML email template. Users can create a letterhead that includes attributes like background color, logo, font size, and font color.

List View

A list display of items (for example, accounts or contacts) based on specific criteria. Salesforce provides some predefined views.

In the Agent console, the list view is the top frame that displays a list view of records based on specific criteria. The list views you can select to display in the console are the same list views defined on the tabs of other objects. You cannot create a list view within the console.

Locale

The country or geographic region in which the user is located. The setting affects the format of date and number fields, for example, dates in the English (United States) locale display as 06/30/2000 and as 30/06/2000 in the English (United Kingdom) locale.

In Professional, Enterprise, Unlimited, Performance, and Developer Edition organizations, a user's individual `Locale` setting overrides the organization's `Default Locale` setting. In Personal and Group Editions, the organization-level locale field is called `Locale`, not `Default Locale`.

Long Text Area

Data type of custom field that allows entry of up to 32,000 characters on separate lines.

Lookup Dialog

Popup dialog available for some fields that allows you to search for a new item, such as a contact, account, or user.

Lookup Field

A type of field that contains a linkable value to another record. You can display lookup fields on page layouts where the object has a lookup or master-detail relationship with another object. For example, cases have a lookup relationship with assets that allows users to select an asset using a lookup dialog from the case edit page and click the name of the asset from the case detail page.

Lookup Relationship

A relationship between two records so you can associate records with each other. For example, cases have a lookup relationship with assets that lets you associate a particular asset with a case. On one side of the relationship, a lookup field allows users to click a lookup icon and select another record from a popup window. On the associated record, you can then display a related list to show all of the records that have been linked to it. If a lookup field references a record that has been deleted, by default Salesforce clears the lookup field. Alternatively, you can prevent records from being deleted if they're in a lookup relationship.

M

Manual Sharing

Record-level access rules that allow record owners to give read and edit permissions to other users who might not have access to the record any other way.

Many-to-Many Relationship

A relationship where each side of the relationship can have many children on the other side. Many-to-many relationships are implemented through the use of junction objects.

Master-Detail Relationship

A relationship between two different types of records that associates the records with each other. For example, accounts have a master-detail relationship with opportunities. This type of relationship affects record deletion, security, and makes the lookup relationship field required on the page layout.

Master Picklist

A complete list of picklist values available for a record type or business process.

Matrix Report

Matrix reports are similar to summary reports but allow you to group and summarize data by both rows and columns. They can be used as the source report for dashboard components. Use this type for comparing related totals, especially if you have large amounts of data to summarize and you need to compare values in several different fields, or you want to look at data by date *and* by product, person, or geography.

Merge Field

A merge field is a field you can put in an email template, mail merge template, custom link, or formula to incorporate values from a record. For example, `Dear {!Contact.FirstName},` uses a contact merge field to obtain the value of a contact record's `First Name` field to address an email recipient by his or her first name.

Metadata

Information about the structure, appearance, and functionality of an organization and any of its parts. Force.com uses XML to describe metadata.

Mini Page Layout

A subset of the items in a record's existing page layout that administrators choose to display in the Agent console's Mini View and in Hover Details. Mini page layouts inherit record type and profile associations, related lists, fields, and field access settings from the page layout.

Multitenancy

An application model where all users and apps share a single, common infrastructure and code base.

N

Notes

Miscellaneous information pertaining to a specific record.

O

Object

An object allows you to store information in your Salesforce organization. The object is the overall definition of the type of information you are storing. For example, the case object allow you to store information regarding customer inquiries. For each object, your organization will have multiple records that store the information about specific instances of that type of data. For example, you might have a case record to store the information about Joe Smith's training inquiry and another case record to store the information about Mary Johnson's configuration issue.

Object-Level Help

Custom help text that you can provide for any custom object. It displays on custom object record home (overview), detail, and edit pages, as well as list views and related lists.

Object-Level Security

Settings that allow an administrator to hide whole objects from users so that they don't know that type of data exists. Object-level security is specified with object permissions.

One-to-Many Relationship

A relationship in which a single object is related to many other objects. For example, an account may have one or more related contacts.

Organization

A deployment of Salesforce with a defined set of licensed users. An organization is the virtual space provided to an individual customer of Salesforce. Your organization includes all of your data and applications, and is separate from all other organizations.

Organization-Wide Defaults

Settings that allow you to specify the baseline level of data access that a user has in your organization. For example, you can set organization-wide defaults so that any user can see any record of a particular object that is enabled via their object permissions, but they need extra permissions to edit one.

Outbound Message

An outbound message sends information to a designated endpoint, like an external service. Outbound messages are configured from Setup. You must configure the external endpoint and create a listener for the messages using the SOAP API.

Overlay

An overlay displays additional information when you hover your mouse over certain user interface elements. Depending on the overlay, it will close when you move your mouse away, click outside of the overlay, or click a close button.

Owner

Individual user to which a record (for example, a contact or case) is assigned.

P

Page Layout

Page layout is the organization of fields, custom links, and related lists on a record detail or edit page. Use page layouts primarily for organizing pages for your users. In Professional, Enterprise, Unlimited, Performance, and Developer Editions, use field-level security to restrict users' access to specific fields.

Picklist

Selection list of options available for specific fields in a Salesforce object, for example, the Industry field for accounts. Users can choose a single value from a list of options rather than make an entry directly in the field. See also Master Picklist.

Picklist Values

Selections displayed in drop-down lists for particular fields. Some values come predefined, and other values can be changed or defined by an administrator.

Platform as a Service (PaaS)

An environment where developers use programming tools offered by a service provider to create applications and deploy them in a cloud. The application is hosted as a service and provided to customers via the Internet. The PaaS vendor provides an API for creating and extending specialized applications. The PaaS vendor also takes responsibility for the daily maintenance, operation, and support of the deployed application and each customer's data. The service alleviates the need for programmers to install, configure, and maintain the applications on their own hardware, software, and related IT resources. Services can be delivered using the PaaS environment to any market segment.

Platform Edition

A Salesforce edition based on Enterprise, Unlimited, or Performance Edition that does not include any of the standard Salesforce apps, such as Sales or Service & Support.

Primary Key

A relational database concept. Each table in a relational database has a field in which the data value uniquely identifies the record. This field is called the primary key. The relationship is made between two tables by matching the values of the foreign key in one table with the values of the primary key in another.

Printable View

An option that displays a page in a print-ready format.

Private Sharing

Private sharing is the process of sharing an uploaded package by using the URL you receive from Salesforce. This URL is not listed in the AppExchange. Using the unlisted URL allows you to share a package without going through the listing process or making it public.

Process Visualizer

A tool that displays a graphical version of an approval process. The view-only diagram is presented as a flowchart. The diagram and an informational sidebar panel can help you visualize and understand the defined steps, rule criteria, and actions that comprise your approval process.

Production Organization

A Salesforce organization that has live users accessing data.

Professional Edition

A Salesforce edition designed for businesses who need full-featured CRM functionality.

Profile

Defines a user's permission to perform different functions within Salesforce. For example, the Solution Manager profile gives a user access to create, edit, and delete solutions.

Q

Queue

A holding area for items before they are processed. Salesforce uses queues in a number of different features and technologies.

R

Read Only

One of the standard profiles to which a user can be assigned. Read Only users can view and report on information based on their role in the organization. (That is, if the Read Only user is the CEO, they can view all data in the system. If the Read Only user has the role of Western Rep, they can view all data for their role and any role below them in the hierarchy.)

Recent Items

List of links in the sidebar for most recently accessed records. Note that not all types of records are listed in the recent items.

Record

A single instance of a Salesforce object. For example, "John Jones" might be the name of a contact record.

Record ID

The unique identifier for each record.

Record-Level Security

A method of controlling data in which you can allow a particular user to view and edit an object, but then restrict the records that the user is allowed to see.

Record Name

A standard field on all Salesforce objects. Whenever a record name is displayed in a Force.com application, the value is represented as a link to a detail view of the record. A record name can be either free-form text or an autonumber field. `Record Name` does not have to be a unique value.

Record Type

A record type is a field available for certain records that can include some or all of the standard and custom picklist values for that record. You can associate record types with profiles to make only the included picklist values available to users with that profile.

Recycle Bin

A page that lets you view and restore deleted information. Access the Recycle Bin by using the link in the sidebar.

Related List

A section of a record or other detail page that lists items related to that record. For example, the Stage History related list of an opportunity or the Open Activities related list of a case.

Related List Hover Links

A type of link that allows you to quickly view information on a detail page about related lists, by hovering your mouse over the link. Your administrator must enable the display of hover links. The displayed text contains the corresponding related list and its number of records. You can also click this type of link to jump to the content of the related list without having to scroll down the page.

Related Object

Objects chosen by an administrator to display in the Agent console's mini view when records of a particular type are shown in the console's detail view. For example, when a case is in the detail view, an administrator can choose to display an associated account, contact, or asset in the mini view.

Relationship

A connection between two objects, used to create related lists in page layouts and detail levels in reports. Matching values in a specified field in both objects are used to link related data; for example, if one object stores data about companies and another object stores data about people, a relationship allows you to find out which people work at the company.

Report

A *report* returns a set of records that meets certain criteria, and displays it in organized rows and columns. Report data can be filtered, grouped, and displayed graphically as a chart. Reports are stored in folders, which control who has access. See Tabular Report, Summary Report, and Matrix Report.

Report Type

A *report type* defines the set of records and fields available to a report based on the relationships between a primary object and its related objects. Reports display only records that meet the criteria defined in the report type. Salesforce provides a set of pre-defined standard report types; administrators can create custom report types as well.

Role Hierarchy

A record-level security setting that defines different levels of users such that users at higher levels can view and edit information owned by or shared with users beneath them in the role hierarchy, regardless of the organization-wide sharing model settings.

Roll-Up Summary Field

A field type that automatically provides aggregate values from child records in a master-detail relationship.

Running User

Each dashboard has a *running user*, whose security settings determine which data to display in a dashboard. If the running user is a specific user, all dashboard viewers see data based on the security settings of that user—regardless of their own personal security settings. For dynamic dashboards, you can set the running user to be the logged-in user, so that each user sees the dashboard according to his or her own access level.

S

SaaS

See Software as a Service (SaaS).

Salesforce Record ID

A unique 15- or 18-character alphanumeric string that identifies a single record in Salesforce.

Sandbox

A nearly identical copy of a Salesforce production organization for development, testing, and training. The content and size of a sandbox varies depending on the type of sandbox and the editioin of the production organization associated with the sandbox.

Save As

Option on any standard, public, or custom report to save the parameters of the report without altering the original report. It creates a new custom report with your saved changes.

Save & New

Alternative "save" on most pages with which you can save your current changes and create a new entry.

Search

Feature that lets you search for information that matches specified keywords. If you have sidebar search, enter search terms in the Search section of the sidebar or click **Advanced Search...** for more search options. If you have global search, enter search terms in the search box in the header.

Search Layout

The organization of fields Included in search results, in lookup dialogs, and in the key lists on tab home pages.

Setup

A menu where administrators can customize and define organization settings and Force.com apps. Depending on your organization's user interface settings, Setup may be a link in the user interface header or in the drop-down list under your name.

Sharing

Allowing other users to view or edit information you own. There are different ways to share data:

* Sharing Model—defines the default organization-wide access levels that users have to each other's Information and whether to use the hierarchies when determining access to data.

- Role Hierarchy—defines different levels of users such that users at higher levels can view and edit information owned by or shared with users beneath them in the role hierarchy, regardless of the organization-wide sharing model settings.

- Sharing Rules—allow an administrator to specify that all information created by users within a given group or role is automatically shared to the members of another group or role.

- Manual Sharing—allows individual users to share records with other users or groups.

- Apex-Managed Sharing—enables developers to programmatically manipulate sharing to support their application's behavior. See Apex-Managed Sharing.

Sharing Model

Behavior defined by your administrator that determines default access by users to different types of records.

Sharing Rule

Type of default sharing created by administrators. Allows users in a specified group or role to have access to all information created by users within a given group or role.

Show/Hide Details

Option available for reports that lets you show/hide the details of individual column values in report results.

Sidebar

Column appearing on the left side of each page that provides links to recent items and other resources.

SOAP (Simple Object Access Protocol)

A protocol that defines a uniform way of passing XML-encoded data.

Software as a Service (SaaS)

A delivery model where a software application is hosted as a service and provided to customers via the Internet. The SaaS vendor takes responsibility for the daily maintenance, operation, and support of the application and each customer's data. The service alleviates the need for customers to install, configure, and maintain applications with their own hardware, software, and related IT resources. Services can be delivered using the SaaS model to any market segment.

Source Report

A custom report scheduled to run and load data as records into a target object for an reporting snapshot.

Standard Object

A built-in object included with the Force.com platform. You can also build custom objects to store information that is unique to your app.

Summary Report

Summary reports are similar to tabular reports, but also allow users to group rows of data, view subtotals, and create charts. They can be used as the source report for dashboard components. Use this type for a report to show subtotals based on the value of a particular field or when you want to create a hierarchical list, such as all opportunities for your team, subtotaled by `Stage` and `Owner`.

System Administrator

See Administrator (System Administrator).

T

Tab

A tab is an interface component that allows you to navigate around an app. A tab serves as the starting point for viewing, editing, and entering information for a particular object. When you click a tab at the top of the page, the corresponding tab home page for that object appears. A tab can be associated with an object, a Web page, or a Visualforce page.

Tabular Report

Tabular reports are the simplest and fastest way to look at data. Similar to a spreadsheet, they consist simply of an ordered set of fields in columns, with each matching record listed in a row. Tabular reports are best for creating lists of records or a list with a single grand total. They can't be used to create groups of data or charts, and can't be used in dashboards unless rows are limited. Examples include contact mailing lists and activity reports.

Text

Data type of a custom field that allows entry of any combination of letters, numbers, or symbols, up to a maximum length of 255 characters.

Text Area

A custom field data type that allows entry of up to 255 characters on separate lines.

Text Area (Long)

See Long Text Area.

Time-Dependent Workflow Action

A workflow action that executes when the conditions of a workflow rule and an associated time trigger are met.

Time Trigger

An event that starts according to a specified time threshold, such as seven days before an opportunity close date. For example, you might define a time-based workflow action that sends email to the account manager when a scheduled milestone will occur in seven days.

U

Unlimited Edition

Unlimited Edition is Salesforce's solution for maximizing your success and extending that success across the entire enterprise through the Force.com platform.

URL (Uniform Resource Locator)

The global address of a website, document, or other resource on the Internet. For example, http://www.salesforce.com.

User Interface

The layouts that specify how a data model should be displayed.

V

Validation Rule

A rule that prevents a record from being saved if it does not meet the standards that are specified.

Visualforce

A simple, tag-based markup language that allows developers to easily define custom pages and components for apps built on the platform. Each tag corresponds to a coarse or fine-grained component, such as a section of a page, a related list, or a field. The components can either be controlled by the same logic that is used in standard Salesforce pages, or developers can associate their own logic with a controller written in Apex.

Visualforce Controller

See Controller, Visualforce.

Visualforce Page

A web page created using Visualforce. Typically, Visualforce pages present information relevant to your organization, but they can also modify or capture data. They can be rendered in several ways, such as a PDF document or an email attachment, and can be associated with a CSS style.

W

Web Links

See Custom Links.

Web Service

A mechanism by which two applications can easily exchange data over the Internet, even if they run on different platforms, are written in different languages, or are geographically remote from each other.

Web Tab

A custom tab that allows your users to use external websites from within the application.

Wizard

A user interface that leads a user through a complex task in multiple steps.

Automated Actions

Automated actions, such as email alerts, tasks, field updates, and outbound messages, can be triggered by a process, workflow rule, approval process, or milestone.

Workflow Action

A workflow action, such as an email alert, field update, outbound message, or task, fires when the conditions of a workflow rule are met.

Workflow Email Alert

A workflow action that sends an email when a workflow rule is triggered. Unlike workflow tasks, which can only be assigned to application users, workflow alerts can be sent to any user or contact, as long as they have a valid email address.

Workflow Field Update

A workflow action that changes the value of a particular field on a record when a workflow rule is triggered.

Workflow Outbound Message

A workflow action that sends data to an external Web service, such as another cloud computing application. Outbound messages are used primarily with composite apps.

Workflow Queue

A list of workflow actions that are scheduled to fire based on workflow rules that have one or more time-dependent workflow actions.

Workflow Rule

A workflow rule sets workflow actions into motion when its designated conditions are met. You can configure workflow actions to execute immediately when a record meets the conditions in your workflow rule, or set time triggers that execute the workflow actions on a specific day.

Workflow Task

A workflow action that assigns a task to an application user when a workflow rule is triggered.

X

XML (Extensible Markup Language)

A markup language that enables the sharing and transportation of structured data. All Force.com components that are retrieved or deployed through the Metadata API are represented by XML definitions.

Y

No Glossary items for this entry.

Z

Zip File

A data compression and archive format.

A collection of files retrieved or deployed by the Metadata API. See also Local Project.

INDEX

Index

Notes

Notes

Notes

Notes

Notes

Notes

Notes

Notes

Notes

Notes

Notes

Notes

Notes

Notes